Native Americans in the School System

CONTEMPORARY NATIVE AMERICAN COMMUNITIES
Stepping Stones to the Seventh Generation

Acknowledging the strength and vibrancy of Native American people and nations today, this series examines life in contemporary Native American communities from the point of view of Native concerns and values. Books in the series cover topics that are of cultural and political importance to tribal peoples and that affect their possibilities for survival, in both urban and rural communities.

SERIES EDITORS:
Troy Johnson, American Indian Studies, California State University, Long Beach, Long Beach, CA 90840, trj@csulb.edu

Duane Champagne, Native Nations Law and Policy Center, 292 Haines Hall, Box 951551, University of California, Los Angeles, Los Angeles, CA 90095-1551, champagn@ucla.edu

BOOKS IN THE SERIES
1. *Inuit, Whaling, and Sustainability*, Milton M. R. Freeman, Ingmar Egede, Lyudmila Bogoslovskaya, Igor G. Krupnik, Richard A. Caulfield and Marc G. Stevenson (1999)
2. *Contemporary Native American Political Issues*, edited by Troy Johnson (1999)
3. *Contemporary Native American Cultural Issues*, edited by Duane Champagne (1999)
4. *Modern Tribal Development: Paths to Self Sufficiency and Cultural Integrity in Indian Country*, Dean Howard Smith (2000)
5. *American Indians and the Urban Experience*, edited by Susan Lobo and Kurt Peters (2000)
6. *Medicine Ways: Disease, Health, and Survival among Native Americans*, edited by Clifford Trafzer and Diane Weiner (2000)
7. *Native American Studies in Higher Education: Models for Collaboration between Universities and Indigenous Nations*, edited by Duane Champagne and Jay Stauss (2002)
8. *Spider Woman Walks This Land: Traditional Cultural Properties and the Navajo Nation*, by Kelli Carmean (2002)
9. *Alaska Native Political Leadership and Higher Education: One University, Two Universes*, by Michael Jennings (2004)
10. *Indigenous Intellectual Property Rights: Legal Obstacles and Innovative Solutions*, edited by Mary Riley (2004)
11. *Healing and Mental Health for Native American: Speaking in Red* edited by Ethan Nebelkopf and Mary Phillips (2004)
12. *Rachel's Children*, by Lois Beardslee (2004)
13. *A Broken Flute: The Native Experience in Books for Children*, edited by Doris Seale and Beverly Slapin (2005)
14. *Indigenous Peoples & the Modern State*, edited by Duane Champagne, Karen Torjesen & Susan Steiner (2005]
15. *Reading Native American Women: Critical/Creative Representations*, edited by Inés Hernández-Ávila (2005)
16. *Native Americans in the School System: Family, Community, and Academic Achievement*, by Carol J. Ward (2005)

EDITORIAL BOARD
Jose Barreiro (Taino Nation Antilles), Cornell University; Russell Barsh, University of Lethbridge; Brian Dippie, University of Victoria; Lee Francis (Pueblo), University of New Mexico; Carole Goldberg, University of California, Los Angeles; Lorie Graham (Blackfeet), Harvard Law School; Jennie Joe (Navajo), University of Arizona; Steven Leuthold, Syracuse University; Nancy Marie Mithlo (Chiricahua Apache), Institute of American Indian Arts; J. Anthony Paredes, Florida State University; Dennis Peck, University of Alabama; Luana Ross (Confederated Salish and Kootenai), University of California, Davis

Native Americans in the School System

Family, Community, and Academic Achievement

Carol J. Ward

LIBRARY ST. MARY'S COLLEGE

ALTAMIRA
PRESS

A Division of Rowman & Littlefield Publishers, Inc.
Lanham • New York • Toronto • Oxford

ALTAMIRA PRESS
A division of Rowman & Littlefield Publishers, Inc.
A wholly owned subsidiary of
The Rowman & Littlefield Publishing Group, Inc.
4501 Forbes Boulevard, Suite 200
Lanham, MD 20706
www.altamirapress.com

PO Box 317, Oxford OX2 9RU, UK

Copyright © 2005 AltaMira Press

All rights reserved. No part of this publication may be reproduced, stored in a retrieval system, or transmitted in any form or by any means, electronic, mechanical, photocopying, recording, or otherwise, without the prior permission of the publisher.

British Library Cataloguing in Publication Information Available

Library of Congress Cataloging-in-Publication Data

Ward, Carol Jane, 1951–
  Native Americans in the school system : family, community, and academic achievement / Carol J. Ward.
    p. cm. — (Contemporary Native American communities)
  Includes bibliographical references and index.
  ISBN 0-7591-0608-8 (cloth : alk. paper) — ISBN 0-7591-0609-6 (pbk. : alk. paper)
  1. Indians of North America—Education (Secondary) 2. Indian students—United States—Social conditions. 3. Indian students—United States—Economic conditions. 4. High school students—United States. 5. High school dropouts—United States. 6. Education and state—United States. I. Title. II. Series.
  E97.W27 2005
  373.1829'97—dc22
                                                          2005001810

Printed in the United States of America

∞^{TM} The paper used in this publication meets the minimum requirements of American National Standard for Information Sciences—Permanence of Paper for Printed Library Materials, ANSI/NISO Z39.48-1992.

CONTENTS

List of Figures and Tables vii
Preface ix

CHAPTER ONE American Indian High School Completion:
A Contradiction in Need of Explanation 1
CHAPTER TWO Contributions of Schooling and
Community Research to an Ecological Approach to the
Study of School Outcomes 22
CHAPTER THREE The Northern Cheyenne Reservation:
The Setting for an Analysis of High School Completion 56
CHAPTER FOUR Case Study Approach and
Descriptive Data 80
CHAPTER FIVE Evaluating Ecological Models of School
Performance: The Relative Effects of Individual, Family, School,
and Community Influences 114
CHAPTER SIX Evaluation of School Dropout Models 150
CHAPTER SEVEN Evaluating Models of School Performance
and Completion for Indian and White Students at Colstrip
High School 189
CHAPTER EIGHT Conclusion: Native Capital and Northern
Cheyenne Dropout Rates 208

References 235
Index 257
About the Author 267

FIGURES AND TABLES

Figures

Figure 2.1	Overview of Influences on School Outcomes	23
Figure 8.1	Social and Cultural Contexts in which Indian Students Are Located	222

Tables

Table 4.1	Variable Definitions	98
Table 4.2	Distribution of Students' Background Characteristics and School Experiences	103
Table 4.3	Graduation Status for Indian Students by School Attended and Gender	108
Table 4.4	Mean GPA by School, Community, Gender, and Graduation Status	110
Table 5.1	Logistic Coefficients for the Effects of Community Residence, Gender, and Family Characteristics on School Attended	117
Table 5.2	OLS Coefficients for the Effects of Community and Reservation, Gender, Family Characteristics, School Attended, and School Experiences on Mean GPA	119
Table 5.3	OLS Coefficients for the Effects of Community, Gender, Family Characteristics, School Attended, Interactions Terms, and School Experiences on Mean GPA	121

FIGURES AND TABLES

Table 5.4	OLS Coefficients by School for the Effects of Community, Gender, Family Characteristics, and School Experiences on Mean GPA	135
Table 5.5	OLS Coefficients for the Effects of Student and Family Characteristics, Culture, Community, School Attended, and School Experiences on Mean GPA	146
Table 6.1	Logistic Regression Coefficients for the Effects of Community Residence, Gender, Family Characteristics, School Attended, School Experiences, and School Performance on Dropping Out	152
Table 6.2	Logistic Regression Coefficients for the Effects of Community, School Attended, Gender, Family Characteristics, School Experiences, and Performance on Dropping Out	167
Table 6.3	Students' Graduation Status by School Attended and Community	170
Table 6.4	Logistic Regression Coefficients by School for the Effects of Community, Gender, Family Characteristics, School Experiences, Attended and Performance on Dropping Out	172
Table 6.5	Logistic Regression Coefficients for the Effects of Student, Family, and Cultural Characteristics, Community, School Attended, and School Experiences on Dropping Out	182
Table 7.1	Means and Standard Deviations for Colstrip Students	191
Table 7.2	OLS Coefficients for the Effects of Individual Characteristics and School Experiences on Mean GPA for all Students at Colstrip	192
Table 7.3	Logistic Coefficients for the Effects of Individual Characteristics, School Experiences, and School Performance on Dropping Out for Students at Colstrip	193
Table 8.1	Summary of Individual and Contextual Variable Effects on Dropping Out Using Quantitative and Qualitative Data	228

PREFACE

This research grew out of two complementary sets of interests: Northern Cheyenne educators' interests in understanding and addressing the high dropout rate among their high school students in the late 1980s and early 1990s, and my interests in doing research that would benefit the Northern Cheyenne and meet the requirements for my PhD program in sociology at the University of Chicago. The result of these coinciding interests was the development of a research effort that was collaborative at every stage—from its inception through implementation to this effort to disseminate the results to a variety of audiences. Although any errors in this presentation of the project and its findings rest with me, the research process itself involved many groups and individuals from across the Northern Cheyenne Nation.

This began with my work with Northern Cheyenne education programs from 1981 to 1987 when my husband and I received an invitation from the president of the tribal college (then called Dull Knife Memorial College), Art McDonald, PhD, to work as grant writers and help develop programs at the college. Importantly, the dropout project, which benefited from the guidance of James Coleman and Mary Brinton at the University of Chicago, was funded by the Office of Educational Research and Improvement, U.S. Department of Education. This support was critical to our being able to pursue a complex research program involving the tribal college and three high schools serving the Northern Cheyenne.

Other essential collaborators were the Northern Cheyenne Education Commission (now the Northern Cheyenne Education Department), the

PREFACE

branch of the tribal government concerned with education services and issues. In particular, Norma Bixby, chair of the Education Commission and now director of the Education Department, was instrumental in establishing the need for the dropout research through her work with students, parents, advisory committees, and teachers. Mrs. Bixby continues to work to improve schooling for American Indian students in Montana as a representative in the Montana legislature, and her recent efforts have focused on new legislation that calls for monitoring school completion rates of American Indian and other students at risk of dropping out.

Three school districts serving Cheyenne high school students—Busby Tribal School, Colstrip Public Schools, and St. Labre Catholic Mission Schools—were important partners in this research. Knowing that the research could identify weaknesses as well as strengths in schooling practices, the superintendents, school boards, and principals in each system willingly participated. Administrative staff, counselors, and liaisons worked closely with the dropout project to ensure the accuracy of the data collected for each student cohort, 1987–1989.

Other important collaborators included the Northern Cheyenne Talent Search coordinator at the time of the project, Zane Spang; the Crow Talent Search coordinator, Alda Goodluck; the Northern Cheyenne Adult Education program director, Juanita Lonebear; and Ted Risingsun, a member of the Dull Knife board of trustees and long-time advocate for education. These three individuals provided particularly important insights and guidance to the project concerning students' schooling, cultural, family, and community experiences. These facets of the project set it apart from more narrowly defined dropout studies. A number of Dull Knife students contributed to the study by doing the hundreds of mundane, but significant, tasks related to schooling research—Mamie Stump, Kathy Harris, and Lorna Sioux, especially, and many community members helped to conduct the Northern Cheyenne Educational Household Census in 1989.

These and other contributors to the research process offered information that was relevant not only to the data collection, but also to the data analysis and interpretation. In countless conversations, individuals discussed their (or their children's) experiences, views, and ideas about schooling that clarified how specific schooling experiences affect students, how schooling had changed, and its relations to family and community life.

PREFACE

The purpose of this book is to support the efforts of the Northern Cheyenne Nation and educators by providing a permanent, public record of the Northern Cheyenne dropout project to a range of audiences that may benefit from the important lessons learned through this collaboration. Zane Spang, now director of student services at Chief Dull Knife College, offers this view of the value of the dropout research: "I think that the information presented in the research is very beneficial and does reflect the situation on the Northern Cheyenne Reservation. This information can be used in a positive way to begin alleviating the dropout problem in this area."

Although not directly involved in the dropout research, two other Cheyenne educators provide remarks that help to place it in the larger context of American Indian education research. Richard Littlebear, PhD, linguist, and president of Chief Dull Knife College since 1995, offers an overview of the kinds of issues that such research should address and calls for more research that examines the multiple historical and contemporary processes shaping Native American schooling. Specifically, he calls for efforts to address a "missing" element, what he describes as "the historical hurt that all Native Americans have experienced when venturing out into the world of mainstream society." He continues:

> The above is about as close as I can come to describing this "missing something." It has to do with having teachers who do not look like Native American students. It's American history that does not relate to tribal history. It is learning lessons couched in a foreign language. It is learning about religions that are not theirs. It is about being denied expressing a spirituality that had more than sufficed for their ancestors for centuries. It is learning about traditions that replaced theirs. It is all about a disconnect between being Native American and what the mainstream society requires. I think this is difficult to measure because I think Native Americans have a difficult time articulating this historical hurt, as I call it. Until there's a convergence between what Native American students experience and what occurs in the classroom, we will continue to experience these dismally high dropout rates.

This study attempted to address, at least in part, these important influences on the schooling experiences and outcomes of Northern Cheyenne students. About the Northern Cheyenne dropout study, Dr. Littlebear

PREFACE

comments, "I think we need these kinds of studies to keep emphasizing that there is this issue of high dropout rates among Native Americans, in general, and the Northern Cheyenne students, in particular. It was informative to read this study, especially since it dealt with a population of which I am a part and dealt with a topic that must be continuously addressed by our schools and parents." Alonzo Spang, EdD, former Bureau of Indian Affairs education specialist, Dull Knife president from 1992 to 1995, and current adjunct professor at the college, also calls for continuing research as well as attention to the role of racism in the schooling of Northern Cheyenne students. "Dr. Ward's research makes clear there are complex problems in the educating of Indian students on or near reservations. Her study shows the need for more research as well as the urgent need to design and implement curricula to address these issues."

Another Northern Cheyenne educator involved in the dropout project, Juanita Lonebear, director of Northern Cheyenne Adult Education, points to some of the most important findings and impacts of the project.

> As an adult educator I feel that the impact this report will make in regard to Native American education is infinite. I have worked in the adult education field for twenty-six years and have observed young person upon young person enter our program who are as bright as any, but show low, low skills and no motivation. This report reinforces the fact that local schools are blatantly failing our Native American students. It is documented proof that we, as parents and especially as a Tribe, need to expect more out of schools for our children. Evidence in the report that I am especially excited about is the fact that schools and communities working together can, and in some cases here, do make an impact. This is really important in culturally traditional communities such as ours. The dropout project report proves too, that Cheyenne culture distinctly has a positive effect. Finally, probably the most prominent and exciting result of this study is the establishing of a Lame Deer High School District.

As suggested by Mrs. Lonebear's comments, important outcomes of this project include not only the distribution and publication of project results, but also actions taken by the Northern Cheyenne Nation to expand and improve secondary school for Cheyenne students. Specifically, a committee of tribal leaders and educators petitioned the state of Montana for a new public high school district on the reservation, basing their argument

PREFACE

on this dropout study and evidence provided by the reservation community. Beginning in the mid-1990s, having a public high school in Lame Deer, Montana, meant that for the first time Cheyenne students no longer had to leave their community or reservation to receive a public high school education. Northern Cheyenne educators have continued to monitor the dropout and school completion rates of Cheyenne students.

My hope is that by building on such efforts as these, educators serving the Northern Cheyenne can create partnerships among local schools, families, and communities that will bring about the kinds and quality of schooling experiences that Cheyenne students deserve. I also hope this research provides the impetus for more research by local educators on the needs and experiences of students in this and other rural, minority communities.

Early in this project I benefited enormously from working with several mentors at the University of Chicago: William Julius Wilson, Mary Brinton, Charles Bidwell, and James Coleman. American Indian sociologists Matt Snipp and Gary Sandefur also provided invaluable advice. I am indebted as well to a number of people who helped bring this project to completion. Those providing much-needed technical expertise for the quantitative analyses were Nan Astone, Joe Olsen, and Suzanne Maughn. I am also deeply grateful for the encouragement and support of my colleagues in the sociology department at Brigham Young University, especially Lynn England, Keith Warner, and Howard Bahr; for the research support provided by the College of Family, Home and Social Sciences; and for the remarkable assistance of graduate students Yodit Solomon and Ben Gibbs on analysis and editing tasks, and Raechel Lizon for indexing. I owe endless thanks to my husband and daughter, David and Kate Wilson, for their inspiration, love, and patience. Finally, I am forever indebted to the educators who taught me through their words and actions how schooling can and should be—my parents, Dayton and Betty Ward; my father-in-law, Paul Wilson; and members of the Northern Cheyenne Nation, to whom this book is dedicated.

CHAPTER ONE
AMERICAN INDIAN HIGH SCHOOL COMPLETION: A CONTRADICTION IN NEED OF EXPLANATION

Thirty years ago Senator Edward Kennedy called American Indian education "a national tragedy" in a summary report for the Special Senate Subcommittee on Indian Education (1969). Today, many would say that despite vast changes in federal policy and resources for education, vestiges of the "tragedy" of Indian education can still be seen in the school attainment patterns of American Indians. Recent research shows that American Indian adults have reached virtual parity with the majority of Americans in average school attainment (Ward and Snipp 1996). However, evidence also indicates that dropout rates remain high among American Indian high school students (Snipp 1989; National Center for Education Statistics 1994, 34; Young 2003). Interestingly, despite insights gained from research in this area, much remains to be understood (Swisher and Hoisch 1992; Deyhle and Swisher 1997). Responding to Vine Deloria's statement that "Indian education does not need another shallow report" (Deloria and Wildcat 2001, 161), this study moves beyond a recital of education failures and offers a more holistic framework—incorporating history, cultural context, and individual actions—to examine contemporary Indian schooling. My research on Northern Cheyenne schooling, conducted from 1987 to 1995, explores relevant social and cultural influences and assesses their impacts on school completion.

Much sociological research has been devoted to the role that education plays in the quality of life attained by different ethnic and racial groups in the United States. The prevailing view concludes that the importance of

CHAPTER ONE

education is due to the connection between educational credentials and participation in the labor market. That is, the bridge between these institutions is crossed as a result of specific types and levels of educational attainment that lead to entry into certain jobs and advancement up career ladders during the course of a person's lifetime participation in the labor force. Moreover, levels of educational achievement shape occupational attainment, which determines, to a large extent, a person's socioeconomic status (i.e., social status, occupational prestige, and wealth) and affects other social outcomes such as attitudes toward and participation in cultural, social, and civic life (Kingston et al. 2003). Thus, the tragedy of American Indian education refers to the difficulty of navigating through and between these institutions and achieving the preferred social statuses conferred by these institutions.

While converting school credentials to employment is relatively more difficult in the United States than in other industrialized nations (Brint 1998), it is even more challenging for racial and ethnic minorities, especially those in rural locations. This suggests that an important distinction concerns levels of educational attainment as opposed to converting education into occupational or job-related rewards. The research presented here addresses educational attainment as a prerequisite to labor force participation, hence, a prior source of stratification. Therefore, high school completion is the central issue.

Dropping out of high school is a serious concern for both individuals and society. Personal costs may include diminished self-esteem or prestige as well as financial loss. Economic costs are typically calculated as estimates of an individual's lost income: the difference between lifetime earnings of high school graduates (ages 25 to 64) and dropouts has been estimated at $300,000 for both males and females (for males, $1.4 million for graduates vs. $1.1 million for dropouts; for females, $1.0 million vs. $700,000) (Day and Newburger 2002). Dropping out also results in losses of at least $71 billion of tax revenues by states and other governments (Jordan and Lyons 1992). Other losses include $3 billion in welfare and unemployment expenditures and $3 billion in crime costs (Levin 1972; Smith 1998). For American Indians and other minorities, costs of dropping out may be even greater, as high school education has become increasingly important in gaining access to scarce opportunities in inner city and rural labor markets.

School Completion Patterns among American Indians

Despite overall improvements in educational status from 1960 to 2000, American Indians are still much less likely to reach the highest levels of educational attainment than most other ethnic groups. A brief review of empirical evidence showing ethnic group differences is presented in the next section, followed by a discussion of schooling patterns among American Indians.

Secondary and Postsecondary School Attainment and Completion

C. Matthew Snipp's comprehensive examination of educational attainment using census data compares patterns for American Indians and Alaskan Natives, African Americans, and Whites for 1970 and 1980 (Snipp 1989) and then 1990 (Snipp 1995; Ward and Snipp 1996). In the first analysis comparing 1970 and 1980 measures, Snipp shows that the lag of Indians behind other groups in educational attainment is attributable in part to the substantial percentage of the Indian population that achieved less than five years of school and the small percentage that completed four or more years of college. As recently as 1980, more than 8.4% of American Indians and Alaskan Natives did not complete fifth grade, compared to 8.2% of African Americans and 2.6% of Whites. While 17.1% of Whites completed college degrees and advanced to graduate training, only 8.4% of African Americans and 7.7% of Indians and Alaskan Natives advanced this far in their schooling.

However, the percentage of American Indians and Alaskan Natives completing high school increased from 22% in 1970 to 55.5% in 1980. By comparison, White high school completion increased from about 55% in 1970 to almost 67% in 1980. In 1970, both African Americans and Indians had 9.8 years of schooling (as indicated by the median) while Whites had 12.1 years. African Americans lagged behind both groups in 1980 with a 51.2% high school completion rate. By 1980, all three groups were at or above a median of 12 years of schooling: 12.0 years for African Americans, 12.2 years for Indians and Alaskan Natives, and 12.5 years for Whites.

Comparing the completion rates of these groups in 1990 shows that the percentage of American Indians with a high school diploma (29.4%) exceeded that of African Americans (28%) but was less than that of

Whites (31.4%). American Indian college attendance (36.6%) again exceeded the rate for African Americans (35.2%) but was considerably below the rate for Whites (47.6%). However, African American (32%) and White (46%) college students were much more likely than American Indian college students (26%) to complete a four-year degree or higher (Ward and Snipp 1996).

In contrast to this evidence of overall improvements in educational attainment, results of the High School and Beyond study by the National Center for Education Statistics (NCES) show that recent cohorts of American Indian students dropped out of high school at a higher rate than other groups, 35% in 1988 (Frase 1989). National figures for minority groups cited by Kunisawa (1988) identify American Indians as having the highest dropout rate (42%) followed by Latinos (39.9%), African Americans (24.7%), and Whites (9.6%). More recent research by the National Center for Education Statistics (1994, 34) indicates that 25.4% of American Indian and Alaska Native students who should have graduated from high school in 1992 dropped out, the highest percentage for all racial/ethnic groups in the United States. Young's (2003) analysis of NCES Common Core data shows that Native American dropout rates remained high in 2001.

Sources of Variation in American Indian Educational Attainment Patterns

Using census data, Snipp (1989) identifies several important types of variations related to school attainment within the Indian population. The first concerns elementary school enrollment patterns: 1980 data for American Indian and Alaskan Native children indicate that most begin school around age 5 or 6, and primary school attendance is almost universal (94%). Similarly, the percentage of Indian students ages 7 to 14 enrolled in school is no less than 94%. However, enrollment begins to decline during the high school years. By ages 17 and 18, only about 60% of urban and rural Indian youths are enrolled in school. Enrollment data for 17- to 19-year-olds, which indicate that only about one-third are enrolled, suggest that the dropout rate is more than 40%.

Snipp also uses 1980 enrollment data to examine "school progress," or school attainment by age and grade level. Estimates of "school progress" are based on assumptions that most Indian students start school by age 5 or 6 and are promoted one grade each year; thus, by age 17 or 18 they would be enrolled in or have completed grade twelve. Snipp's analysis, however, shows that the percentage of students behind in grade level increases dramatically each year but varies by place of residence. For example, in reservation and other nonmetropolitan areas in 1980, only 6% of the 7- and 8-year-olds were behind in school; by ages 11 and 12, 15% were behind in school; and by ages 17 and 18, 41% were behind in school. In contrast, in 1980, a third of Indian students in metropolitan and nonreservation areas who should have been juniors or seniors were below this grade level or had dropped out. In 1990, the percentage of Indian 17- and 18-year-olds in nonmetropolitan areas who were behind in school or had dropped out increased to 48% (Ward 1995).

Snipp's findings show that location and age are two sources of significant variation in school attainment patterns. Concerning location, differences in school achievement between Indian residents of nonmetropolitan/reservation areas and metropolitan/nonreservation areas are as high as 20%. For example, percentages of the population in nonmetropolitan/reservation areas with twelve years or more of school range from 37% to 71%, while metropolitan and nonreservation population percentages range from 52% to 75%. Concerning age, intergenerational gaps are consistent throughout the population; like other ethnic and racial groups, young American Indians and Alaskan Natives are better educated than their elders. More than 70% of the Indian population ages 25 to 30 has completed at least twelve years of education, with a range of 70% to 79% across rural and metropolitan areas. High school completion among adults ages 36–40 ranges from 50% to 75%; for adults ages 46–50 it ranges from 32% to 63%; and for Indians ages 70 and above, high school completion rates range from 13% to 29% (Snipp 1989, 197). Despite the decline in the dropout rate to about 30% for adults ages 25–30, however, the dropout rate for youth ages 17–19 is markedly higher.

These figures indicate some of the perplexing patterns of American Indian educational attainment. While variations in school attainment continue to be affected by rural, reservation, and urban location, an emerging pattern related to age represents an important contradiction. Secondary schooling attainment has increased overall among each adult age group, but high school completion rates now are lowest among Indian youth. Thus, contrary to general patterns and expectations for American

CHAPTER ONE

youth that their high school completion rates will surpass those of adults, contemporary Indian youth are falling further behind.

The Importance of Residence Patterns for Assimilation

The effect of rural or urban location has been the subject of several research efforts addressing the assimilation of American Indians. According to Sandefur and Tienda (1988, 9),

> Despite substantial increases in educational attainment over the past few decades, many Native Americans remain unprepared to compete in a highly technical and bureaucratized world of work. . . . This situation may improve as larger shares of Native Americans complete postsecondary. However, to the extent that job possibilities on reservations remain limited while larger shares of Native Americans reside on them, the prospects for economic parity with whites will not be realized. Moreover, within the American Indian population, sharp differences in relative economic status between reservation and nonreservation residents will remain.

In his research on minority poverty, Gary Sandefur (1988) examines how such attributes as educational attainment and employment contribute to poverty rates. Comparing Indians with Whites, African Americans, and Hispanics using 1980 census data, Sandefur shows that unemployment was higher for American Indians in rural areas (15.3%) than in central cities (12.3%)—their rural unemployment rate being the highest of any group. Sandefur concludes that while studies of urban poverty are important, studies of processes affecting the rural poor are equally important. In particular, we need to better understand the processes by which the educational system allocates rural Indians to lower positions in the labor market, or excludes them altogether.

Other research (Snipp and Sandefur 1988) confirmed that the income levels of American Indians in nonmetropolitan areas were related to both human capital and labor market conditions. Of special significance was the lower level of educational attainment among Indians in nonmetropolitan areas (10.6 years compared to 12.3 years for metropolitan residents). However, lower income among Indian workers was also affected by poorer job opportunities in these areas. Studies in the 1990s (Gregory, Abello, and Johnson 1996; Brown et. al. 2001) indicate that despite increased human capital among American Indians, recent economy-wide changes have contributed to continuing barriers to Indian employment, especially in rural, reservation communities. These findings point to the need to identify both individual characteristics and social and economic conditions of specific locales that shape the attainment process for Indian people.

Implications of Reservation Residence

The location of American Indians on reservations has important implications for the allocation of both educational and economic opportunities. The reservation system represents the special trust relationship between American Indians and the U.S. government initiated through military conquest. Of particular consequence for Indian individuals and families have been policies resulting from this relationship. Although the early policies that made American Indians wards of the state have long ended, Indians continue to experience the results of, first, paternalistic and, then, assimilationist practices that located them on reservations, delayed citizenship for many until well into the twentieth century, created congressional trusteeship, and led to social and economic isolation as well as urban relocation (Snipp 1986, 1988; Cornell and Kalt 1990). Snipp (1988) describes the history of policy changes for Indian peoples as a movement from "captive nations" to "internal colonies," suggesting that in the process of recent "development," economic exploitation has been added to political dependency. That is, federal policies that failed to assimilate Indians led to recent efforts to promote "self-determination." However, these policies also have generally left in their wake lower educational attainment, insufficient levels and types of participation in the labor force, poor health conditions, and impoverishment (Wax, Wax and Dumont 1964; Jorgensen 1978; Talbot 1981; Sandefur and Scott 1983; Snipp and Sandefur 1988; Snipp 1989; Cornell and Kalt 1990; Snipp 1995; Ward and Snipp 1996).

Understanding the impact of federal policies and their changes, however, requires recognizing the diversity of American Indian cultures, resources, and interests. American Indian responses to being incorporated into the American political economy and culture range from resistance to acceptance. Thomas Hall (1986, 1988) asserts that a group's status at any

CHAPTER ONE

point in time reflects both the group's power relative to other groups and its economic and cultural adaptations to specific sets of circumstances. An excellent example is provided by Duane Champagne's (1996) analysis of the responses of two different tribes to opportunities to develop their coal resources for profit, one resisting and the other accepting this type of natural resource exploitation.

Cornell's (1988) analysis of American Indian political resurgence emphasizes that increased opportunities in several political arenas have contributed significantly to improvements in American Indians' social status. In particular, political action at multiple levels—tribal, regional, and national—has led to increased attention to the social and economic needs of Indian people and greater American Indian influence on federal policies (Cornell 1988). Nagel (1996) concludes that recent cultural renewal seen in many American Indian communities was fueled and given momentum by the Red Power movement that occurred primarily in the 1960s and 1970s. Thus, indigenous efforts to resist domination—both political and cultural—not only have persisted, but they have expanded in recent years.

One important area in which political efforts have resulted in improved resources and opportunities for Indians is education. While even the earliest federal policies concerning American Indians provided for education, strategies for achieving Indian education goals have varied tremendously. Indian students initially were placed in federal and mission schools, but if these schools were unable to accommodate, they were sent to public schools or boarding schools (Fuchs and Havighurst 1972; Nabokov 1978; Szasz 1974). In spite of the differences in structure, approach, and orientation among these schools, they had a common purpose in Indian education; in support of the government policy to assimilate American Indians, they each attempted to eliminate the use of native languages and religious practices. Boarding schools were especially effective in this pursuit since they also separated children from their families and communities for long periods of time. However, in the late 1960s and early 1970s, political pressures by American Indians resulted in a decline in the sanctions against students' use of their native languages and other cultural expressions in schools.

Congressional enactment and funding of Indian education initiatives (1972, 1975) provided for a new cultural sensitivity to Indian education (cultural awareness programs) as well as more public education opportunities for Indian children (college scholarships, tribal colleges on reservations, adult education, and avenues for greater involvement of Indian administrators, teachers, and parents through Indian-controlled schools). Additionally, bilingual education programs developed educational practices for incorporating native language and cultural instruction into Indian classrooms (Crawford 1987). Despite general support for these policy changes in Indian education, their implementation frequently met with resistance from those most invested in assimilation of Indian students (Szasz 1974). Thus, the types of schooling found in Indian communities include a variety of educational settings and approaches: Bureau of Indian Affairs (BIA) and tribally controlled schools, public schools, Catholic and other private schools, and alternative Indian schools.

Current variation in American Indian schooling, especially on reservations, has important consequences for educational attainment. For reservation populations, which still experience the legacy of the special status of American Indians in all facets of their lives, it is important to consider the range of school experiences that contribute to diverse school outcomes.

Summary

The information presented above provides a brief overview of research comparing the educational attainment of American Indians to other racial and ethnic groups. For more than a hundred years, federal policies have implemented a variety of approaches to "assist" Indian people in assimilating into the American social system, especially education programs. Yet ethnic group comparisons show that while American Indian adults have generally reached parity with Whites and African Americans in terms of high school completion, there are persistently high dropout rates among high school–age students. Differences in educational attainment are related to age as well as reservation/rural and urban residence.

Despite differences within the Indian population and between Indians and other groups, very little recent research has systematically addressed the sources of either Indian/non-Indian differences in high school completion or the bases for intragroup differences among American Indian high school students. A particularly interesting phenomenon that has yet to be addressed is the recent decline in high school completion among younger cohorts of American Indian students. While the school attainment of previous generations of Indian students was below that of Whites, school completion increased with each age group, resulting in higher overall adult education levels today. In contrast, the data presented above show that the recent Indian high school dropout rate is both higher than that of White students in the same cohort and higher than previous cohorts of Indians, thus reversing the previous pattern.

Understanding why high school dropout rates increased through the 1980s and into the 1990s requires looking more closely at the processes affecting a particular population of American Indian students. Holding one structural source of differentiation constant—reservation location—allows examination of other social and cultural influences on educational outcomes. This allows for investigating the following general research questions: What are the sources of educational stratification and the processes affecting school completion rates for rural American Indians? Are these different from processes affecting other ethnic groups? What processes differentiate rural Indian students from other rural students? Additionally, what are the processes that produce intragroup differences within a particular population of Indian students?

A Case Study of American Indian High School Completion

The first and central issue of this research is high school completion among rural American Indian students. To address this issue, this research examines social and cultural processes affecting the schooling of a specific rural population located on and around the Northern Cheyenne reservation in southeastern Montana. Specific questions to be addressed include: What are the cultural and social sources of differences in Cheyenne students' school outcomes? How do individual and family characteristics, school contexts, and school experiences affect students' educational performance and completion? This study extends previous work on the effects of type of school attended (public or private), an important influence on school completion identified by recent education research. It also adds new insights about the nature and effects of students' cultural resources, their families, and their communities on schooling.

A second objective involves comparing the school completion patterns of Indian and White students who attend one of the schools serving the Northern Cheyenne reservation. Comparing these two groups will highlight differences and similarities in the processes affecting their school outcomes.

An Ecological Approach to the Study of Minority Schooling

The approach taken in this study identifies multiple sources and levels of influence (micro and macro) on minority school outcomes; consequently, it is more ecological than earlier approaches that focus on either individual traits or contextual factors for understanding inequalities in education. Specifically, relevant social structures, locales, cultural contexts, processes, and group histories, as well as individual attributes and actions, are important influences on school completion. In the sections that follow I outline the major ideas drawn from several sociological literatures that inform the ecological perspective.

My approach builds on the recent work of scholars who clarify the relationship of cultural resources, contextual factors, and social processes to individual traits and actions for schooling outcomes. For example, in his comparison of individual-oriented, human capital and status attainment approaches with context-oriented, conflict/cultural capital perspectives, Farkas (1996) concludes that the views typically associated with this polarity are inadequate when each is considered alone. His synthesis provides, on the one hand, a more contextual (and realistic) view of the lower educational "investment" by poor and minority group members (a shortcoming of the human capital emphasis) while, on the other hand, it assesses the levels and types of skills developed through education (elements that contextual views tend to disregard) (1996, 10). In this view, cultural resources (i.e., skills, habits, and styles), formed at young ages and essentially without conscious intent, are central to educational stratification (Farkas 1996, 11–12). This view suggests a greater focus on the cultural resources and skill development of Indian students.

Starting from the need for synthesis, my approach begins with the "Wisconsin model" of status attainment, or human capital development model, and incorporates a range of contextual factors relevant to the study of minority schooling. Initially, the status attainment approach compared the effects on schooling and occupational outcomes of individual-level traits, such as ascribed statuses and socioeconomic background traits. Although subsequent researchers added social psychological and other intervening variables, this research has consistently found that measures of ability remain among the best predictors of students' academic attainment and school completion (Rumberger 1987). However, ability measures continue to be highly correlated with the social class and race or ethnicity of the student (Brint 1998). Thus, critics who point to the narrow focus on "atomistic individuals" of this approach recommend much greater attention to students' social and educational contexts (Apple and Weis 1986).

To address these problems, my approach draws on the concept of social capital to represent important social relations and processes within social class and cultural groups that affect human capital formation and status attainment. Social capital is the aggregate of actual or potential "social connections" or other resources available to members of a durable network of relationships. Thus, it includes the network of parents, family, and community members who provide practical and moral support for schooling to students (Coleman 1988). Because access to and availability of social capital are critical elements of socializing students (Furstenberg and Hughes 1995), deficiencies in social capital among minority students may contribute to failure and dropping out (Coleman and Hoffer 1987).

Although difficult to incorporate into human capital and status attainment models, the analysis of cultural capital is also important for explaining the role of cultural resources in stratification. Central to this approach is the idea that student ability levels are strongly affected by family members' investments of time and class resources in the socialization of their children (Bourdieu 1979). Thus, cultural capital, which encompasses the amount of schooling as well as specific attitudes, preferences, and behaviors characterizing social groups, is embodied capital that may be converted into other forms of capital, and it represents a hidden form of the transmission of capital from one generation to another. For example, upper- and middle-class parents use their human capital and cultural resources to support their children's educational achievement and to provide access to the specific credentials required for upper- and middle-class positions (Bourdieu 1986) and a broad range of social and cultural settings (Erickson 1996). In contrast, lower-income groups are seen as less effective in socializing their children than affluent groups because they have little access to socially powerful networks and do not instill the attitudes or provide the range of relevant experiences necessary to help their children become upwardly mobile. Gambetta's (1987) research supports this view of the importance of economic assets and social class lifestyles for students' educational aspirations and achievement. Specifically, his findings show that students of different classes evaluate their school performance, labor market opportunities, and expected benefits and use their assessments to form divergent life plans and preferences. Thus, the concept of cultural capital is useful for clarifying the processes by which social class values and interests affect school outcomes (Bourdieu 1993).

While early research in the critical theory tradition proposed direct linkages between social class and schooling outcomes (Bowles and Gintis 1976), other research emphasizes cultural difference—how the distance between ethnic students' cultures (in particular, the cultural processes for establishing social status) and the school's culture affects their social integration into the school (Bourdieu and Passeron 1977). The latter approach suggests that if minority and poor parents' cultural practices are seen as less relevant and holding less economic value, their children will be at a disadvantage (Snipp et al. 1993). This view is particularly useful for understanding the effects of minority cultural practices that diverge sharply from the standards of modern Western culture. Thus, in the approach for this study I have moved the analysis of cultural practices of schools and communities to the foreground, focusing on the "negotiated" informal and implicit social rules and meanings that actors use (Apple and Weis 1986).

The concept of cultural discontinuity unites elements of critical theory and cultural difference theory by emphasizing how both cultural resources and structural factors influence American Indian school outcomes (St. Germaine 1995). This view suggests that the clash of native cultures with the school's majority culture and the student perception of restricted opportunities (Reyhner 1992a; Tierney 1992) leads Indian students to neglect school requirements and pursue alternatives (including failure) to preserve their culture of origin. Teachers' misinterpretation of students' language and behaviors and communication of lower expectations for minority student performance are central elements in this process (Hurn 1993; Fine 1991; Powers et al. 2003). In his analysis of these approaches

CHAPTER ONE

to minority schoolings, McLaughlin (1994) concludes that an emphasis on the power relations in schools is essential for explaining minority students' school failure and creating meaningful changes in schooling.

Also useful for my approach are studies that clarify how the political and social dynamics in a specific cultural context affect schooling. Mary Brinton's (1993) comparative research on human capital development systems examines the normative aspects of human capital formation and school completion processes by incorporating the cultural values and practices of the students' family, school, and community. In her analysis of Japanese and American educational achievement, Brinton (1988) identifies the key "actors"—students, parents, school authorities, and employers—who influence school outcomes through their resources, interests, and value orientations. Specifically, actors' support for particular cultural norms, such as gender roles, the timing of marriage, family responsibilities, and work roles, as well as their access to the opportunity structure, shapes the schooling decisions and trajectories of students. Epstein's (1990) work also supports the need to empirically examine how relevant social groups—family, peer, and school—affect schooling.

Research on the cultural resources of status groups adds an important dimension to my approach by suggesting that minority ethnic groups have particular values, social relations, cultural practices, and meanings that are autonomous from (or have unique relationships to) the dominant culture of American, urban, middle-class society (Hall 1992). These groups provide to students particular views of the value of knowledge (obtained in formal schooling) and school participation, which Bowles and Gintis (2002) suggest may be disadvantageous to students to the extent that they do not lead to success in the dominant system.

However, recent research on immigrants (Portes and Sensenbrenner 1993; Fernandez-Kelly and Schauffler 1996) offers insights into how unique social mechanisms operating in these communities can support schooling outcomes. These include value orientations, reciprocal exchanges, bounded group solidarity, and enforceable community-trust relations. While these authors focus on the social and cultural dynamics of ethnic immigrant (voluntary minority) communities, for my study, it is useful to consider how they might apply to other (involuntary) minority communities. Specifically, experiences with discrimination and prejudice, the networks of community relations, and the levels of unique and high-quality resources that minority communities command are likely to be salient factors shaping social capital resources in American Indian communities. Additionally, identification with the community, the ability to exit their community or access resources outside it, and the ability to obtain benefits within their community are especially likely to affect reservation communities—unique American Indian "ethnic enclaves." These ideas extend the framework for this study by specifying the influences of social structures and social and cultural capital located within specific groups. They also build on Coleman's (1988) work on the effects of different levels of social capital and relations within families, communities, and different types of schools—public and private (Coleman and Hoffer 1987).

Other authors provide useful concepts for understanding how ethnic community circumstances, such as isolation, opportunity structures, and organization, affect schooling. Wacquant and Wilson (1989), for example, demonstrate that the social isolation of Black ghetto residents at the level of the household, social network, and neighborhood impedes their access to opportunities for improving economic circumstances. Their findings indicate that despite the efforts of some adults to support educational achievement, the isolation experienced at the three levels identified may be overwhelmingly detrimental to educational achievement. Schools located in these poor communities have little effect on changing or enhancing the opportunities and attainment of the poorest Black students. In recent efforts to test this contextual perspective, Elliott et al. (1996) confirm that neighborhood disadvantages are important factors in understanding adolescent behaviors. Features of social organization, such as informal control, affect neighborhood rates of adolescent pro-social competence, appropriate friendships, and problem behaviors. Sampson's work (1998) reminds us that the concept of social capital includes dimensions of nurturing (which exist as potential elements of social relations) and networks that must be activated to affect achievement.

Whereas much of the research on education in the last few decades has addressed the effects of urban neighborhoods on students, DeYoung (1987) suggests that there are very good reasons for the resurgence of interest in rural communities and schools. One of these is related to the benefits that "small" schools can bring to the students, especially community support, higher teacher expectations, and rapport. In fact, small rural schools may test and demonstrate models for "effective schools." On the other hand, a serious issue for rural education is the inequality of educational and labor market opportunities for ethnic groups (Hobbs 1995; DeYoung 1987).

While these authors have specified the social and cultural processes within racial or ethnic communities, others focus on the social structural barriers that shape minority opportunities. For example, Ogbu (1988) suggests that central to the study of minority schooling outcomes is recognizing the effects of forced assimilation and the specific types of isolation Blauner (1972) described for colonized or castelike ethnic minorities. This approach focuses on minority student responses that may involve internalizing the dominant group's rejection (Lamont and Lareau 1988), engaging in conflicts with representatives of the dominant group, and developing ambivalent identities and oppositional cultural frames of reference. Specifically, these authors point to the need to understand how such structural conditions affect both students and the school setting.

To better conceptualize school-community dynamics, Erickson (1987) synthesizes communications and labor market explanations with the implications of resistance theory. His view suggests that while crucial elements of relations between students and teachers are trust, legitimacy, and interests, important messages about social relations outside the school establish boundaries between cultural, class, and gender groups. However, the pedagogical process determines whether or how cultural (or racial), class, and gender differences become meaningful in school. Thus, a more complete explanation of school failure or success involves addressing how cultural and structural processes intersect in the school setting. Wehlage, Lipman, and Smith (1989) also assert that students' school membership is affected by their school adjustment, academic performance, and perceived social involvement or isolation, which, in turn, influences investment in school-related success. However, Mickelson's (1990) work on the "attitude-achievement" paradox among Black adolescents indicates that despite supportive attitudes toward schooling held by lower-class Black parents and adolescents, these attitudes do not necessarily accompany concrete behaviors related to school success.

The ecological approach for this study incorporates several aspects of community and social structures that provide important influences on schooling: rural location, cultural orientations to schooling, social organization of the community, relations between the school and community, and community members' agreement with school goals and practices. The meaning of schooling and educational attainment to the ethnic group members must be identified and related to relevant social and cultural processes, such as the specific processes by which children are socialized, the roles of parents and other adults, and the types and levels of social control and sanctions provided by the ethnic community. Values, expectations, and practices associated with schooling must be understood in relation to other important institutions such as the family and the economy. Moreover, how education practices and outcomes relate to acquiring social status within the ethnic group must be determined in order to understand the implications of education for participation in community social institutions. Finally, structural features of the community and surrounding area, such as labor market opportunities and the degree of social isolation, influence family and community support for education and participation in schooling. Thus, the perspective used here identifies multiple types and levels of influences—family, community, and social structural—as well as the salience of each type or level of influence operating in particular school and community contexts.

Also important are school context influences such as the size and types of schools, school policies toward minority students, pedagogical practices, curricular organization, and assignment processes. Additionally, identifying school organizational features, sources of control of the educational process, and the ideologies of key actors helps to determine how ethnic community members' orientations fit school practices. Where school orientations differ substantially from those of the minority group, the intersection of these divergent views has special implications for educational outcomes. For example, the meanings given to schooling may range from positive to negative and lead to acceptance, adaptation, or rejection, all of which may directly affect students' school performance and attainment, which, in turn, will then influence their participation in important social institutions of the community and society. Thus, an important benefit of the approach taken in this study is the ability to trace the influences at each of the levels identified and assess their relative impact on school outcomes.

CHAPTER ONE

The Importance of Integrating Quantitative with Qualitative Data

Accomplishing my research objectives involves two approaches: the use of quantitative methods as well as ethnography. The first is necessary for analyzing individual-level student data, while the second provides qualitative data required for exploring relevant patterns in student experiences and the social and cultural structures associated with school, family, and community life. Together these two approaches identify much more about the multiple influences on dropping out of school than either approach alone. Reasons for combining these approaches are related to critiques of two sociological research traditions. The first involves a critique of the status attainment or "achievement" tradition in which individuals are the unit of analysis for analyzing models of schooling outcomes. Such research, emphasizing social-psychological influences, background characteristics, and school effects, has been criticized for not fully incorporating social and cultural dynamics and their effects. The second debate is related to the attribution of status differences among various groups to structural and historical processes. An important criticism is that the actions of individual actors are not sufficiently accounted for by the focus on macro-level processes.

This research both utilizes and critiques the "achievement" approach by identifying the types of information that it does and does not contribute to an understanding of dropout behavior among American Indian students. To address the shortcomings and difficulties in interpreting school outcome models, this research also incorporates several types of contextual data concerning relevant social and cultural processes. Such information contributes insights into the multiple influences on students as they live and make decisions in the ever-changing and "contested" arenas of the school, family, and reservation community. I use these two approaches not to force an adjudication between the two but rather to form a more comprehensive analysis of the problem.

This strategy follows precedents established by scholarship developing the "embeddedness" paradigm (e.g., Granovetter 1985; Mingione 1991) for the study of economic status, development, and poverty. Other scholars have focused on the cultural resources of minority students and their families in the study of human capital formation and stratification (e.g., Farkas 1996; Hall 1992). For this study, the embeddedness approach is useful in specifying how American Indian populations have developed unique social and cultural adaptations to their changing political and economic conditions. Specifically, this approach highlights ways in which social relationships among Native Americans affect the distribution of opportunities and resources to their community, and how these relationships and macro-structural forces intersect to influence schooling. It explores the concept of *native capital* as a means for representing how local cultural practices mediate these social processes.

The first approach involves a quantitative analysis of data for three cohorts of students (1987–1989) attending three high schools—public, private Catholic, and tribally controlled—on and near the Northern Cheyenne reservation. Models of the school completion process identify the effects of specific influences, using data on student characteristics, family background, school type, school experiences, and performance. A comparative analysis then identifies differences in the relative importance and effects of independent variables for Indian and White students attending one of the three schools.

These analyses are interpreted with qualitative data collected for the case study population through extensive participant observation and interviews as well as from historical and other data sources. The second approach, therefore, provides relevant information on the cultural, social, political, and economic processes affecting the schooling of reservation students that is essential for interpreting the patterns identified in the schooling models.

The Northern Cheyenne Case

The Northern Cheyenne reservation in southeastern Montana provides a good setting for this case study for three reasons. First, information at the time of the study suggested a severe dropout problem among Indian students in this population. A report presented to the Northern Cheyenne Education Commission provided evidence that 183 (37.9%) of 483 high school–age Northern Cheyenne tribal members living on the reservation were not in school as of October 1986 (Bryan and Yellowtail 1985). Additionally, a 1985 survey designed to ascertain residents' views of the educational systems serving Northern Cheyenne reservation children found that the majority of respondents agreed there was a problem with "student dropout" (67%) and "student attendance" in the local schools (74%).

CHAPTER ONE

To put this information into perspective we can compare the dropout rates of different age groups of Indians on the Northern Cheyenne reservation with Indians nationally. Similar to the national findings, results of the 1989 Northern Cheyenne Educational Census show that the rate of high school completion is declining among recent generations of Indian reservation residents: the graduation rate of adults ages 25–44 is 80%; for adults ages 19–24 it is 64%; and for the 1987–1989 high school cohorts, the graduation rate is about 55%.

Additional support for this research population concerns its representativeness of Montana reservations on several social indicators. For example, the Northern Cheyenne reservation had a substantial percentage of persons and families below the poverty level in 1990, with 48% of adults and 44% of families living in poverty. The median income of both households and families as well as per capita income fell in the middle of the range for the seven Montana reservations. An unemployment rate of 50% placed the Northern Cheyenne reservation in between the highest rate (Rocky Boy reservation at 66%) and the lowest rate (Flathead reservation at 20%) (Montana 1994).

Like those of other reservations, the communities within the Northern Cheyenne reservation vary in several important ways: opportunity structure, human capital characteristics, how residents interact and participate in community and reservation social life, and the extent to which residents speak Cheyenne and practice traditional cultural activities. For example, in 1989, the Busby community had a somewhat higher proportion of adults with secondary education credentials than Ashland or Lame Deer, while Lame Deer had a higher rate of unemployment. Busby also had a higher percentage of Cheyenne speakers than either Ashland or Lame Deer (Ward and Wilson 1989). These variations represent different social and cultural environments where students learn the meaning and value of schooling.

Finally, the high level of interest of Northern Cheyenne educators in understanding the dropout problem provided the opportunity for this research. Funding from the Department of Education's Office of Educational Research and Improvement (1988–1989), and access to the schools serving the Northern Cheyenne reservation and surrounding area and the communities associated with these schools, permitted an in-depth study of high school completion in this rural population.

Summary

Although this project takes as its point of departure the "Wisconsin model" of status attainment, it goes beyond the model's traditional parameters—adding qualitative data for school and community contexts—to explain high school completion among American Indian students. Such an approach not only adds structural dimensions to a statistical model of school completion, but it also examines intragroup variation and stratification by focusing on the effects of the social and cultural features of local reservation society. It addresses the criticism of "omitted variables" for human capital and contextual explanations. The use of both quantitative and qualitative methods for this case study is intended to provide new insights for developing theoretically and empirically sound explanations of the processes that differentiate American Indian students that may prove useful for the analysis of other cultural and racial groups as well. The concept of *native capital* is developed to facilitate understanding of how social and cultural practices mediate the effects of macro-structural forces on high school completion.

CHAPTER TWO
CONTRIBUTIONS OF SCHOOLING AND COMMUNITY RESEARCH TO AN ECOLOGICAL APPROACH TO THE STUDY OF SCHOOL OUTCOMES

The following review of relevant schooling and community research will further explore and extend the approach for this study of Northern Cheyenne schooling. The discussion will identify factors and processes that differentiate minority schooling, particularly of American Indians, and their schooling decisions. Lines of inquiry reviewed below include student and family characteristics and resources, school experiences, and school and community contexts and relations. This review of empirical research on ethnic minority school attainment and completion, and Indian education studies in particular, where appropriate, will reveal deficiencies in the literature that this study will address.

A central feature of this chapter is the development of a more comprehensive conceptual framework for understanding the schooling outcomes of American Indian students as shaped by the multiple social groups and cultural processes in which they are located—the "nested structures" relevant to schooling (Powers et al. 2003). This approach builds on the synthesis of perspectives discussed in chapter 1 by incorporating research that addresses the specific processes that stratify American Indian educational outcomes. The specific statements of expected findings accompanying the proposed conceptual framework draw on a wide variety of theoretical and empirical materials and delineate two areas for investigation: the processes of American Indian educational completion and the comparison of Indian and non-Indian school completion. Thus, the research statements directly correspond to the research objectives outlined in chapter 1. Figure 2.1 summarizes the influences on school outcomes.

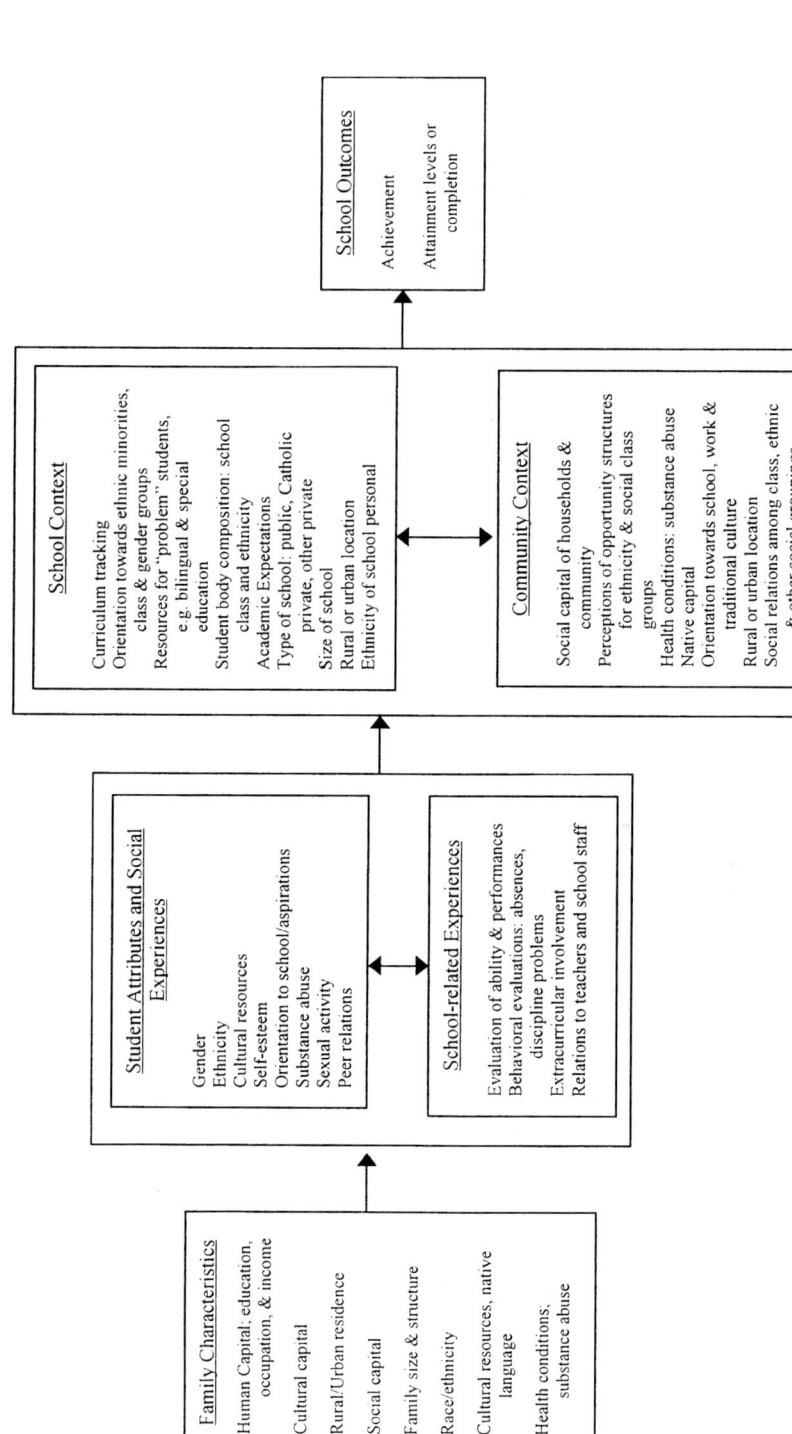

Figure 2.1. Overview of Influences on School Outcomes

CHAPTER TWO

A note of explanation is in order concerning this strategy. The combination of quantitative and ethnographic approaches in this study makes necessary the presentation of general statements rather than specific hypotheses. While quantitative analyses are typically preceded by a review of selected variables that are to be included in the evaluation of models, in this case a somewhat more comprehensive review of the influences on relevant school outcomes is required. The qualitative data included in the case study point to important areas of the family, school, and community contexts that are not measured at the individual level or included in the statistical tests. For example, descriptive statistics and ethnographic information indicate the relevance of the following contextual areas: school climates, resources, and orientations in the three types of schools; student and parent relations to the schools; differences in school experiences of graduates and dropouts; and the effects on students of the local social structures, cultural practices, and family and community relations. Therefore, statements about expected findings take into account not just the types of variables for which there are individual-level student data, but also the full range of variables that are meaningful for this case study.

The Role of Individual Attributes and Actions

Influences on Individual Educational Attainment and Completion

Education research has identified a number of individual-level influences on students' decisions to stay in school through graduation or leave school early. Although this type of research focuses on individual students' attributes, attitudes, social relations, and behaviors, it typically includes a number of other variables in order to assess their relative influence. Consequently, this review also will identify how individual attributes, attitudes, and behaviors relate to other variables often analyzed.

In addition to the significance of socioeconomic status and minority group membership for schooling outcomes (Brint 1998) discussed previously in chapter 1, gender is another student attribute identified as important to schooling. Analyses of gender differences in school performance, however, show somewhat mixed results. While studies indicate that girls often have higher grades in school than boys, standardized test data have shown girls to have lower levels of performance in math and science, although these gaps have narrowed somewhat in recent years (deMarrais and

LeCompte 1995). Other studies suggest that problems leading to dropping out may be more prevalent among ethnic minority girls than boys (Velez 1989; Jordan, Lara, and McPartland 1996). Family-related problems were the reasons given most frequently by females, while alienation and suspension were the primary reasons cited among male students. Additionally, many dropouts leave school to get married or because of pregnancy (Ekstrom et al. 1986; Wehlage and Rutter 1986; Rumberger 1983).

Students' decisions to leave school typically are based on economic and personal reasons (Wagenaar 1987). Many dropouts have reported that they left school because they wanted to or felt that they had to in order to help their families financially. Personal reasons for dropping out are related to students' lower levels of self-esteem and having less control over their lives than other students. Dropouts also have poor attitudes about school and low educational and occupational aspirations, and they are often less involved in school activities (Wagenaar 1987). Conversely, higher academic orientation as well as involvement leads to school success for both White and minority students. Other attitudinal traits of dropouts include their values concerning autonomy, such as having their own money; work; and involvement with the local community (Ekstrom et al. 1986).

Among the most relevant findings of education research are the effects of peer relations on student attitudes and decisions about schooling. This research shows that students tend to have similarities with their friends, for both social background and selection reasons, which include educational aspirations. Even though the influence of friends, particularly as academic resources, changes during schooling, it has been found repeatedly to be important for high school performance (Kerckhoff 1986; Crosnoe, Cavanagh, and Elder 2003). Research by Ekstrom et al. (1986), Jones (1977), and Quay and Allen (1982) shows that dropouts are more alienated than stayers and are more likely to have friends who are alienated as well. The effects of encouragement from peers, parents, and teachers to attend college, however, have been shown to vary by school performance level and with student aspirations, although the reciprocal effects of these influences are unclear (Bidwell and Friedkin 1988).

School performance is central to the process of school completion (Rumberger 1987, 1995; Roderick 1993). A profile of the characteristics and conditions associated with dropouts typically includes poor performance levels, low verbal ability, an external locus of control, less home support for education, low educational aspirations by the student's mother, and less parental involvement in selecting a high school curriculum. Such traits are thought to indicate lack of integration by the student and his or her family into the school (Ekstrom et al. 1986). In contrast, Dumais (2002) found that both boys' and girls' school performance benefited from higher aspirations for occupational achievement. In fact, this influence was just as important as their socioeconomic status.

Not only is language proficiency an important cultural variable, but it is particularly relevant to school performance and completion among language minority students. For example, speaking a language other than English (Steinberg, Blinde, and Chan 1984) has been found to play a crucial part in the educational attainment process: language provides the medium for meaningful learning and also contributes to the underlying basis for participation in schooling (Giddens 1979; Sahlins 1976).

Alcohol or drug consumption and abuse also contribute to higher rates of "failure" or dropping out among high school students. Mensch and Kandel's (1988) research on the influence of drug involvement on dropping out of high school found that dropouts showed significantly higher rates of use of all classes of drugs than did other students. In particular, they found that use of any drug at any age increases the propensity for dropping out, but the earlier the students initiate their drug use, the greater the likelihood of leaving school without a diploma.

Mensch and Kandel's (1988) findings also show the strong, negative impact of early sexual activity and pregnancy on school completion. Their data suggest that adolescent participation in a variety of deviant activities because they oppose societal or age-related norms greatly increases the risk of dropping out of school. Additionally, participation in one deviant activity increases the propensity of participating in others and reduces the commitment to conventional institutions, for example, schools.

Although these studies pertain to individual attributes, attitudes, and behaviors, they also point to the important effects of socially defined roles, relations, and structures on students' school experiences. Such studies indicate that students' relations to peers and adults within the school environment, as well as their interaction within communities and social networks outside school, have important influences on individual school performance, a factor crucial in decisions to stay in or leave school. What are less clear are the specific mechanisms by which social relations and experiences shape students' attitudes and orientations toward school performance and completion. As some critics have suggested (e.g., Tierney 1992), a research emphasis on individual rather than social aspects of schooling has made the school a "black box" in much of education research.

Influences on American Indian Achievement and School Completion

Empirical findings for American Indian school achievement and attainment generally parallel the general patterns discussed in the previous section. For example, analyses of Indian students' academic achievement from the Title IV Indian Education program evaluation (Development Associates 1983) provide information concerning the patterns of student performance in public schools over a forty-year period. The results show that progress has been irregular. The favorable academic achievement levels of the 1950s deteriorated in the 1960s and 1970s, but the indicators for the 1980s again approach those of the 1950s. Although the reasons for the apparent drop and upsurge in achievement scores are not clear, the data show that despite increases, achievement scores overall remain well below national norms.

Several studies reviewed by Crawford (1987) suggest that the lack of English skills among American Indian students negatively affects their academic achievement. Other studies similarly find that traditional cultural affiliation, often indicated by native language fluency, affects school performance (Backes 1993; Dodd and Nelson 1989; Kroskrity 1986; Scott 1986; Greenbaum 1985; Philips 1983). James et al. (1995) argue that the remnants of native grammatical syntax and styles tend to limit English fluency even among students who do not speak their tribal language well. Based on her review of studies of learning styles, however, Hale (2002, 90) concludes that "Native American students reflect all possible modes of learning. What does need to be remembered is that these learning modalities are mediated by a particular cultural orientation. Cultural orientation, especially in terms of language, continues to influence the learning and perceptions of Native American students."

Research on American Indian populations also has identified individual characteristics important for understanding the school completion of Indian students. Examining dropout behavior, authors of the 1983 report of the evaluation of Title IV, Part A, Indian Education Projects, LaFromboise and Rudes (1981), found that earlier studies showed the characteristics of Indian dropouts to be similar to those of non-Indian dropouts, although there appeared to be an equal prevalence among Indian males and females. The typical profile included the following characteristics: 17.5 years of age with 6.4 siblings (one previously a dropout), single rather than married, between the tenth and eleventh grades, arrested one or more times, and never contacted or helped by a social service agency after leaving school (Davids 1963; Scott 1967). Later characterizations of dropouts showed that they were more likely to come from reservations, rural areas, and urban inner cities (Snipp 1989) and that females were more likely than males to drop out (47% vs. 27%) (Frase 1989). Bowker (1992) found a similar pattern among Northern Plains Indians. Recent research by Alberta Gloria and Sharon Robinson Kurpius (2001) and Ness (2002) on school persistence among American Indian college students provides evidence for the importance of high self-esteem as well as strong social support and sense of self-efficacy. Achievement motivation is also important for Native American students (McInerney and Swisher 1995), which Benson's (1996) research suggests may be problematic among some native youth.

Substance abuse has been found to be a common behavior among Indian youth and has specific implications for their success in school. Studies of Indian adolescents (Takie, Lynch, and Charleston 1988) and adults (May 1996) have found that there is considerable variation among Indian communities in reported drinking behaviors. Among youth, the degree of attachment to either parents or friends and the extent of drinking in these two groups are directly related to drinking behaviors among both teenagers and their younger siblings. A third study (National Institute on Drug Abuse 1987) found that substance abuse among Indian youth occurs at levels that are substantially higher than among non-Indian youth, and that such behavior is highly correlated with school failure as well as dropping out of high school. Takie, Lynch, and Charleston (1988) indicate that Indian youth do not necessarily view drinking behavior positively. In fact, the majority of adolescent drinkers in their study assessed drinking negatively for both youth and adults. The authors' explanation points to contradictory norms attached to drinking: since drinking is legally restricted for youth, it is an "adult" behavior that confers higher status on those youth who participate. In fact, societal norms attached to adult independence and drinking as well as peer pressures may provide youth with the incentive to drink. In a recent study of minority students that included students of all academic performance levels, Beauvais et al. (1996) found that dropouts were the group most frequently involved with drugs.

In summary, research on Indian student characteristics shows, first, that motivation and performance affect dropout behavior in similar ways in Indian and non-Indian student populations. Other studies show the importance of cultural orientations to learning, location in traditional, rural, or urban communities, and peer and adult influences related to behaviors and experiences that either detract from schooling or that support school achievement and completion. However, most studies in this line of inquiry have not established clear links between students' school performance and the social and cultural contexts in which attitudes toward learning and school are formed. Research identifying Indian students' attitudes toward and experiences with schooling, as well as relations to significant others, comes closest to clarifying the social and cultural processes relevant to school outcomes. An important question for this research concerns how individual characteristics, social relationships, and cultural experiences, particularly language proficiency, differentiate Indian schooling outcomes.

Expected Research Findings

American Indian students' sociocultural characteristics are expected to have important effects on their orientations to and involvement with school. In particular, poor skills in the language of instruction contribute to lower performance levels, thus indirectly affecting school completion; students with language problems may not fully understand academic expectations, which hinders their participation in class and completion of assignments. Gender will also have an important effect on school completion: girls will be more likely to have successful school performance and will also be more likely to drop out of school. Other important influences on school completion include peer relations, attitudes, substance abuse, and conflict with authorities.

Expected research findings are summarized in the following statements:

1. Understanding or speaking their tribal language will negatively affect students' school performance and indirectly increase the chances of dropping out.

2. Being female will increase school performance and increase the chances of dropping out.

3. Higher levels of student contact with or conflict with authorities as well as substance abuse will increase the chances of dropping out. (See figure 2.1.)

The Effects of Family Characteristics

Family Influences on Ethnic Minority School Outcomes

Several areas of research provide insights into the effects of family background characteristics on ethnic students' school outcomes: status attainment, socialization within the family, and educational stratification by social class and race. First, research in the status attainment tradition has shown the effects of ascribed compared to achieved characteristics of students and their families (Apple and Weis 1986). Additionally, research in this tradition has addressed questions related to the intergenerational transmission of social class.

Several exogenous variables have been found by status attainment research to have a direct bearing on educational as well as occupational outcomes of children: father's and mother's educational attainment; father's and mother's occupation and race/ethnicity; and family size, income, and assets (Rumberger 1987; Hauser, Tsai, and Sewell 1983; Jencks, Crouse, and Mueser 1983). In spite of evidence that educational attainment gaps between ethnic groups have closed during recent history (Mare 1979, 1981), differentiation of educational attainment continues to be influenced by social class origins. For example, parents' socioeconomic status directly affects student educational and occupational aspirations (Hauser, Tsai, and Sewell 1983; Bidwell and Friedkin 1988). However, parents' education levels and aspirations for their children have the greatest effects on students' attainment, and these effects are seen not only at the end of their school "career" but at the elementary level as well (Alwin and Thornton 1984; Looker and Pineo 1983). Research by Cheng and Starks (2002) shows the importance of the effects of different kinds and levels of support from parents, extended family, friends, and teachers on minority student school aspirations.

Another important characteristic of the student's family is its structure. For example, children from single-parent families are more likely to exhibit signs of early disengagement from school and less likely to complete high school (Astone and McLanahan 1991). However, growing up in a stepparent family has similar negative effects on children's educational attainment.

Studies of social class and ethnic patterns of socialization of children help explain the effects of family background on schooling. These studies (Kerckhoff 1986; Kohn and Schooler 1969; Dornbusch et al. 1987; Rumberger 1987; Parcel and Dufur 2001) have focused on the form and content of interaction, communication skills, permissive versus authoritarian parenting styles, cultural and material aspects of the home, and experiences with education and occupations that are transmitted to the student. One of the best predictors of children's achievement levels, in fact, is the amount of reading materials in the home, a factor that is highly correlated with socioeconomic status (National Assessment of Educational Progress 1985). However, in recent research attempting to identify the specific mechanisms that produce such effects, Farkas (1996) found important mediating variables in the relationship between social class/racial background and reading ability as measured by standardized tests. The results show that basic cognitive performance measures explain most of the relationship between social class background and reading ability, and all of the relationship between Black minority status and reading ability (1996, 31). Thus, they provide direct empirical evidence for the importance of linguistic culture for lower-class and African American achievement levels in reading.

In studies concerning family influences on adolescent problem behaviors including dropping out, various types of stress on families (e.g., financial, emotional) have been found to negatively affect parenting behaviors, especially supervision of children (Barber 1992). In contrast, when parents (as well as other family and community members) actively support children's learning and are engaged with their schools, school performance tends to be higher (Epstein 1990; Furstenberg and Hughes 1995; Coleman 1988; Lareau 1989; Parcel and Dufur 2001). However, recent research found that parents of minority students in a remedial track initially showed higher levels of involvement in their children's schooling compared to parents of other students. Nevertheless, this involvement declined sharply over time, thus limiting the overall support students received from parents (Crosnoe 2001).

CHAPTER TWO

Although research on the role of social class resources, cultural capital in particular, addresses a significant social process relevant to students' school experiences, it is concerned only with social class distinctions; that is, it does not identify the nature or effects of family resources, support, and attitudes toward schooling that occur within other status or ethnic/cultural groups. It essentially reflects attempts to assess how closely students' family-based class resources match the practices and expectations of middle-class educators and school personnel. Thus, use of the concept of cultural capital for assessing the cultural resources of ethnic minority families is potentially very limiting.

The problem is illustrated by an approach developed for assessing parents' involvement in children's schooling. Among the five types of parent involvement identified by Epstein (1990), three of the types (home conditions that support schooling, direct parent involvement at the school, and parental monitoring of learning activities at home) involve activities based on middle-class, Anglo assumptions about parenting responsibilities, cultural knowledge of appropriate activities, and cultural norms regarding parent relations to schools and school personnel. Epstein's call for better research on "hard-to-reach" families, including language minorities, suggests that the relative effects on school outcomes of resources present in minority families, especially social relationships and parenting styles, have not been adequately examined. Furstenberg and Hughes (1995) also suggest the need for further research on how family social relations and resources affect students' academic success, behavior, and well-being (590).

As mentioned briefly in chapter 1, Ogbu's (1978, 1988) research emphasizes the influence of minority status on children's schooling. He asserts that limits on the level of participation of racial and ethnic minority parents in the local economy and labor market negatively affect their socioeconomic status as well as the educational and occupational experiences they can share with their children. Students belonging to "involuntary" minority racial and ethnic groups typically are less motivated and prepared for higher-status jobs often portrayed as closed to them. Additionally, the lower levels of family assets associated with lower socioeconomic status often mean the lack of resources available to finance higher education for children. Other research points to the limits on practical information that ethnic group members, especially students' parents and other family members, have about schooling (Mickelson 1990), occupations, jobs, and other means of access to economic opportunities (Kim 1981).

Minority perceptions of opportunity may lead to a variety of strategies for schooling. Although Ogbu found that "involuntary" minorities (e.g., Blacks, Mexican Americans, and American Indians) were most likely to develop oppositional attitudes, Foley's (1991) research indicates that working-class and middle-class Mexican American students develop higher achievement orientations and behaviors when they perceive support and labor market opportunities that reward their school credentials. Stanton-Salazar and Dornbusch (1995) found that unlike other Mexican American students, bilingual Mexican American students more successfully accessed school personnel (or others outside their homes who had needed resources) and had more trust in the schooling system.

Research on ethnic student achievement also addresses the cultural attributes of minority students and their families. As suggested previously, speaking a language different from that of teachers may present problems for communication and participation in classroom activities. Additionally, cultural practices of the family and ethnic group may have the effect of making students *appear* to have less ability than is really the case (Bowles and Gintis 1976; Collins 1977; Cicourel and Mehan 1985; Ogbu 1988). Alternatively, cultural values of an ethnic minority group may enhance the achievement of students. Hirshman and Wong's analysis of Asian students (1981) identified specific values that mediated the effects of structural variables such as parents' labor force participation and social status, suggesting that both structural and cultural factors are useful for explaining the higher educational attainment of Asian American students.

These studies indicate the value of considering a "sociocultural perspective" (Schmid 2001) that gives attention to both the social and cultural dimensions of minority family contributions to minority schooling experiences and stratification. Additionally, while comparative research identifies factors that distinguish ethnic groups, studies involving a single group often reveal meaningful bases for internal differentiation.

The Effects of Family Influences on American Indian School Outcomes

Although studies of Indian populations (such as those cited in chapter 1) have identified a range of factors contributing to the low status attainment of Indians overall, much of the research does not directly address the relationship between family characteristics and the educational outcomes of Indian students. Exceptions include Eberhard's (1989) research showing that family mobility and tribal affiliation affected dropout behavior among urban Indian high school students. In contrast, a study by Sack et al. (1987) examined family background variables and found that those most closely associated with children's school achievement included family structure, parents' education and employment history, degree of involvement in a social network, frequency of parental contact with the school, and level of parental interest in acculturation into the majority culture. These studies uphold earlier findings pointing to the importance of family stability (Brown 1973) and family size (LaFromboise and Rudes 1981) for school outcomes.

Research in reservation settings confirms that lack of parental encouragement and problems at home influence dropout behavior (Bowker 1992; Coladarci 1983; Platero et al. 1986; Giroux 1997). Recent qualitative studies also have found that dropouts often have problems at home that make school performance difficult (Davis, Anderson, and Jamal 2001; Kitchen, Velásquez, and Myers 2000). The lack of parental involvement, particularly in American Indian contexts, may be related to parents' discomfort with the educational system. It may also reflect some Indian parents' ambivalence toward formal schooling, or perhaps their own negative experiences with schooling; in particular, many adults of previous generations have experienced separation from family, harsh treatment, and forced assimilation at boarding schools (Szasz 1974). Finally, less parental involvement in school may represent a particular parenting style, typical of many American Indian communities, which includes protective guidance, but noninterference in adolescent decisions (Yellowbird and Snipp 1994; Bowker 1993). Importantly, Deyhle's (1991, 1995) research indicates that while traditional Navajo treatment of teenage children may differ from the public school approaches, especially in terms of the level of direct adult supervision, the cultural integrity that Navajo students experience in traditional families positively affects their school participation and success. This finding is supported by Coggins, Williams, and Radin's research (1997) on the effects of traditional Ojibwa parental values on school performance.

The concept of cultural discontinuity or "mismatch" (i.e., dissonance between the cultural background of Indian students and that of mainstream schools) has been central to Indian education studies of achievement and dropping out (e.g., Philips 1983; Reyhner 1992a). In contrast, several studies suggest that neither traditional orientations nor traditional cultural identities of students are strongly associated with school failure or dropping out (Brandt 1992; Deyhle 1992; James et al. 1995). Ledlow (1992) and Wood and Clay (1996) conclude that cultural discontinuity alone does not lead to poor performance; rather, its coexistence with structural barriers contributes to academic problems among American Indian students.

Other research findings that do not directly address educational achievement nevertheless have implications for the study of family background influences on students. In particular, studies indicate that such factors as poverty and poorer health conditions have important consequences for Indian students' school outcomes. Sandefur and Sakamoto (1987) examined two factors related to the high level of poverty among Indian families: structure and size. Their research shows that Indian households are significantly larger than Black and White households, have younger household heads, and are more likely than either Black or White households to be located in nonmetropolitan areas. Comparisons of the effects of household structure and size reveal that Indian household incomes suffer somewhat more from larger households. Additionally, while single mothers with children are the most likely of any household type to be below the poverty line, Indian couples with children constitute a larger proportion of the poor in this group.

Snipp's analysis of census data (1989) confirms the continuing use of non-English languages among American Indians. Although a large percentage of Indians are English speakers (70% of persons ages 11 to 20), 23% speak both English and their native language. Increasingly small percentages speak their native language exclusively. As with educational attainment, native language use is affected by residence and age: older people and rural residents are more likely to speak their native language. Indians living on reservations and in traditional communities are especially likely to speak their native language and to have limited English proficiency.

To summarize, studies of American Indian populations indicate that important social factors affect the social position and quality of life of students and their families in Indian communities. These include parents'

CHAPTER TWO

labor market participation, educational levels, rural/reservation or urban location, income levels, speaking a native language, and health conditions. Social characteristics of Indian parents and families have important implications for Indian students' socialization, achievement, and school completion. Important questions can be raised, however, about how family characteristics, interactions, and cultural orientations contribute to the differentiation of Indian students' school outcomes.

Expected Research Findings

In this research, primary focus is given to family background characteristics related to social status, in particular the levels of attachment of adults in the household to educational and economic institutions. Human capital characteristics of parents or adults in the home, specifically, education and employment status, are expected to affect students' school outcomes. Also significant for explaining Indian students' school completion is family structure, in particular, the presence of at least two adults in the household, and the integration of adults and nuclear family units into traditional social groups, such as extended families and communities.

Additionally, traditional cultural orientations of families and communities are expected to positively affect school outcomes because of cultural values that generally support the acquisition of knowledge and wisdom and, specifically, the development in children of learning skills important to family and community life. This is consistent with the perspective of Northern Cheyenne traditional leaders, such as Chief Dull Knife and more recently John Woodenlegs, who advocated for education for Cheyenne people, not for the purpose of assimilation (cultural replacement), but rather as a resource for survival in a world dominated by a different culture.

On the other hand, negative effects on students' school outcomes can be expected from parental attachments to the drug and alcohol subculture as well as poor school experiences, poverty, and unemployment. However, the specific social and cultural dynamics operating within Cheyenne families and communities and their relation to schooling remain to be clarified. (The effects of cultural orientations of adults will be discussed further in the last section of this chapter, concerning the interaction of multiple influences on students.)

Expected findings are summarized as follows:

4. Parents' high school completion will negatively influence dropping out.
5. Employment by at least one adult in the student's household will negatively affect dropping out.
6. Having only one adult in the student's household will increase the likelihood of dropping out.
7. Higher levels of parental involvement and support for schooling will decrease the chances of dropping out.
8. Higher levels of traditional cultural resources among adult family members will reduce students' chances of dropping out. (See figure 2.1.)

The Effects of Students' Experiences with Schooling

The Role of School Experiences in School Achievement and Completion

Students' experiences with schooling and their assessments of the punishments and rewards associated with the learning situation encountered in the school are particularly important influences on school outcomes. While some researchers have examined the effects of student involvement in school activities, other research has focused on students' evaluations of schooling. For example, Bidwell and Friedkin (1988) assert that certain aspects of the educational setting may provide for pressure, demands, and stress while others bring personal satisfaction and rewards. However, it is the ratio of perceived punishments to rewards that determines the student's self-confidence and motivation to continue with schooling. In this view, the choice to continue with schooling is strongly affected by two aspects of the classroom and the school: first, the student role is that of a novice who is subordinated to the expert teacher and, second, students are taught in groups in which their performance is submitted to public evaluation and invidious comparison with other students, which promotes competition. In such an environment, students' decisions about educational attainment become a function of "tolerance for education," that is, the ability to adapt to stresses induced by schooling (Bielby 1981). Additionally, Smerdon's (2002) research shows that students' sense of school membership, which in turn affects their school engagement and performance, is shaped by their treatment within the school. Participation in extracurricular activities, however, has been shown to mediate these effects and positively influence school performance and completion. Recent research also shows that the value of specific types of activities varies by school and community context; for example, sports participation has a different meaning in lower-class and minority schools than in middle-class schools (Guest and Schneider 2003).

In research concerned with school participation and behavior in school, school experiences have been identified as the best predictors of the decision to leave school or not (McDill, Natriello, and Pallas 1986). Highly correlated with dropping out generally is poor academic performance as measured by grades, test scores, and grade retention, as well as behavioral problems such as absenteeism, truancy, and discipline problems (Wehlage and Rutter 1986; Ekstrom et al. 1986). Numerous studies have indicated the higher incidence among both lower-class and ethnic minority students, especially Blacks, Latinos, and American Indians, of poor school experiences that contribute to dropping out (Wagenaar 1987; deMarrais and LeCompte 1995). (Possible reasons for such poor experiences will be discussed in the next section.) In comparative studies, minority groups have generally shown lower levels of performance as indicated by standardized tests, although some studies have shown social class to have more important effects on school performance outcomes than ethnicity (Wagenaar 1987; Coleman and Hoffer 1987).

Student responses to poor school experiences may include continued acceptance of schooling requirements, negotiation, or resistance (Valli 1983). John Ogbu's (1989, 197–200) research on involuntary minority students suggests a wider range of strategies for coping with school experiences: assimilation; focusing on individual success rather than racial identity; accommodation without assimilation; success in school as well as minority activities; setting upper-class goals; conformity to school demands but also navigating street culture; ambivalence; and rejection of school learning or "acting white." Akom's (2003) research with high school–age female Nation of Islam members, however, suggests the need for further elaboration of Ogbu's approach to include greater attention to strategies for high achievement among involuntary minorities that reject the oppositional attitude and redefine school success as supporting minority goals. Research by Fordham (1996) and Horvat and Lewis (2003) also demonstrates the diversity within involuntary minority groups with respect to orientations to success. Their findings reveal that students may "manage success" in ways that resist both the "acting white" label and lower expectations for minority student achievement.

The Role of School Experiences in American Indian School Achievement and Completion

American Indian research has focused on identification of "cultural differences"—not cultural deficit (Deyhle and Swisher 1997)—as important influences on Indian students' school experiences. In an attempt to understand more about the reasons for Indian students' poor performance, Dodd and Nelson (1989) identified several relevant types of obstacles to learning: problems with language and temporal orientation, and learned helplessness, which may be based in social or cultural processes rather than physical handicapping conditions. Additionally, differences between non-Indian and Indian students have been found in attitudes toward or commitment to success in school, discipline, orientation toward group versus individual learning processes, learning styles, and views of and responses to teachers' authority, all of which may be related to the degree of involvement in or attachment to native culture (Backes 1993; Kroskrity 1986; Scott 1986; Greenbaum 1985; Philips 1983; Fuchs and Havighurst 1972). Differences in orientation to school affect the learning process and may contribute to the development of poor academic skills; poor communication, listening, and memory skills; withdrawal; developmental lags in learning; and a broad range of learning disabilities (Dodd and Nelson 1989). However, research by Huffman (2001) and Whitbeck et al. (2001) indicates that traditional culture can positively affect school performance both at the early grades and in college. (This is discussed in more detail in later sections.)

Evaluations of Indian education nationally (Development Associates 1983) show that Indian dropouts demonstrate many of the same characteristics and motives as their non-Indian counterparts. Students are least likely to complete school if they have poor grades, poor attendance, and disciplinary problems (Swisher and Hoisch 1992; Eberhard 1989; Platero et al. 1986; Coladarci 1983). For example, in Brandt's study of Navajo students

(1992), absenteeism was strongly correlated with dropping out. According to Jordan, Lara, and McPartland (1996), students who continually experience problems at school or failure (e.g., suspensions, low grades) become detached from school and eventually drop out altogether.

Other influences on Indian students' school experiences include their view of the relevance of the curriculum (Szasz 1974; Coladarci 1983; Deyhle 1992) and the lack of reward for high school completion (Kleinfeld 1973). However, Indian education studies also show that Indian students' engagement with school and extracurricular activities enhances their performance and chances of graduation (Swisher and Hoisch 1992; Deyhle 1992; Coladarci 1983). LaFromboise and Rudes (1981) suggest that the types of schools Indian students attend should be examined for their influence on Indian students' school engagement, success, and graduation.

Expected Research Findings

Indian students' school experiences, such as attendance, extracurricular activities, and discipline problems, indicate their level of involvement with schooling and can be expected to affect their performance levels and school completion.

Expected research findings include:

9. Negative relations to or experiences with school, as indicated by suspensions, poor attendance, transfers to other schools, and conflicts with authorities, will increase the chances of dropping out.

10. Higher levels of school performance and participation in extracurricular activities will reduce the probability of dropping out. (See figure 2.1.)

The Effects of School Context

Contextual Influences on School Outcomes

A more in-depth examination of the role of schools in the socialization of students reveals crucial contextual contributions to schooling outcomes. In this line of research key influences include assessment of student ability, the form and content of curriculum, the type and organization of school settings, teaching approaches, and the school population and climate. Its focus on the organizational dimensions of learning within the school environment distinguishes the school context approach from the achievement tradition discussed above. However, Rosenbaum (1986) draws on human capital and structural theories of mobility as well as "signaling" theory to analyze the effects of schools on students' educational careers. In this view, an important element of the educational setting is the assessment of key "attainments," such as test scores, passing from one grade level to another, and so on, in order for movement to occur into positions available within the school. In this process of student performance, assessment, and movement, the "ability" of the individual is defined by school authorities. The cumulative effects of this signaling process determine the status conferred on the individual and the potential for mobility, both through the educational institution and subsequently in the job market. Consequently, how schools evaluate student ability and use these evaluations to form ability groups is paramount to student success.

This approach is especially useful for specifying a mechanism for ethnic stratification in the educational setting: assessing individual traits (e.g., "ability," cultural/ethnic characteristics, or age) as deviant from the optimal traits designated by the conventional wisdom and assessment tools in use. Hence, ethnic group members' routine allocation to lower ability groups (because they "don't measure up" to the typically used school criteria) takes on the appearance of fair evaluations of progress.

The effects of ability grouping have received a substantial amount of attention in education research. Many studies show that placement of students in ability groups is highly correlated with achievement levels. Research findings also show that differential treatment (on the basis of social class, race and ethnicity, and gender, especially) is a significant factor in student performance and attainment patterns as well as curriculum track placement (Cicourel and Mehan 1985; Van Fossen, Jones, and Spade 1987).

In research focused on the process of tracking by Gamoran and Mare (1989), both achievement and graduation differences were accounted for largely by students' previous achievement levels and socioeconomic status. The authors conclude that students would generally fare better if they were all assigned to the college track; that is, their achievement as well as their graduation rates would be higher. In essence, their research suggests that tracking reinforces students' initial achievement differences.

Another area of research addresses the effects of ability grouping based on learning disabilities, a "deficiency" often associated with minority status. According to studies including minority children for whom English is often a second language (e.g., American Indian and Latinos), minority children are typically overrepresented in special education classes (Dodd and Nelson 1989; O'Connell et al. 1987). In fact, data presented by O'Connell et al. (1987) show American Indians to compose the largest percentage of any ethnic group in the category of learning disabilities within a comprehensive classification of handicapping conditions. That there is a disproportionate number of ethnic minority and poor children with learning disabilities suggests to Carrier (1986) that the learning disability category provides for reproduction of class differences in less stigmatized ways than designations of retardation or physical handicaps.

Ethnographic research on language minorities provides some insight into the school processes that limit ethnic group access to educational resources and inhibit performance levels. For example, Cicourel and Mehan's research (1985) found that minority children frequently express "bicultural ambivalence," or shame for their native culture and hostility toward the new culture, which presents them with images about the inferior status of their native culture. In these situations educators can "empower" or "disable" language-minority children by the approach they take toward the use of native language and cultural materials in instruction (Crawford 1987).

Another relevant dimension of school organization concerns the effects of the composition of the student body. Research findings show that academic ability and social status distributions within the student body affect educational outcomes (Alexander and Eckland 1975). Other research, which is particularly relevant to the analysis of ethnic group attainment processes, has examined the effects of desegregated school climates. While some studies have found academic and social benefits for minority students that derive from attending desegregated schools (Braddock, Crain, and McPartland 1984), others have found that desegregation has not always led to social integration. Where such practices as tracking reinforce racial or cultural group differences, students often remain segregated (Wax 1980; Schofield 1982). Johnson, Crosnoe, and Elder (2001) show that minority students' school attachment and engagement benefit from their being in schools with larger proportions of other members of their own groups.

Looking at the context of the school even more broadly, others have identified aspects of the "climate" of the school as important to educational plans and academic performance; in these studies the most important aspects of school climate were the degrees of parental involvement and commitment to the school (Coleman 1961; McDill, Rigsby, and Meyers 1969). Public and private schools also have been found to provide different types of school climates and structures that affect school experiences and outcomes (Coleman and Hoffer 1987; Lee and Bryk 1988). (See discussion of school type in the next section.)

"Effective schools" literature suggests the importance for student achievement levels of such organizational elements as administrative leadership, especially as it facilitates agreement on educational goals and methods among faculty, students, and parents and supportive working relationships among teachers. Additionally, it shows the following features of school organization as important to student outcomes: overall support for innovation in providing responsive learning opportunities and services for students at risk of dropping out; high levels of expectations and support for low achievers; and opportunities for close interaction between faculty and students (Wehlage, Lipman, and Smith 1989).

Contextual Influences on American Indian School Outcomes

Empirical research in the "cultural difference" tradition has provided some important insights into the gaps between typical schooling practices and American Indian cultures. Such research has shown that in spite of the changes that have allowed for cultural differences to be acknowledged in the curriculum, Indian students still experience the vestiges of long-term policies that have denigrated and handicapped them: lack of identification with school personnel, other students, the school curriculum, and the demands of school life. Additionally, perceptions of prejudice from school personnel and non-Indian students continue. Many Indian students on reservations attend schools in which they have non-Indian teachers who know little, if anything, about the culture or language of the students, in which instructional practices are unfamiliar to the students, and in which parents have little influence or involvement (Kroskrity 1986).

CHAPTER TWO

The effects of these circumstances have been documented in research on Indian classrooms: Greenbaum (1985) reports that Indian students in regular (non-Indian) classroom settings interacted very differently with non-Indian teachers than did non-Indian students, the effects of which were detrimental to learning. Similarly, Philips's study of Warm Springs Indians (1983) revealed that classroom contexts and practices were very different from the social settings with which Indian children were familiar: the classroom demanded individualized performance and emphasized competition among peers. Indian children, on the other hand, performed more effectively when the classroom contexts were organizationally similar to local Indian contexts that emphasized cooperation and sociality.

Other case studies have focused on the level of cultural integration of American Indian students in particular school settings. Deyhle's (1986) study of Navajo students found that they resisted the racist school culture and developed alternative ways of participating and modifying their social status in the school. McDonald also found that Indian students often experience a kind of culture shock that can result in poor performance and dropping out (1978).

Two and a half decades ago, Antell (1979) found that dropping out among Indian students occurred at a higher rate in public schools (30%), where 70% of Indian children were educated, than in BIA schools (6.5%) or private schools (1.9%). Such findings suggest the possible importance of differences in school contexts. Consistent with the earlier studies, research conducted by the BIA also shows some evidence that the federally funded schools may be more effective for Indian students than other types of schools (General Accounting Office 2001). However, findings from a study by Kleinfeld, McDiarmid, and Hagstrom (1989) reveal that the shift from boarding schools to small public high schools dramatically reduced rural Alaskan Native dropout rates.

Since more American Indian students are enrolled in state-run public schools now, these schools have the primary responsibility for addressing language and cultural integration problems. However, O'Brien's analysis of "the demise of Indian education" (1990) suggests that the reality of the situation is that the public school system is not meeting the needs of Indian students, as demonstrated by the high Indian dropout rate nationally (35.5%) reported by the National Center for Education Statistics in 1988 (Frase 1989). A particular problem with public schools is the lack of "English as a second language" programs for Indian students who come to school with poor English skills.

Other school context factors contributing to the educational stratification of American Indian students are related to the organization of instruction, in particular, ability grouping. The data presented in the preceding section about the learning disabilities of Indian students compared to other cultural groups show that problems with learning, which result in channeling students to special education and remedial services, disproportionately affect Indian students. Dodd and Nelson (1989) suggest that American Indian students are overclassified as learning disabled and placed in remedial programs or lower ability groups. Although factors other than physical handicaps (e.g., cultural, environmental) may contribute to these conditions, schools typically respond by providing remediation in order to improve school performance.

In summary, some evidence suggests that while resources have been allocated to minority schooling for the purpose of improving educational opportunities, improvements are still offset by contextual effects that may act as punishments or otherwise have negative repercussions for minority students. Specifically, the adjustment problems of language and cultural minority students point to social and cultural aspects of schooling that negatively affect their educational achievement. Studies presented above show that Indian students participate in school settings and show different degrees of "tolerance" to cultural incongruity. Their divergent responses to schooling may provide the basis for educators' stereotypes of and relationships with minority students that, in turn, may affect their integration and performance. However, some students with traditional identities also perform well and graduate. Such diversity among students suggests the need for research on how the range of cultural orientations and identities affect school performance and dropping out.

Despite the research findings indicating the importance of examining connections among family, community, school, and social conditions affecting Indian students, little research has taken this more comprehensive approach. For example, in spite of the fact that most reservations are served by several types of schools—public, private Catholic, and tribally controlled—there is no research that makes sufficient, systematic comparisons among types of schools to determine either the extent or nature of the differences among them or the reasons for their effects on student

CHAPTER TWO

achievement. Nor are there studies of the effects of Indian community social structures and cultural orientations on school outcomes, or the interaction of these with schools and labor market structures. In particular, studies are needed on how different social conditions and cultural orientations of Indian communities relate to various types of schools and differentiate school outcomes. Although ambitious, such studies hold the most promise for understanding the schooling processes and outcomes of ethnic minority students, especially American Indians in reservation communities, who may differ sharply from other students.

Expected Research Findings

Tribal and/or private schools are expected to have a more positive effect on Indian students' completion than the public schools due to the goals and mandates of tribal and private schools serving Indian communities for meeting the special needs of their students. However, such effects may be modified by the level and allocation of resources; because these schools are typically smaller, they may not have the resources to adequately meet student needs. Additionally, orientations of school personnel toward ethnic minorities will influence their effectiveness in retaining minority students through graduation. Agreement of community members and schools on educational goals and methods and local cultural support for education are also expected to have important contextual effects. The responses of Indian communities in terms of acceptance, adaptation, or rejection of the meaning and practices of education are crucial to the kind and level of social support for education provided by the different schools.

In a desegregated public school context, due to the potential for increased prejudice and ethnic conflict, ethnic minority group membership will have an important influence on school outcomes. Indian students also may have more negative school experiences due to adjustment problems, academic difficulties, and less involvement in school activities.

Expected results are summarized in the following statement:

11. Enrollment in the tribally controlled and Catholic Indian schools will have more positive effects on school outcomes than enrollment in the off-reservation, non-Indian, public high school. (See figure 2.1.)

School and Community Relations

Connections between School and Community Contexts

Research by Coleman and Hoffer (1987) indicates the strength of school context effects but also emphasizes the effects of relations between the school and the community on students' educational outcomes. Students were positively affected by the orientation of the school when that orientation was strongly supported by parents and families or the community of the students. In particular, the Catholic school orientation helped to decrease the likelihood of dropping out of school by students from traditionally disadvantaged families as well as from "deficient" families, that is, families with such characteristics as single parenthood or two working parents. "At-risk" students, or those with poor academic performance, frequent absences, and disciplinary problems, were much more likely to drop out of school if they attended either public schools with no strong orientation or, to a lesser extent, other private high schools with weaker orientations than Catholic schools. Further research has confirmed these findings generally but has pointed to the relevance of other aspects of the school organization such as the fact that small, private schools are less likely to use curriculum tracking than larger public schools (Lee and Bryk 1988).

The concept of "social capital" suggested by Coleman and Hoffer (1987) is especially useful for explaining the school outcomes of ethnic minority students. Coleman (1988, S119) identifies three forms of social capital: obligations and expectations that depend on trust relations in the social environment, information-flow capacity of the social structure, and norms accompanied by sanctions. These aspects of social capital were found to be important for the formation of human capital as measured by graduation from or dropping out of high school. Coleman's findings indicate that students' school outcomes are influenced not only by the relationships within the family but also by the degree to which community members express and reinforce attitudes and behaviors about schooling. Thus, to the extent that ethnic minority families and communities do not have social capital that supports schooling and relations with the schools their children attend, ethnic students may be disproportionately disadvantaged.

Further elaborating the mechanisms by which social capital affects school attainment and other social outcomes, Portes and Sensenbrenner

(1993) identify four different dimensions of social capital operating in minority immigrant communities—bounded solidarity, enforceable trust relations, value orientations, and reciprocal exchange—relevant to the study of reservation communities having similar structural features. Zhou and Bankston (1994) show that higher levels of community social capital facilitated the school success of second-generation Vietnamese youth in New Orleans, thus revealing the importance of school–community linkages. These research efforts indicate that students' integration into community networks and conformity to cultural expectations supporting school goals positively affect students' performance and graduation and improve their access to local opportunities and resources.

Beaulieu and Israel's (1996) analysis of dropout behavior shows the significance of social capital within both families and communities. While each type of social capital varies in effects and significance for urban, suburban, and rural populations, an important finding is the power of the combination of family and community social capital for school completion across all three populations. Critical to each type of social capital are processes within families and communities that provide support for school completion and constrain behaviors that detract from school attainment. Other considerations of importance include the levels of both human resources and opportunities available to families and the communities in which they are located. Supporting previous research (Seipel 1996; Beaulieu and Mulkey 1995; Hobbs 1995; Lichter, Cornwell, and Eggebeen 1993), these findings indicate that rural populations remain vulnerable due to the deficiencies of both resources and opportunities at levels that now often rival the needs of urban centers.

American Indian Community Research

As suggested in chapter 1, rural/reservation versus urban residence is an important source of stratification of American Indians. Cornell (1984) suggests that other sources of internal differentiation for American Indians are related to their differing levels of attachment to cultural, social, political, and economic structures of tribal communities. Such consideration of the structural and cultural differentiation within ethnic groups makes analyses of influences on schooling more complex. However, it also provides the bases for a more complete understanding of the relationship of family and parental characteristics to students' school outcomes. This more comprehensive approach also addresses the connections between school and community influences on the schooling of ethnic minorities.

Research on American Indian communities has demonstrated the economic isolation of families and communities, particularly on reservations, which has been suggested to negatively affect school achievement levels. Of particular relevance are empirical studies showing the poor labor market opportunities and generally lower incomes among Indian individuals, families, and communities. For example, recent studies have indicated that the economic status of Indian adults, based on employment or income levels in rural or reservation locations, did not improve dramatically over a ten-year period, 1979 to 1989 (Gregory, Abello, and Johnson 1996). Cornell and Kalt (1990) report that in 1980 nearly 45% of reservation Indians lived in households with incomes below the poverty level, and 14% of the households had incomes less than $2,500, according to census data. These authors also report that the unemployment rate for Indians on reservations in 1989 was 40% nationally, compared to an unemployment rate of 5% for the United States as a whole. According to Snipp (1989), while older Indians living in urban areas (or who had more than sixteen years of schooling) had a greater chance of having a white-collar occupation, the majority of Indians held jobs in lower-paying occupations. Thus, American Indian socioeconomic status is related to human capital levels and labor market opportunities, both of which are relatively lower in rural and reservation areas (Snipp and Sandefur 1988).

Jensen and Tienda's research (1989) further substantiates the effect of rural residence on Indian poverty. Their findings indicate that while rural Indians, overall, have seen long-term improvements in economic status, they remain vulnerable to economic downturns that dramatically reduce work and other economic opportunities. During such times, Indian populations are less likely than other minority groups to take advantage of welfare programs to offset economic hardships. Instead, they often rely on scarce family and community resources for assistance. The result is often a deepening of poverty for many Indian families.

Huff's (1997) analysis of Indian education in reservation and White border communities reveals that local opportunity structures play a significant role in shaping student perceptions of the relevance and use of school credentials. Importantly, her research shows that the extent to which Indian community members are involved in school organization and decision making affects rural Indian students' participation and success. Where Indian community members are prevented from involvement in schooling, except in nominal ways, and where opportunities for Indians to transform school credentials into meaningful employment are scarce, Indian students' school achievement and completion suffer.

Although research by Deyhle (1992) supports other research showing the importance of local opportunity structures, her findings show that despite the poverty of Indian communities, local social networks and cultural processes may have positive effects on students' school attainment. For example, in her study including Navajo and Ute students, those living in poorer, traditional Indian communities did not have the highest dropout rates. In fact, these students were among the most likely to be integrated in traditional Indian families, have strong Navajo identities, and have the family and reservation community support they needed to graduate. Deyhle (1991, 1995) concludes that the "cultural integrity" of Indian students often provides them with important social and cultural resources needed to succeed at school and in other community settings (especially off the reservation) where "racial warfare" and poor economic resources in general often severely limit opportunities for Indians. Her research is also significant in comparing the benefits of traditional family culture to the misunderstandings of school personnel who often perceive native traditions and Indian parenting practices as negative. Other researchers, such as Bowker (1993) and LaFromboise, Heyle, and Ozer (1990), support these findings regarding the positive effects of students' integration in their native culture and family networks.

These studies indicate an important feature of Indian community–school relations that has not been captured well by research emphasizing either "culture discontinuity" or structural deficiencies. This research shows that American Indian students, their parents, and other members of their communities participate in two different sociocultural contexts that may overlap at times and, at other times, may conflict. The discontinuity approach suggests that students facing this dilemma are destined to fail because they enter schools controlled by the dominant group, which has more "cultural capital." On the other hand, research emphasizing structural deficiencies suggests that Indian students' perceptions of racism and lack of opportunities lead to their "rational" rejection of both traditional identities and schooling.

CONTRIBUTIONS OF SCHOOLING AND COMMUNITY RESEARCH

However, Deyhle's research shows that Navajo students who succeeded in school resolved the dilemma by accepting school as valuable to their future ability to support themselves and their families but rejected the pressure to assimilate—that is, to give up their traditional cultural identity, family, and community life. Similarly, studies by Tierney (1992) and Huffman, Sill, and Brokenleg (1986), which document the range of strategies used by American Indian students to cope with college life, also indicate the choice of many Indian students to maintain their cultural integrity. While the responses of some Indian students include rejection of the educational system, others find creative ways to resist complete acculturation and remain integrated in their families and communities while participating in the educational process (Huffman, Sill, and Brokenleg 1986). These studies are exceptional, however; most studies of Indian educational retention and completion fail to fully address either the resources or the competing demands on Indian students from within their school, community, family, and social networks.

The significance of this line of research lies in its implications that efforts to explain minority school failure and dropout behavior as resulting solely from the lack of social capital or cultural capital, at least in part, are misplaced. There is some evidence that social capital deficits are important: Deyhle and others have found, for example, that students disconnected from school, family, and community support are the most vulnerable and "at risk" for failure. However, the focus on social capital does not recognize two important situations of minority students: first, the success of Indian students who do not acculturate and, second, the tremendous amount of social and cultural capital often available to Indian and other minority students that does not fit the expectations of educators. In other words, social support for Indian students may be invisible to outside observers of minority communities. Additionally, although the cultural resources of Indian students, which help to ensure success within their families and communities as well as in their schooling, may be viewed as having little relevance to outsiders, such orientations and practices remain quite valuable and meaningful to Indian students and their families.

Nagel and Snipp's (1993) efforts to explain recent changes in American Indian identity and tribal affiliation are suggestive of the approach needed to consider the influences on American Indian populations adapting to the intersection of Indian and non-Indian societies. Their analysis shows that recent identity changes (largely a reidentification with Indian tribes) have occurred through processes of "ethnic reorganization" that allow a group to maintain its integrity while modifying its structural and cultural forms. For some populations, adaptations have resulted in new forms that represent extensive accommodations to the culture of the dominant group in order to survive. For other populations, adaptations represent resistance to cultural and economic assimilation. For example, Wilma Dunaway's (1996) analysis of Cherokee adaptation to American efforts to incorporate the tribe into an expanding capitalist economy shows how creative ways were found to maintain significant elements of tribal culture and economic structures even in the face of tremendous force. Many American Indian communities continue this process of resistance through creating new ways of participating in both American institutions (such as the school and labor market) and the institutions indigenous to their communities.

For this study, the concept of *native capital* is proposed for the purpose of shedding light on how American Indians in a particular context, who face circumstances common to other reservation populations, adapt and create new responses to their participation in modern American institutions, particularly schooling. Claus Offe's neo-Marxist theory of late capitalism (as summarized and discussed by Münch 1994, 82–88) is useful for understanding the types of contradictions affecting populations, such as American Indians and other minorities, who are culturally marginalized and concentrated in nonproductive sectors. For American Indians residing in reservation communities, two contradictions—or a double contradiction—become apparent. The first contradiction involves the fact that American Indian communities are minimally incorporated into capitalist production; this derives from the historical relations of American Indians to the state and economy that have resulted in poor development of economic activities and opportunities in reservation communities. Consequently, American Indians participate primarily in public sector activities. This means that they have been incorporated into the reserve labor force, while many also act as guardians of potentially valuable natural resources. Thus, while American Indians experience the contradiction of being part of a system in which production is social, but privately appropriated by capitalists, they also occupy positions within nonproductive sectors from which they may critique this political economic system.

CONTRIBUTIONS OF SCHOOLING AND COMMUNITY RESEARCH

A second contradiction involves the fact that American Indian reservation residents maintain (to varying degrees) cultural values and practices that place priority on (1) production for use value and (2) exchange that often involves the redistribution of wealth, as well as (3) a de-emphasis of personal accumulation of wealth for prestige. Thus, American Indians also experience a cultural contradiction that provides the tools for some degree of resistance to further incorporation into the capitalist system.

The term *native capital* represents the cultural resources of native peoples, the particular ways in which American Indian community members internalize tribal values and orientations, engage in social relations and cultural practices, and develop skills and abilities needed to achieve success within their own communities. This aspect of native capital indicates the potential for resistance to assimilation and incorporation into a market-based economic system. However, to the extent that these values, relations, practices, and skills overlap or are compatible with those of the dominant society and therefore are reinforced in schools and valued in market exchanges, they also support the acquisition of human capital (school credentials, etc.) and participation of American Indians in a competitive capitalist system. Thus, the term *native capital* itself represents the ways in which a group's unique social relations and cultural knowledge mediate the capitalist processes of human capital formation and labor market participation.

This conceptual approach is consistent with recent studies of rural minority economic conditions—including more comprehensive analyses of minority institutional effects on both human capital resources and labor market demand—which allow for addressing both the complexity and the constraints experienced by rural populations. These studies suggest the importance of data on both individual economic activities (formal and informal) and the reservation or enclave economy as a whole. Such an approach is well represented by Mingione's (1991, 1994) research that explored the ways in which economic patterns are embedded in particular social, economic, and political institutions. His "embeddedness" approach begins with the notion that work is located within regulatory systems in which norms of reciprocity shape the dynamics of a competitive market. Social units relevant to the study of work in such contexts include those in which reciprocal relations occur, such as the household (in which mutual obligations are aimed at meeting the survival and other needs of members) and the community, especially ethnic communities, in which

CHAPTER TWO

specific cultural traditions, values, and history play important roles in creating social obligations and relationships among members. Within these social units, normative social relations include specific ways in which individuals and groups behave in the labor market and economy, including the criteria employers use for hiring; how employers and employees relate to each other; what meaning education credentials and employment have for individuals, families, and communities; what types of economic activities are valued; consumption standards; and the expectations that individuals, families, and communities have for the local economy.

The "embeddedness" approach is especially useful for understanding reservation communities that vary considerably in terms of their social and cultural practices as well as their natural and economic resources. On the other hand, what most reservation populations have in common is that families (including households, clans, or bands) and communities on reservations are powerful social units that mediate the effects of historical and structural forces on reservation economies. Thus, contextual analyses are intended to improve our understanding of how specific populations have been affected by political economic shifts that increased poverty in the late 1980s and early 1990s. In particular, they reveal how rural reservation residents have survived economic and political changes by drawing on their unique cultural resources and social networks. Additionally, they reveal how specific cultural orientations and adaptive practices interact with both the legacies of historical conditions and contemporary social structures to narrow the pathways out of poverty.

By shedding light on the means by which a particular ethnic group survives forced assimilation and incorporation, this conceptual approach also has implications for understanding sources of intragroup differentiation. Indian tribes may experience changes in social organization if subtribal groups develop different levels of attachment to or meanings for "traditional" practices or adapt differently to external circumstances and pressures. Applied to the schooling of Indian youth, this approach suggests the need to identify differences in meanings, values, and behaviors regarding education among the subgroups within a tribal population and the bases for such differences. The development of such internal group diversity as a result of American Indian interaction with dominant group institutions as well as local cultural and social processes suggests important questions about the specific causes and mechanisms by which differentia-

CONTRIBUTIONS OF SCHOOLING AND COMMUNITY RESEARCH

tion occurs and its effects on Indian students. Other questions of interest concern the potential effects of such differentiation for the maintenance of the sociocultural integrity of the tribal group or Indian community and the role of schooling in this process.

Expected Research Findings

Despite the few studies conducted to date regarding the effects of American Indian community dynamics on school outcomes, evidence suggests that traditional communities may have positive effects to the extent that local social structures and resources support schooling. Therefore, expected results include the following:

12. Students' residence in communities with stronger social networks and traditional cultural resources along with greater opportunities to use schooling credentials will decrease the chances of dropping out. (See figure 2.1.)

In the next chapter, a description of the Northern Cheyenne reservation community—its history, culture, and political, social, and economic life—provides the basis for consideration of the empirical evidence presented in subsequent chapters on school completion. In chapters 4, 5, and 6, quantitative and qualitative analyses are presented that address the direction and relative effects of key sources of influence in educational processes. Specifically, quantitative analyses answer questions regarding influences that differentiate Indian students within the Northern Cheyenne reservation setting, focusing on such sources as individual and family characteristics and community and school contexts. Qualitative data obtained for the case study explore in detail the nature of the processes affecting performance levels and school completion.

CHAPTER THREE
THE NORTHERN CHEYENNE RESERVATION: THE SETTING FOR AN ANALYSIS OF HIGH SCHOOL COMPLETION

In the following description of the Northern Cheyenne case study setting, I will provide an overview of the political and economic history of the Northern Cheyenne Tribe and other information specific to the late 1980s and early 1990s when this study was conducted. Descriptive data will address the tribe's social, cultural, and economic characteristics and community dynamics affecting the three schools serving the majority of the Northern Cheyenne students. This information provides insight into the contextual influences relevant for interpreting the school completion process.

The Northern Cheyenne Tribe has structural similarities to many other Indian tribes, especially its experiences with federal policies toward Indian reservations and the assimilation of Indian people. The Northern Cheyenne also have a unique combination of resources from which they have forged opportunities for survival and the continuation of their peoplehood; additionally, they possess a unique repertoire of cultural practices on which to base their adaptation to the constraints imposed by the reservation system. These factors have influenced the availability of schooling, school resources and organization, Northern Cheyenne attitudes toward schooling, and students' educational achievement.

The Northern Cheyenne Social Structure

The Northern Cheyenne reservation was established in southeastern Montana in 1884 by an executive order that set aside 371,200 acres for the

THE NORTHERN CHEYENNE RESERVATION

tribe. With subsequent modifications to this land base, the reservation now includes 447,000 acres spanning thirty-six miles from east to west and twenty-three miles from north to south. It is located in both Rosebud and Big Horn counties. A description by Steve Chestnut (1979, 3) captures the essence of the terrain.

> The reservation lies within the northern Great Plains region. It consists of grassy, high plains capped by sandstone ridges. There is a thin and fragile covering of topsoil. About one-third of the reservation consists of low hills covered by irregular stands of pine, while the streams are bordered by cottonwood. The reservation landscape is a composite of ridges, plains, hillsides, valley bottoms, and stream courses resulting from thousands of years of natural weathering erosion, without interference by man. The result is a balanced natural landscape, sufficient to provide life-support to its human and animal populations. . . . A recent report estimates that a total of 23 billion tons of coal, in seven coal beds, lies beneath the reservation. Of these, perhaps 5 to 10 billion tons are suitable for stripping. This deposit constitutes a portion of the Fort Union formation. The value of the Northern Cheyenne coal reserve is reckoned in terms of billions of dollars. . . . However, there has been no commercially significant coal mining on the reservation.

The social organization of the tribe structures the actions and activities that tribal members pursue and shapes the way individuals and groups relate to each other in the reservation communities. Several characteristics of communities that have been found to be useful in understanding social organization include diversity and complexity, outside ties, distribution of resources, coordination and cooperation among residents, and patterns of personal interaction (Feeney et al. 1986). In the following paragraphs I briefly describe some of the basic aspects of Northern Cheyenne social organization.

Northern Cheyenne tribal members have a strong sense of tribal identity based on shared language, culture, history, political organization, social organization, and values. An important factor in the maintenance of their identity is the physical isolation of the reservation. However, several changes in reservation life have contributed to the increasing diversity of the population. Such changes include improved roads, increasing availability of television via satellite and cable, and growth in this rural region. Additionally, Northern Cheyenne tribal members have become more mobile;

CHAPTER THREE

it is very commonplace to leave the reservation for extended periods for military service, work, or education opportunities. Most people also leave for short trips for shopping and recreation that increase interaction with people who live outside the reservation. In spite of the increasing presence of non-Indians and members of other tribes on the reservation, the Northern Cheyenne still make up the majority of the reservation population. According to community studies included in an Environmental Impact Statement by the Bureau of Land Management (BLM, Department of the Interior 1989), there is no other reservation where the tribal members constitute a majority of the population. The result is that Northern Cheyennes have more opportunities for interaction with members of their own tribe than do most other tribes.

In general, social diversity now characterizes the reservation population as a result of greater experience off the reservation and changes in organizations and institutions located on the reservation. Social diversity can be seen in the various degrees of attachment tribal members have to traditional institutions such as ceremonies, tribal social events, religious affiliations, and traditional medicine, as well as new institutions such as government, education, and the labor market (BLM 1989). Tribal members often rely on new community institutions, such as social services and the tribal court, to help resolve disputes and change behaviors, rather than depend on traditional sanctions. There are a wide variety of social groups to which people may belong based on their interests and participation in traditional or nontraditional activities. For example, adult tribal members may maintain ties to the warrior societies as well as belong to one of many churches on the reservation, or other groups such as Alcoholics Anonymous (AA), business, professional, and farm or ranch organizations. Some statuses unique to the reservation context include those based on blood quantum (e.g., full-blood, mixed Indian and non-Indian, mixed tribes) and traditionality (traditional, nontraditional), while other statuses relate more to the larger American context, such as employment status.

Kinship, however, remains a major force shaping the status and social relationships of Northern Cheyenne tribal members. Extended family members still often choose to live close to each other (BLM 1989). However, more families live in single-family homes and are more scattered across the reservation. Nevertheless, individuals often maintain close ties with extended family living in separate households.

THE NORTHERN CHEYENNE RESERVATION

Residence patterns of the five districts (Ashland, Birney, Busby, Lame Deer, and Muddy Creek) of the Northern Cheyenne reservation still follow, to some extent, the settlement patterns of the bands moving to the reservation in the 1880s. According to Moore (1987), the five districts originated with the settlements of the following bands: the Ree band, the White River people, Little Wolf's band, the Black Lodges, the Scalpers, and the Totoimana. The Ree band settled on the middle reaches of Rosebud Creek, while the White River people settled on the headwaters. Today, these bands are represented in the districts of Muddy and Busby respectively, although descendants of the Ree band also live in Lame Deer district. Little Wolf's band is also included in Muddy district. The largest band, the Black Lodges, settled on Lame Deer Creek near the federal agency headquarters that became the district and town of Lame Deer. The Scalpers settled the Birney district, near what is now the town of Birney, on the southern boundary of the reservation. This community is said to be the only place where a particular dialect, "Sutaio," is still spoken. The fifth settlement was composed of the Totoimana band, or the Ashland people, a group that had lived with the Oglala Sioux at Pine Ridge but moved to the Cheyenne reservation when it was established (Moore 1987).

The five original districts now include communities that formed as families moved closer to transportation, jobs, and schools and expanded as housing developments were built by government agencies. The town of Busby, located in the western part of the reservation, known for its community cohesion, is the home of Busby Tribal School. It is composed of many descendants of the White River people. The town of Ashland, located on the eastern edge of the reservation, is the home of the St. Labre Catholic Mission, which includes a high school. The town of Birney is located on the southern edge of the reservation, is very small, and has the reputation of being a traditional community. Muddy Creek, between Lame Deer and Busby, is a residential area still inhabited by some descendants of Little Wolf's band. Lame Deer, located in the center of the reservation, is the largest, most diverse community, and includes descendants of the Ree and Black Lodge bands. It is the location of the tribal government offices, the Indian Health Service clinic, the Bureau of Indian Affairs, other tribal programs, small businesses and services, several Head Start centers, Lame Deer Public School, and Chief Dull Knife College. The majority of the Northern Cheyenne Tribe lives in Rosebud County

CHAPTER THREE

and composes about a quarter to a third of that population. A much smaller proportion lives in Big Horn County.

Community Characteristics

The community of residence is important for the Northern Cheyenne students because the five different communities on the reservation (Lame Deer, Busby, Ashland, Muddy, and Birney) represent not only different geographic areas but distinctive social and cultural environments. Communities have different proportions of Cheyenne speakers, levels of unemployment, educational attainment, and sources of jobs and other valued social and cultural resources. These intrareservation variations are not typically included in schooling studies. However, ethnographic research suggests the likelihood that community factors affect school outcomes.

The analyses presented in the following chapters include the effects of the three largest communities in which the students live, Lame Deer, Busby, and Ashland (insufficient data were available to include the other communities). Data from the 1989 Northern Cheyenne Educational Census (Ward and Wilson 1989) provide more information about the differences among these communities at the time of the dropout study. We found that while 45% of Busby's population had some fluency in Cheyenne, Lame Deer and Ashland had smaller proportions (38% and 33% respectively) of Cheyenne speakers. Additionally, 77% of Busby's adult population completed high school or a GED, compared to 71% in Ashland and 68% in Lame Deer; thus, almost a third (32%) of the adults in Lame Deer did not complete their secondary schooling, compared to 29% in Ashland and less than a fourth (23%) in Busby. In Busby, 58% of the working population earned an annual income of $12,000 or less, compared to 53% in Lame Deer and 68% in Ashland, while more workers in Lame Deer (20%) earned over $20,000 compared to Busby (13%) and Ashland (9%).

The relative sizes of the three communities are another important characteristic in this analysis that indicates the opportunity for community members to know and interact with each other. In 1989, Ashland had the smallest Indian population of the three communities, with several hundred Northern Cheyenne residents. Busby had about eight hundred residents, while Lame Deer was about twice the size of Busby. From this

THE NORTHERN CHEYENNE RESERVATION

descriptive data, we may distinguish the three Northern Cheyenne communities for the analysis as follows: Of the three, Busby had the highest level of traditional cultural resources as well as a relatively larger amount of human capital (e.g. educational credentials) although somewhat lower income. Lame Deer had comparatively less human capital and modest traditional resources, although income levels are somewhat higher. Finally, although Ashland had somewhat higher human capital, its traditional resources were modest, while income levels were very low. Drawing on Portes and Sensenbrenner's (1993) formulations of social capital (especially reciprocal exchanges, resources, and trust relations), a comparison of the three communities that considers size, traditional and other resource levels (e.g., human capital and income), and opportunities for interaction produces the following ordering from highest to lowest: Busby, Ashland, and Lame Deer.

Northern Cheyenne Language Use

Information from the 1989 Northern Cheyenne Education Census provides additional indications of the importance of native culture to tribal members, especially native language use: 38% of the respondents (914 persons) reported that they speak or understand Cheyenne. As reported previously, the percentage of Cheyenne speakers varied among the communities on the reservation, ranging from 29% in Muddy district to 45% in Busby. Importantly, the use of Cheyenne increased with age: about 13% of preschoolers, 16% of school-age children, 32% of young adults ages 19–24, and 51% of persons ages 25–44. In the two oldest age groups, 68% of those ages 45–65 spoke Cheyenne, while 77% of persons 66 years and older spoke Cheyenne. Interestingly, however, the largest percentages of Cheyenne speakers was among 25- to 44-year-olds (41%) and 45- to 65-year-olds (24%).

Educational Attainment Patterns

Measures of educational achievement of the reservation population indicate the effects of educational policies for the Northern Cheyenne Tribe and suggest how credentials relate to labor force opportunities. For example, educational achievement of the Northern Cheyenne reservation population has been fairly high: in 1980, 55% of the adult population had

CHAPTER THREE

completed high school, compared to 53% of the Fort Belknap population, 52% of the Crows, and 50% of the Blackfeet population. This rate of high school completion for the Northern Cheyenne was at the median for all Indians in the country in 1980 (Snipp 1989), although lower than for all residents of Montana (74%). Similarly, while 17.5% of Montanans had completed a baccalaureate degree in 1980, only 2.7% of Northern Cheyennes had completed a college degree.

Since 1980, school completion rates have changed. Data from the 1989 Northern Cheyenne Educational Census (Ward and Wilson 1989) show that 50% of Indian people on the reservation had received a high school diploma, although 19% had received a GED; about 31% of adults had neither type of secondary education credential. While about 40% of adults had attended college, only about 25% had finished a degree program. The largest percentages of high school/GED graduates were found in Muddy district (84%), Busby (75%), and Ashland (71%). The smallest percentages of high school/GED graduates were found in Birney (54%) and Lame Deer (68%).

As indicated in the overview in chapter 1, the levels of educational attainment of the Northern Cheyenne are similar to national patterns (Ward and Wilson 1989). Until recent cohorts, each age group increased its proportion of high school graduates: 17% of those 65 and older had twelve years of school, compared to 50% of adults 45–65 and 80% of adults ages 25–45. However, young adults ages 19–24 showed a decline, with 64% having completed twelve years of school, and the youngest age group (students who received their secondary schooling in the early to late 1980s) had an even lower rate of completion (60%) than the previous age group. This reversal from the previous increase in educational attainment suggests that, like other American Indians across the nation, the Northern Cheyenne are experiencing a generational change in schooling patterns (Snipp 1989).

Moreover, each generation of Northern Cheyennes has experienced different conditions on the reservation related to changing political and economic circumstances as well as change in institutions such as schooling. To understand more about the differences in educational experiences by generation requires that we examine the recent history of reservation schools. The Northern Cheyenne, like other tribes, have been served by several different types of schools—public and private—but have also experienced in their earlier history a lack of schools for tribal members to attend. In fact, some older members of the tribe reported in the 1989 educational census that they only received a third-grade education because there were no higher grades to attend. Several of these people even went to the third grade several times because they wanted to continue to go to school. Each of the three high schools serving the reservation during this study (St. Labre Catholic Mission School, Colstrip Public School, and Busby Tribal School) as well as the tribal college will be described in the sections that follow.

St. Labre Catholic Mission School

Both Catholic and Mennonite missions were established to educate and "assimilate" the Northern Cheyenne. However, only the St. Labre Catholic Mission offered both day school and boarding facilities for Northern Cheyenne and Crow students in Ashland, Montana, just east of the Northern Cheyenne reservation. St. Labre Catholic School is still part of the St. Labre mission founded a century ago. It is a privately administered Roman Catholic school that serves an almost exclusively Indian population. Students attending the school from the Northern Cheyenne reservation are primarily from the Ashland and Lame Deer communities.

St. Labre is probably the best known of the schools serving the reservation because of its successful national direct-mail fund-raising activities. Once an impoverished mission, over the last several decades it has built a large and relatively stable endowment from private donations.

As a Catholic school, St. Labre emphasizes spiritual as well as academic development. The history of St. Labre is interesting in that it closely parallels national priorities in Indian policy. In the earlier years of its history, missionaries at St. Labre appear to have favored an assimilationist perspective in their dealings with Indians. Older Cheyennes relate how some tribal members, inspired by the sermons of St. Labre missionaries, roamed the reservation on horseback, roping and pulling down sweat lodges (Risingsun 1989). While some recall harsh or negative experiences in this boarding school, others express gratitude for the care they received during difficult times on the reservation (Rowland 1994; Baird-Olson and Ward 2000). Today, the St. Labre staff emphasizes integration of the values of their Roman Catholic sponsor with respect for the traditions of the

CHAPTER THREE

community (Rowland 1989). In fact, some St. Labre clergy participate in sweat lodge activities with members of their parish. Due to its commitment to provide educational programs with private funding, St. Labre no longer allows federally funded special education programs to be offered. However, it does provide some remedial instruction with the intent to mainstream students as quickly as possible.

An important part of the history of the school is the change in governance of the school in 1975. From 1975 through 1985 St. Labre School operated under a contract with the Bureau of Indian Affairs. During that time, a community-elected school board governed the school, and the facilities were leased from the St. Labre Mission. In 1985, however, the Catholic diocese of Great Falls, Montana, resumed governance. A community advisory board, elected mostly from the reservation area but including one member from the Crow Tribe, provided community input to the management of the school (Bryan and Yellowtail 1985). Accompanying these changes were declining enrollments: in 1985, the enrollment of high school students was 140, but the 1987 cohort enrollment decreased to 27. In the 1988 and 1989 cohorts, however, enrollment increased again to 39 and 57 respectively. Along with these changes came a shortening of the school name to *Labre* for a period and then a return to *St. Labre* as the school's links to the Catholic Church were reestablished.

Funding for the school changed radically when it became a private Catholic school again. As a contract school, it received federal monies of about $400,000 per year, but with the change to private status, its budget increased to $1.7 million. At that time, St. Labre charged a minimal tuition but had a scholarship program for students in need. In 1985, the composition of the faculty and staff was primarily non-Indian (Bryan and Yellowtail 1985); there were one Cheyenne and one Sioux teacher, one Cheyenne counselor, and fifteen Cheyenne paraprofessionals.

Generally between one-third and one-half of the students attending St. Labre Catholic Mission School were from the Crow reservation, located just west of the Northern Cheyenne reservation in Big Horn and Yellowstone counties. Crow students come from a reservation in which the culture and social organization differ from that of the Northern Cheyenne. Although certain aspects of the social organization of the two tribes are similar, such as access to off-reservation experiences (e.g., for work, education, and military service) and the presence of non-Indians and other tribal members, as well as new institutions, there are some important differences. For example, the Crow Tribe is somewhat larger, with a reservation population of about 7,600 in 1987 (BLM 1989). In fact, the Crow people compose at least 50% of the population of Big Horn County. In terms of cultural differences, a larger percentage of Crow tribal members (about 70% according to Talent Search sources [Goodluck 1988]) speak their native language fluently, and students often receive their early academic instruction in their own language in reservation schools. Additionally, family organization is clan based and matrilineal. Unlike the Northern Cheyenne, the Crow have a larger reservation, but tribal members are a minority within its boundaries. Also, unlike the Northern Cheyenne, the Crow Tribe chose to exploit their coal reserves, resulting in additional revenues for the tribe. However, unemployment and poverty remain serious problems for members of this tribe as well (BLM 1989).

Colstrip Public School

When public schools were allowed to offer schooling to the Northern Cheyenne, the public school district in Colstrip, Montana, just north of the reservation, admitted reservation students. While there has been a settlement in one form or another at Colstrip since early in the century, the modern town has been built, for the most part, since the energy boom of the early 1970s. Although residents resist the description of Colstrip as a "company town," the town was primarily planned and built by the Montana Power Company to provide a comfortable, attractive, and model community for the employees of the four power plants located there. The recipient of a municipal planning award, Colstrip boasts carefully manicured parks, scrupulously clean streets, and an active and positive community spirit. It also maintains one of the wealthiest school districts in the state, which prides itself on an abundance of academic and athletic facilities and a wide variety of learning opportunities for its students. Colstrip schools are governed by a six-member school board elected district-wide, including one board member elected from the Northern Cheyenne reservation. Faculty and staff composition in 1985 included fifty-one teachers and staff in the high school. Three American Indians worked for the school district, one as a counselor, one as the home-school coordinator, and one as an elementary teacher (Bryan and Yellowtail 1985).

CHAPTER THREE

The budget for Colstrip High School increased from $936,515 in 1980 to $2,785,472 in 1985. Additional funds for Colstrip schools were provided by Public Law 874, which authorized funding for reservation students in lieu of taxes from residents, and from the Johnson-O'Malley program, which provided special funding to school districts with Indian student enrollments (Bryan and Yellowtail 1985).

Colstrip's student body reflects the population of the town and surrounding area—primarily White, middle- and working-class families. Livelihoods of these families include primarily mining-related work, service jobs, and ranching. However, in the late 1980s about a third of the students were from the Northern Cheyenne reservation, primarily from Lame Deer, although there were students from Busby as well. Some students lived as far as seventy-five miles from the school. Although the Indian students constituted a minority of the student body, this group represented the single largest concentration of Indian students in the three schools that served most reservation residents.

Enrollment of Indian students in the high school increased from forty-seven in the 1987 cohort to sixty-three in the 1989 cohort and composed from 28% to 38% of the total high school enrollment. Unlike the Indian student enrollment, total enrollment in Colstrip High School declined sharply over the period 1982–1989. The decline in students reflected primarily the loss of population from the Colstrip area with the end of construction on local power plants in the mid-1980s. High school enrollment was as high as 452 in 1985 but decreased by more than half (to 168) by 1987 (Ward 1992).

Busby Tribal School

Finally, as tribes won the right to provide educational services to their members in 1972, the Northern Cheyenne Tribe contracted with the BIA to administer its own school. Thus, the Tribe transformed the BIA boarding school at Busby, called the Tongue River Reservation Boarding School, to Busby Tribal School (Bryan and Yellowtail 1985). In its early years as a boarding school administered by the BIA, Busby School's history included strict and sometimes abusive policies directed at the boarding school students. Today, there are no longer boarding facilities, but the school continues to be affected by the negative image re-

THE NORTHERN CHEYENNE RESERVATION

sulting from the early assimilationist policies of the school. Memories of experiences at the Busby boarding school are still strong among older Northern Cheyennes. Ted Risingsun (Northern Cheyenne Follow Through 1980, 8) recalled the effect of attending the school:

> I remember Busby School and how it used to be because I went there as a child. Everything was like in the military. I was a little boy, and with the other little boys, we would get up when the whistle blew, dress when the whistle blew, go out and "police" the grounds picking up little pieces of paper and things so we would learn to be "responsible." We went to breakfast when the whistle blew, and we stood behind our chairs and couldn't sit down until the whistle blew. We were punished if we spoke to each other in Cheyenne and we were made to feel ashamed that we were Indians, and ashamed of our families. When I got a chance to go home, I cried that I did not want to come back. But my family said that I must go back. So I became deaf. I have been told that it was not a physical problem, but hysterical deafness. But I could not hear and my family could not send me back to the school. I still, today, have trouble with my hearing sometimes. I think it goes back to what happened to me as a child. The Indian schools have done terrible things to Indian children.

Mr. Risingsun, quoted by Crawford (1987, 44), describes his experience in relation to being forbidden to speak his native language: "I'd never spoken English, but at school I was expected to use it. I didn't even know that my name [in English] was Ted Risingsun. I hung my head. If there had been a bilingual [or multicultural] teacher there, things would have been different."

While Busby School (now called the Northern Cheyenne Tribal School) has changed a great deal since the 1930s when Mr. Risingsun attended the boarding school, it has had many other problems. Among the three schools in this study, Busby has the smallest resource base with which to provide comprehensive services for grades K through twelve (Bryan and Yellowtail 1985). In the 1985–1986 school year, Busby received about $650,000 from the BIA for administration of the school and about $332,000 in federal grants for special programs such as bilingual education, Chapter I, special education, and Title IV Indian education. However, high staff and faculty turnover, low morale, and political turmoil have affected this school as well in recent years.

CHAPTER THREE

Busby Tribal School's high school enrollment declined dramatically from 207 in 1972 to 80 students in 1985. Changes continued with the enrollment of 30 students in the 1987 cohort, 18 in the 1988 cohort, and 30 again in the 1989 cohort (Ward 1992). Declines in the early 1980s were related to the suspension of operations because the building was assessed as hazardous due to the lack of funding for adequate maintenance (Bryan and Yellowtail 1985). During this time, Busby School was governed by a five-person board elected within the portion of the reservation located in Big Horn County, the westernmost part of the reservation. Students attending Busby School were primarily from Busby, but a substantial proportion was bused from Lame Deer.

Chief Dull Knife College

The Northern Cheyenne Tribe also has its own tribal college that serves the postsecondary education needs of the reservation. Consequently, students from local high schools can attend two years of college without leaving the reservation. The college began in 1972 as an Indian Action Program that offered vocational training. Located in Lame Deer, Montana, in the center of the Northern Cheyenne reservation, it was named for Chief Dull Knife, one of the leaders of the Northern Cheyenne Tribe who first asked for schools to be built for Cheyenne children to learn *tsemoná*, "a new way of life." As programs were developed and the school diversified, it established the foundations for a postsecondary educational institution. When the Indian Self-Determination legislation in the early 1970s paved the way for tribally controlled community colleges, the Indian Action Program at Northern Cheyenne became one of the first of thirty-four two-year colleges established on Indian reservations. For more than twenty years now Dull Knife Memorial College (now known as Chief Dull Knife College) has been offering a two-year liberal arts curriculum and associate's degree, which provides for transfer to a four-year college, as well as vocational programs and certifications. Among the special vocational programs Dull Knife Memorial College has offered are paraprofessional training for child-care workers, special education paraprofessional training, substance abuse counselor training and certification, law enforcement training, welding, carpentry, computer literacy and graphics design, natural resources management, and secretarial and basic business accounting skills. The college serves not only the tribe but also areas off the reservation that have no other access to postsecondary education.

Political and Economic Organization of the Reservation

Economic and political structures of the Tribe have important implications for opportunities available to tribal members. A brief overview of these structures will be followed by a discussion of the economic characteristics of reservation residents.

An important factor affecting economic conditions on the Northern Cheyenne reservation is the development of natural resources. Like other tribes that have substantial deposits of nonrenewable minerals and other resources, the Northern Cheyenne Tribe has had to make decisions regarding the exploitation of these resources as well as the control of their development by outside agencies, both private and public. Although the Tribe had agreed in the 1960s to allow the development of coal resources, it later reconsidered the decision and successfully undertook actions to halt this activity. In one of the most important assertions of tribal sovereignty in the last four decades, the Tribe used a number of legal options to protect the reservation environment and create some work opportunities for tribal members. First, the Tribe received from the Environmental Protection Agency a Class I air quality designation that served to curtail the polluting mining and power plant operations in the immediate vicinity of the reservation. However, a compromise to which the Northern Cheyenne Tribe later agreed provided the go-ahead for additional power plant construction north of the reservation in exchange for installation of scrubbers in the power plant smokestacks and funding for monitoring reservation air and water quality (Ashabranner 1982).

Second, the Tribe utilized the Indian preference provisions of the Indian Self-Determination Act of 1975 as well as affirmative action to establish employment opportunities for Northern Cheyenne tribal members in energy-related enterprises operating near the reservation. The Tribe believed that in this way the Northern Cheyenne could learn about energy development and plant operations, and the Tribe could continue to have

CHAPTER THREE

communication with energy developers for the purpose of negotiating benefits and resolution of other issues related to the impact of further development of coal resources. Although it is a subject of some controversy among tribal members, especially those who see coal development as a potential remedy to the persistent poverty on this reservation, the decision not to develop coal remains in force today. Sustained tribal effort has been required over almost forty years to protect the reservation environment and its coal resources. Such efforts would not have been possible without the backing of the Northern Cheyenne people and the Council of Forty-four, which was instrumental in the Tribal Council's decision making to reject proposed coal development (Spang 2004). This support has been demonstrated at critical points through the use of referendum votes (Ashabranner 1982). The basis for such support lies in both the cultural beliefs of the Northern Cheyenne about their land and their understanding of the effects on reservation life of coal development activities (Nordstrom 1977).

The development of timber and water resources has also involved difficult decisions and actions by the Tribe. For example, timber resources were depleted by fires in 1988 (28,000 acres were lost in fires that occurred at the same time as the fires in Yellowstone Park) and through what some tribal members believe was mismanagement by the Bureau of Indian Affairs. This has caused some members to want to increase the Tribe's involvement in the management of this resource. Increased pressures on water resources resulted in the need to quantify Northern Cheyenne water rights. Although it took almost fifteen years to negotiate an agreement with the State of Montana, the Northern Cheyenne Tribe is one of the few tribes to have successfully completed a tribe–state compact for water rights, which gives the Tribe ownership of 91,330 acre-feet of water from the Tongue River and Big Horn reservoirs near the Montana–Wyoming border, as well as the Rosebud Creek drainage (Montana 2003). In July 1995, the Tribe celebrated the final phase of completion of the compact agreement.

In relation to land ownership and control, the Northern Cheyenne Tribe also represents a relatively unusual situation in Indian country in that the Tribe has maintained an exceptionally high degree of control. Unlike some tribes that have lost large amounts of land resources following the allotment of reservation lands to individuals who subsequently sold their property rights to non-Indians, the Northern Cheyenne Tribe established an unprecedented land policy that allowed it to regain its lost lands. In the 1970s the Tribe began to buy back from individuals lands that were part of the reservation. By 1990 about 98% of the reservation was owned by Northern Cheyenne tribal members, the Tribe itself, or other Indians residing on the reservation (Lopach, Brown, and Clow 1990).

In spite of the strength reflected in the precedent-setting economic policies that reestablished tribal control over a good part of the natural resources of the Northern Cheyenne Nation, the establishment of a strong political foundation for the Tribe has been difficult to accomplish within the context of the reservation system. In 1936, the Northern Cheyenne Tribe accepted the Indian Reorganization Act (IRA) government structure that provided for a tribal council governing body and a tribal court system. Following the establishment of the reservation in 1884, U.S. agents established a tribal police. The new system adopted in 1936 diverged sharply, as it did for many tribes, from the governance structure of the Tribe prior to the reservation system. In contrast with the previous structure of the Council of Forty-four, which included the heads of the various bands and clans, the much smaller Northern Cheyenne Tribal Council is elected from the five districts on the reservation. Despite recent structural changes (e.g., the separation of powers by constitutional amendment) and occasional challenges by tribal members, the government continues to protect the welfare of the Tribe overall and experiences cohesion and solidarity when the tribe or its homeland is threatened (Lopach, Brown, and Clow 1990; Risingsun 1989).

An important responsibility of the Northern Cheyenne Tribe is the operation of programs and services for reservation residents. Trends in federal funding for tribal programs and services in the late 1980s and early 1990s, however, negatively affected educational programs as funding cuts forced choices in favor of the most crucial social services to families. The only programs to receive funding increases in 1988 were the tribal courts, social services, credit and financing, agriculture, and real estate appraisals and services. Overall, the Tribe lost almost a half million dollars of funds for programs serving the Northern Cheyenne. An analysis of the funding losses and gains by agency, that is, BIA versus the Tribe, shows that the dollar increases were concentrated in the BIA-operated programs while the Tribe gained funding in only two areas, social services and the tribal courts (Northern Cheyenne Tribal Committee on 638 Funding 1988).

CHAPTER THREE

Labor Force and Income Patterns

The level of federal and other resources and their allocation to tribal and BIA programs directly affects the opportunity structure of the Northern Cheyenne reservation. On this reservation, as on many others, the vast majority of jobs are in the public sector. The 1989 Northern Cheyenne Educational Census (Ward and Wilson) revealed that only 44% of adults worked either full- or part-time. Additionally, the majority (69%) of employed adults worked in the public sector: educational programs supported by public funds (31%), the federal government (19%), the tribal government (17%), and the county or state (2%). Only 11% of adults working were employed in businesses off the reservation, while a little more than 8% were employed by businesses on the reservation. (For a more detailed analysis, see Ward 1998b.)

Comparisons of unemployment figures for 1980, 1983, 1985, and 1989 show that employment reached its lowest level in 1985, but it then increased somewhat by 1989. Data from the U.S. Census Bureau showed unemployment to be 16% in 1980, but BIA figures differed greatly; they showed 48% unemployment in 1983 and 60% in 1985. Such discrepancies are largely related to measurement differences for the two data sources. Census data have been criticized due to problems with enumeration on reservations. However, the validity and reliability of BIA data have been questioned as well. The Northern Cheyenne household census in 1989 (Ward and Wilson 1989) showed unemployment to have subsided to 49%, or about the 1983 level.

Such figures give some indication of the fluctuation in employment on the reservation that corresponds, to some extent, with private sector jobs but primarily reflects budgets of tribal programs and agencies. With the completion of major construction projects in the area (e.g., power plants, highway repairs, and the Tongue River Dam), public sector opportunities remained important through the late 1980s and into the 1990s. Although Northern Cheyenne adults with high school diplomas were as qualified as adults in Big Horn and Rosebud counties for lower-skilled jobs, the unemployment rate on the Northern Cheyenne reservation has been consistently higher than the rates for these counties overall (BLM 1989; Ward 1998b).

Data on adult employment patterns provided by the 1989 Northern Cheyenne household census (Ward and Wilson 1989) show that only

34% of the adult respondents were working full-time, while 10% worked part-time. Almost 35% of working adults reported their work income as ranging from 0 to $7,000. A little over 26% reported earnings of $12,000 to $20,000, while over 21% reported work incomes of $7,000 to $12,000. Finally, almost 18% reported earning over $20,000. Combining responses for the two lowest income categories, over half of the working adults (56%) reported incomes of $12,000 or below. However, the distribution is bimodal, with larger percentages in the lowest and next to highest categories, revealing the earnings gap between the professional employees in public administration and the large number of persons in low-wage jobs. More than half of the low-income workers lived in Lame Deer. Although Lame Deer also had a large percentage of the highest income earners, Muddy district has the largest proportion overall.

Per capita household income levels, estimated by the Bureau of Land Management's study (1989) of the Northern Cheyenne reservation, were much lower in 1986 than levels for the rest of the region: $4,280, or 39% of the regional per capita household income of $10,877. Census data show that in 1979 the median Indian household income ($7,473) in Rosebud County was 38% of the White household income ($19,500). However, in 1989, the median Indian household income ($14,203) was 43% of the White median household income ($33,079) (Montana 1994). These data show that Northern Cheyenne households gained little spending power between 1979 and 1989 (BLM 1989).

The U.S. Bureau of Land Management's analysis of the relationship between household income and business activity identifies two mutually reinforcing conditions that contribute to the poor economy of the reservation. First, the low income levels of individuals and families, which result in low levels of consumption, do little to support businesses located on the reservation. Second, the low level of business activity on the reservation, in turn, provides few opportunities for income to circulate on the reservation. As a result, income is spent off the reservation rather than supporting the Northern Cheyenne economy. This situation provides for little expansion or new development of business activity. Two major obstacles to business development identified by the U.S. Bureau of Land Management analysis include a lack of capital and a lack of collateral. Because of complex legal jurisdictions affecting property on the reservation,

CHAPTER THREE

Cheyennes can use their allotted property as collateral for bank loans, with BIA authorization of this use of trust land. However, off-reservation banks have often been reluctant to make such loans and have required applicants to have a very good financial track record. Although the long-term effect has been to impede business growth on the reservation (BLM 1989), the recent establishment of a bank on the reservation is now helping to support more local businesses.

Poverty, Dependency, and Age Distribution

Information on poverty and dependency of the tribal and local area population provides evidence of the effects of the political economic organization of the reservation. Data concerning public assistance claims by the reservation and county populations show the increasing needs of families and children. BIA General Assistance clients on the Northern Cheyenne reservation averaged 83 clients per month in 1982, but the numbers increased to 112 in 1983 and 173 by 1984—representing an increase of over 200% in that three-year period (Montana 1985). This increase was the highest in that time period for any tribe in Montana. Tribal Social Services reported increases of up to 1,166 recipients of general assistance by the first quarter of 1985 as well as increases in the demands placed on child welfare services (BLM 1989). Similarly, the number of Indian recipients of Aid to Families with Dependent Children (AFDC) in Rosebud County in 1980 had almost tripled by 1984. Census data by county (U.S. Census Bureau 1993) show that over the decade from 1979 to 1989, the poverty rate increased for American Indians from 45% to 48%; among persons with children, the poverty rate increased from 49% to 54%. By 1989, the gap between poor White and Indian families had grown as well: among White families, the percentage in poverty having minor children fell by almost 25%, from 90% in 1979 to 65% in 1989, while among Indian families in poverty, the percentage with minor children increased from 86% to 100%. Thus, the Indian population in this county saw their economic conditions worsen considerably over the decade compared to Whites.

Other structural characteristics are suggested by the age distribution of the Northern Cheyenne population. One aspect is particularly important for understanding the pressure on economic and social resources: 47%

THE NORTHERN CHEYENNE RESERVATION

of the population was age 18 or younger in 1989 (Ward and Wilson 1989). The U.S. BLM study (1989) reported that the median age on the reservation was 19.1 years, compared to 29.6 years for the state. Additionally, the larger proportion of Indians in childbearing years resulted in a higher Indian birthrate in 1980–1983 in Rosebud County (42.6 per 1,000 people), compared to 37.6 for all Indians in the state and 24.6 for non-Indians in Montana.

Adding the proportion of elderly (ages 65+) to the proportion of minors in a population shows the extent of burden on adults eligible to work (ages 19–64) for supporting dependents. The dependency ratios calculated for Rosebud County in 1990 show that American Indians had a substantially higher ratio than whites (1.0 vs. 0.7). Moreover, 1990 figures for average household size show that American Indian households had roughly one more person than White households (3.84 vs. 2.77), and Indian families were larger (4.1) than White families (3.3). These data showing both a high dependency ratio and a high unemployment rate clarify why pressures increased on Cheyenne family resources and public assistance. These figures also suggest an important impact on housing conditions: tribal housing is often overcrowded.

Health Characteristics

Health characteristics of the Northern Cheyenne population not only indicate structural inequalities in reservation communities, but they also point to obstacles for worker participation in the labor force. One indication of the health status of the Northern Cheyenne population is the death rate. Comparing Indians to non-Indians in Rosebud County (Montana 1985), the Indian death rate for 1980 to 1983 was 9.5, compared to 6.5 for non-Indians. Indian Health Service (IHS) data for 1981 to 1985, however, show that the overall death rate for the Northern Cheyenne and Crow tribes together was lower (684 per 100,000) than the rate for all Indians in the Billings service area (817) and the United States as a whole (862) in 1984.

Indian Health Service data for 1981 to 1983 show that the Billings area tribes ranked third in deaths due to diabetes mellitus, 33.8 deaths above the national average for all races, and 17.9 deaths over the national Indian average. Comparing the combined figures for the Northern

CHAPTER THREE

Cheyenne and Crow tribes to all the Billings area tribes and the United States for 1961 to 1985, we see that these two tribes together had higher mortality rates (23.5) for diabetes mellitus than both the area (22.4) and the country (15.5). In 1987–1989, the mortality rate for diabetes mellitus increased to 30.9 for these two tribes, compared to 30.17 for all service units in the state and 11.3 for the U.S. population. The Crow and Northern Cheyenne service unit also had the highest mortality rates for accidents (155.6) compared to all Montana service units (110.1) and the United States (33.5) as well as for alcoholism (17) compared to all Montana service units (11.68) and the United States. (6). However, this service unit had rates lower than the Montana averages for liver disease and cirrhosis and heart disease, although these rates were considerably higher than the U.S. rates (Montana 1994).

While authors writing about the Northern Cheyenne Tribe often mention alcoholism and related problems, they rarely discuss how removed this behavior is from the traditional Cheyenne values and practices. However, Ashabranner (1982) provides a clue as to the importance of health and well-being that reportedly provided much of the motivation for the tribe's pursuit of clean air standards and other efforts to protect the reservation population and resources. He quotes a tribal elder, Sylvester Knows His Gun (1982, 131), speaking about the values underlying the campaign to save reservation resources: "Cleanliness is woven into all the rest of our culture. Clean body; we still purify ourselves in sweat lodges, just as our ancestors did. Water unpolluted. Minds uncluttered; some Cheyenne still make the trip to Bear Butte in remembrance of the teachings of Maheo and to purify their minds and spirits. The air must be pure to breathe and clear to see the brightness of the sun and stars." And yet, in spite of the emphasis on purity, substance abuse and addiction and the accompanying health and social problems are believed to affect all the Northern Cheyennes; that is, everyone is affected either directly or indirectly. Reasons for such problems are related to conditions of poverty, unemployment, and the frustration resulting from exclusion from economic and other opportunities. However, analyses of the substance abuse problems of the Northern Cheyenne youth (National Institute on Drug Abuse 1987) suggest the relevance of generational differences in the conditions that foster substance abuse.

Problems with Schooling among Northern Cheyenne Youth

Information about recent students attending high schools serving the Northern Cheyenne reservation indicates some of the factors that may be associated with the changing pattern of school completion among Indian students. One important area of information is provided by a study funded by the National Institute on Drug Abuse (1987). The report, entitled "Drug Use among Indian Students on the Northern Cheyenne Reservation," presents the results of a 1987 survey of 278 students attending grades six through twelve at Colstrip, Lame Deer, Ashland, and Busby schools. A major finding of the survey shows that about 60% of high school students were seriously involved with drugs or alcohol. While the students' use of drugs was not continuous, it was sufficiently heavy to cause risk to students' physical and/or emotional health.

The situations for students in these schools are very different today than they were for earlier generations of students. And yet, there are still vestiges of the earlier problems with education that affect Northern Cheyenne students attending these schools. Community sentiments about the problems persisting in education for reservation students are evident from responses to a 1985 survey conducted by the Adult Education program at Chief Dull Knife College (Ward and Wilson 1985). When asked what factors respondents believed contributed to educational problems on the reservation, 13% cited problems related to the school systems, for example, that education is imposed on Indian children; racial discrimination by teachers and others; teachers who do not care; insufficient facilities; that rules are too strict; insufficient activities for children; lack of funding for educational programs; insufficient transportation; and teacher deficiencies.

The largest category of reasons for school problems was related to substance abuse: 27% of the respondents cited abuse of narcotics and alcohol as a major factor contributing to low educational attainment. The second largest category concerned problems with motivating children: 25% cited a lack of interest in school as indicated by high rates of truancy, dropping out, no motivation to finish, giving up on school, lack of awareness of opportunities for education and subsequent opportunities afforded by education, and lack of awareness of educational resources. In a related category, 15% identified personal problems as the basis for educational problems: conflict with the non-Indian culture, despondency over living on the reservation, a sense of hopelessness and lack of control, and the belief that education had nothing to offer. Additionally, 11% pointed to family problems such as little parental guidance, little personal support for students, and alcoholism.

After the survey in 1985, additional information was collected from parents, students, and teachers in local schools that have a BIA Johnson-O'Malley program (Northern Cheyenne Education Commission 1990). In 1990, 103 students, teachers, and parents of Indian students in the Colstrip district responded to a survey questionnaire that asked respondents to identify problems facing Indian students in school. The most frequently mentioned problems were poor study habits, drug and alcohol use, poor self-image, family problems, and personal problems. Again parents and students identified the need for teachers and other school personnel to relate positively to the students' culture as well as their academic problems. Important education-related needs included both better academic instruction and assistance with personal and social needs, such as help cultivating a positive self-image, respect for their native culture, guidance concerning adaptation to White culture, and help with drug and alcohol or family problems. These responses were consistent with the findings of the educational census (Ward and Wilson 1989), which included a question about the extent to which adults felt that the use of drugs and alcohol affected the performance of schoolchildren in the community. Almost 91% agreed that drug and alcohol abuse influenced their children's schooling.

Summary

Information on the social, cultural, political, and economic conditions of the Northern Cheyenne reservation helps to establish several important attributes of the families and communities of the students included in this research: This reservation includes a large population of children and young people, large numbers of unemployed people, people with low incomes as well as people who have not received educational credentials, and large segments of the population who continue their Cheyenne traditions and practices, such as speaking their native language. There are also many affected by substance abuse and health problems. In spite of the large proportions of people with little education or few economic resources, there

THE NORTHERN CHEYENNE RESERVATION

is also a substantial proportion who have postsecondary schooling and who work, especially for tribal programs, schools, and educational programs. Overall, the data indicate substantial support for and concern about educational achievement.

The question posed for this research effort, then, is, why does such a large proportion of Indian youth fail to complete high school? The next chapter begins to address this question with presentations of relevant descriptive data collected on several recent cohorts of students attending three high schools serving the Northern Cheyenne reservation. After establishing some basic characteristics of the student population, the following chapters present analyses of the processes that affect students' school completion.

CHAPTER FOUR
CASE STUDY APPROACH AND DESCRIPTIVE DATA

Analyses of American Indian high school completion are complicated by factors that bring both homogeneity and heterogeneity into the analytical frame of reference. That is, research involving American Indian populations must address the structural forces that have shaped and continue to shape the lives of individuals of Indian ancestry in the United States. And yet, Indian communities also have unique cultures and have adapted to the pervasive historical and structural influences in a wide variety of ways, creating diversity within the population that complicates analyses of American Indians as a group.

To explore the effects of structural forces without sacrificing recognition of the singularity of a particular Indian schooling, I take a case study approach to examine schooling on the Northern Cheyenne reservation. The research will utilize data for several social units—individuals, families, schools, and communities—in an effort to capture as fully as possible the nuances of the process of Indian high school completion. Quantitative analyses will evaluate models of educational performance and completion, specifying the relevant influences for Indian students. Analyses will also examine differences in schooling processes among the three schools serving the Northern Cheyenne reservation and compare processes for Indian and White students for one school in which there is a mixed student population. Models of the schooling processes to be evaluated include variables identified in previous research on ethnic educational stratification as well as new variables identified by research on Indian communities and Indian education, and through fieldwork on the Northern Cheyenne reservation.

Qualitative data will contribute detailed information to the interpretation of relationships among variables identified in the models. Ethnographic methods were used initially to identify problems associated with school completion as a priority research concern to Northern Cheyenne educators and community residents. Additionally, qualitative methods were used to explore patterns identified in the analysis of schooling data as well as to clarify social, economic, and cultural influences on schooling outcomes. The details of the qualitative methods used are described below, followed by a discussion of the quantitative methods, data sources, and variables. Concluding this chapter is a presentation of selected descriptive data on characteristics of the case study population and distributions on the dependent variables, school performance and completion. The evidence presented is intended to answer some basic questions about the students included in the study and to offer some insights about the dependent variables prior to discussion of the multivariate analyses of school completion models presented in chapter 5.

Qualitative Methods

In this section I will describe my fieldwork on the Northern Cheyenne reservation. The primary qualitative method I used was participant observation while I lived on the reservation and worked for the Northern Cheyenne tribal college for three years. Additionally, I conducted over 150 in-depth interviews and had ongoing interactions and discussions with key sources including both reservation community members and school personnel. First, I will provide some background information about my selection of the Northern Cheyenne as the case study. Then I will discuss some salient aspects of school and community life illuminated by the fieldwork. This information will be used extensively in the interpretation of quantitative analyses of school performance and completion in chapters 5 and 6.

Selection of the Northern Cheyenne as the Case Study

I became acquainted with the Northern Cheyenne as a result of my work from 1981 to 1983 with Native American Research Associates, an American Indian consulting company located in Lawrence, Kansas. While working on projects with this consulting group, I developed working relationships with

CHAPTER FOUR

staff members of Dull Knife Memorial College (now known as Chief Dull Knife College), the two-year tribal college located on the Northern Cheyenne reservation. My work with this organization provided the opportunity for establishing a relationship with the Northern Cheyenne Tribe that has continued for more than twenty years.

From 1981 to 1987, I worked on a number of projects for the college, including development of grant applications for various types of instructional programs as well as research and evaluation activities. Working on these projects gave me the opportunity to make several trips to the reservation and see first-hand what the reservation schools were like.

I maintained contact with the Northern Cheyenne Tribe and Chief Dull Knife College when I returned to graduate school at the University of Chicago in 1984 and continued to develop my interest in educational issues affecting American Indian populations. When it came time to select a research topic, I discussed specific education-related interests and issues with the staff and faculty of Dull Knife and found that they were quite supportive of my doing research that would have some benefit to the schools and the tribe in terms of information as well as policy direction. I was especially interested in educational achievement and its role in the stratification of the Northern Cheyenne. Taking jobs as grant writers with the tribal college, my husband and I moved to the Northern Cheyenne reservation on July 4, 1987. After the first year, we assumed faculty positions in addition to our other responsibilities, bought a house, and lived on the reservation until August 1990. Although we no longer live in Montana, we continue to work closely with the tribal college and spend one to two months there each year.

Although our experiences were certainly shaped by the fact that we worked at the college, and many of our friends were associated with the college and the other schools, we had a wide range of experiences and contacts with people on the reservation. For example, we continued to do consulting projects with the Northern Cheyenne Tribe and other organizations on the reservation. This allowed us to meet people in other settings, such as Tribal Social Services, the tribe's Cultural Committee, the Follow Through program at the elementary school, the Economic Development Planning Committee, Northern Cheyenne Industries, Northern Cheyenne Fitness Center, and many others. Additionally, we attended the White River Mennonite Church in Busby and went to as many social and cultural activities

CASE STUDY APPROACH AND DESCRIPTIVE DATA

and events as we could. Through our consulting activities, the work at the college, social activities, and friendships, we were able to learn about the social and cultural life of the reservation, and the area political economy.

Participation in the Northern Cheyenne Education Commission

Much of my qualitative and quantitative data collection was initiated through my work with the Northern Cheyenne Education Commission, a tribal organization composed of representatives from six school districts and the tribal community college serving Northern Cheyenne children and adults in the southeastern Montana area. The Education Commission was organized in 1983 to address the educational needs of the Northern Cheyenne Nation. Tribal Resolution No. 33 states that the purposes of the commission are: "to conduct studies and research on educational problems facing the reservation-wide educational system(s), to identify major problems, to compile data and information, to seek alternative solutions and make recommendations to the Tribal Council in accordance with findings and possible solutions for long-range systematic, functional and improved educational systems on the reservation."

The commission members typically met once a month during the school year to share information on the educational needs and problems of the students as well as to develop ways to obtain relevant education data and work together to meet the identified needs. The six schools providing education for the Northern Cheyenne and other communities in the southeastern part of Montana include Lame Deer Public School, Busby Tribal School, Colstrip Public School, Ashland Public School, Hardin Public School, and St. Labre Catholic Indian School. Combined, these schools served approximately 2,600 students in 1990. Of this number, more than half of the students were Indian—predominantly Northern Cheyenne and Crow. The tribal college had an enrollment of approximately 250 students from both the reservation and surrounding areas. Thus, the Education Commission membership represented a diverse group of schools including elementary, secondary, and postsecondary education, and public, private, and religious schools operating both on and off the reservation. And yet all had the common purpose of serving the rural population of the Northern Cheyenne reservation and Rosebud and Big Horn counties.

Meetings of the Education Commission addressed specific issues identified by the commission members. During my three years of attending

CHAPTER FOUR

meetings, activities were directed toward three goals: (1) increasing the information flow among the schools about the needs of students and about the programs and curricula the schools were using to address these needs, (2) improving information on the truancy and dropout problems that had been identified, and (3) improving services to students with drug- and alcohol-related problems.

The problems of truancy and dropout among the Indian students attending local schools have been concerns of the Education Commission since its inception. Drawing on consultant reports indicating parental concerns about dropout and truancy and an estimated dropout rate of 38% in 1986, the Education Commission took several actions to address these problems:

1. Three schools developed a plan for sharing the costs of hiring a single truant officer.

2. The Education Commission members worked together to develop a truancy policy that could be adopted by all the schools.

3. The Education Commission worked more closely with agencies of the tribal government, specifically the law enforcement and court systems, to identify truant students and dropouts.

4. Part of the agenda of each Education Commission meeting was devoted to presentations of programs offered by local schools to address retention problems or needs of the students.

Education Commission members visited each member school during the commission's regular meetings. Thus, each school had an opportunity to make presentations on programs of special interest to the commission. As a result of these meetings, I was able to establish ongoing relationships with the schools, interact with staff and faculty, and learn firsthand about their programs.

Observations of the Three Case Study High Schools

Colstrip Public School

During my initial visits, I was struck immediately by the enormous differences in the three schools. Colstrip public schools were the most af-

CASE STUDY APPROACH AND DESCRIPTIVE DATA

fluent and offered the widest range of programs, many of which were state-of-the-art. For example, two new efforts in the late 1980s emphasized the development of language and critical thinking skills beginning at the elementary level, and the use of a variety of technologies for addressing special learning needs. My first impression was that Colstrip schools were sensitive to the needs of minority students who had learning disabilities or language problems. The overall attitude toward the Northern Cheyenne Education Commission appeared to be positive, if not enthusiastic, and staff seemed willing to work on important issues, such as the high dropout and truancy rates among Indian students.

After considerable contact with Colstrip schools, other important aspects of the school context became evident. For example, many discussions with special education personnel revealed that Indian students were often identified early on as learning disabled. Although this designation provided some resources for dealing with language and other learning problems, it was also difficult to shed. Some teachers also expressed concern that, in some cases, special education resources were used to address behavioral problems. One thing became particularly clear: not many of the Colstrip faculty and staff had much understanding of the Northern Cheyenne reservation, its culture, history, or social life, and its students. However, we eventually discovered a possible explanation. While all Indian students in the Colstrip system attended the middle school and high school as they reached the appropriate grade levels, at that time most Indian elementary students were assigned to only one of the two elementary schools in the district. This effectively segregated the Indian students and other children who lived in outlying areas. The official rationale for this practice was that it facilitated the transportation of children who were bused. However, in 1991 the school district recognized the negative effects of this practice on students' opportunities for interaction across ethnic group boundaries and changed the school assignment process to allow Indian and other children from outside Colstrip to attend the same elementary schools as Colstrip residents. School officials have publicly affirmed the importance of not restricting associations between Indian and non-Indian students and faculty.

The treatment of Indian students by Colstrip schools has been rather hotly debated on the reservation, particularly in the early 1990s. Some Indian parents who attended Colstrip themselves and sent their children there have been strong advocates of Colstrip. However, others have expressed concern about the experiences of their children with prejudice, including negative comments about Indians (for example, belittling their traditional dress), the lack of attention to Indian culture in the curriculum and activities of the school, the lack of support for participation of Indian students in school activities, and indifference to working with the parents of Indian children. During the late 1980s and early 1990s, virtually all school-related problems involving Indian students were assigned to two Indian counselors from the Northern Cheyenne reservation. Otherwise, teachers and administrators appeared to concern themselves little with responsibilities to Indian students, despite some pleas made by school administrators for cultural sensitivity.

St. Labre Catholic Mission School

My impressions of St. Labre were initially quite different from those of Colstrip. My first contact with this school involved a group of St. Labre high school students who participated in a program called Montana Teen Institute. This program was designed to enhance self-esteem through activities such as support groups for students who had drug and alcohol problems themselves or within their families. The Northern Cheyenne counselor at St. Labre who coordinated the program was trained in chemical dependency and was from Ashland, the community in which the school is located. This program was part of a range of services related to chemical dependency and other kinds of mental health needs. Also, a special counseling staff provided services to both students and staff of the school and offered one of the few employee assistance programs in the state. Nothing of this magnitude existed at either Colstrip or Busby high schools despite the fact that both schools had problems with drug and alcohol abuse.

The level of resources available to St. Labre provided for extensive and high-quality facilities and programs. However, it had fewer state-of-the-art programs than Colstrip Public School, but more than Busby Tribal School. Unlike either of the other schools, St. Labre has dormitories that provide housing for students who preferred not to be bused from the Northern Cheyenne reservation or who were from more distant areas, such as the Crow reservation and other communities. Because many of the

CASE STUDY APPROACH AND DESCRIPTIVE DATA

students living in the residential facilities were from the Crow reservation, the student population was distinctly different from that of either of the other schools—a student body comprising two tribal groups (although the Crow students were a minority). As a result, the schools made some efforts to incorporate information about the cultural heritage and histories of these groups. In recent years the school also has sponsored more cultural activities, such as powwows, and the church has included Indian ceremonial items (e.g., sweet grass) in the Catholic masses. In explanation of these changes, school personnel say that their primary emphasis is on the spiritual needs of the students, whether that means Catholic or tribal traditions, or a combination of the two.

I learned about other, perhaps less obvious, aspects of the mission school through interactions with the counseling staff and faculty as well as parents of Indian students attending the school. Several conversations concerned treatment of students and focused on specific incidents involving a new discipline program. A conversation with one of the non-Indian teachers (who constituted a majority in the school) was interesting in revealing the view that since none of the Northern Cheyennes spoke their native language anymore, there was no need for attention to language barriers. This was particularly interesting in light of information from the 1989 Northern Cheyenne household census indicating that almost 40% of the respondents reported that they understood and/or spoke Cheyenne. As we searched for reasons for the discrepancy between the teacher's perceptions and the real situation, several sources pointed out that, for some people, speaking Cheyenne in front of nonspeakers was considered inappropriate. Consequently, facility with the Cheyenne language was not always revealed to outsiders.

Other incidents concerning student treatment were mentioned by a member of the counseling staff and a parent who described some less-than-desired results of a "discipline" program established by St. Labre in the 1980s. Based on a Boys Town model, this program required students to use a certain type of etiquette and speak in prescribed ways to teachers and other authority figures at the school. For example, there were specific greetings and responses to questions or comments from teachers that students were supposed to learn and use. If they failed to respond in the prescribed ways, they were subject to a range of disciplinary actions. The rationale for the program was that it would increase student awareness of

CHAPTER FOUR

polite behavior and appropriate ways to act toward persons in authority. However, the counselor and parent both related incidents in which use of the discipline program served to alienate students from the faculty and administrators because it did not allow students to behave in ways that were genuine or to represent the truth about problem situations to school personnel without fear of reprisal. Both the counselor and the parent independently concluded that the program inhibited students unnecessarily, that it forced "phony" behavior, and that the program was misused by some faculty and staff. Both persons also questioned the cultural sensitivity of the program.

Finally, another parent of a St. Labre student indicated that her child had experienced physical abuse from an older member of the mission school faculty that was so extreme that she could not satisfactorily explain it away or ignore it. As a result, she felt compelled to initiate a lawsuit against the school. Federal authorities also investigated other accusations made against several staff members. Although most of the accusations were found to be "baseless," the general perception among many parents remained that some abuse did occur at the school.

This information suggests that while St. Labre had many efforts and programs in place to serve the unique needs of its student body, the legacy of the rather harsh Catholic boarding school atmosphere had not been shed completely. Additionally, despite its efforts to accommodate the cultural heritages of the students it serves, St. Labre continued to have problems of cultural conflict among students, parents, and school personnel.

Busby Tribal School

Early contacts with Busby School created different perceptions than the ones I subsequently developed. My first impression of Busby was formed in a meeting with the school superintendent, a non-Indian who was temporarily filling the position on an acting basis. He had virtually no knowledge of the community, no awareness of the circumstances of the students, and little interest in addressing their educational problems or needs. For example, his response to my discussion of the need for research on the dropout problem and truancy was one of indifference and reluctance to do anything that might get him in "trouble." He was generally threatened by the request for his help and unwilling to cooperate.

Not too long after this conversation, a discussion I had about the same problems and issues with the next superintendent, a Northern Cheyenne from Busby (an MEd and former president of the Northern Cheyenne Tribe), was quite the opposite. He not only was familiar with the problems but provided additional personal insights into the situation. For example, he listed the types of problems experienced by a number of students attending the tribally controlled school: drug and alcohol abuse, truancy, dropping out, conflicts with authorities, poor attendance, failure to take standardized tests, delinquency, poor self-esteem, poor health and nutrition, weak family support for schooling, abuse at home, and little supervision of either schoolwork or behavior in general by adults in the home (Bailey 1988). His assessment of the situation of the Busby School population was that virtually any kind of problem could be found at the school, and that all students were affected in some way by at least one problem, and usually a combination of several of the problems he listed. This superintendent concluded that the irony of the situation was that although Busby students were especially in need of help, this school was the most poorly equipped of the local schools to address the many problems students brought to the school. His explanation of why the students at Busby had such serious problems was that Busby was compelled to take any student who couldn't make it in any of the other schools. In other words, Busby "inherited many of the problem students of the other schools." This essentially resulted in the school functioning as a de facto alternative school that was required to serve students with a wide variety of needs.

However, Busby's effectiveness in meeting students' needs was limited by a number of factors, some of which could be located in the organization, others in the history and resource base of the school, and others in the community. Organizationally, Busby, like the other schools, was handicapped by the lack of a pool of American Indian teachers certified to teach in reservation schools. Combined with the lower levels of resources available from the Bureau of Indian Affairs, this resulted in hiring a primarily non-Indian faculty for which the turnover rate was very high. Because many teachers came from out of state, and often the East Coast, their motives for teaching in a reservation school often were related to teaching "poor little Indians" or romanticized views of the West, Indian communities, and Indian cultures. Unfortunately, this led to high levels of confusion and frustration as teachers encountered the realities of

CHAPTER FOUR

reservation life. Often the majority of new teachers had to be replaced by the end of the school year. This seemed to be a greater problem for Busby than for either Colstrip or St. Labre.

Complicating this problem, of course, was the turnover in administrative staff as well; Busby School had had a new superintendent every year for four years in a row. This contributed significantly to the lack of cohesion and instability of the school. School personnel were rarely able to reach agreement on or sustain activities related to a unifying philosophy, specific school goals, or the kinds of relationships needed among school personnel and between the school and the community.

In the face of this constant turnover, on the other hand, a small core group of staff and faculty remained at Busby. However, this too was problematic at times in that some of those remaining at the school were known for having undue influence, by virtue of longevity in the community and familiarity with individual school board members. Because of the instability of the personnel situation, the school board sometimes responded by increasing its role in school management or supporting the actions of well-known teachers or staff over new administrative personnel. This created tensions, suspicions, and political turmoil that negatively affected the community as well as the school environment. The degree of suspicion became evident to me in a lengthy discussion with a long-time faculty member who explained why teachers and staff were discouraged from providing "too much information" to students and parents about either their performance or the school: they did not want the community to be upset by standardized test scores, grades, or other aspects of the school that could add to the school's negative image. Therefore, it was better not to disseminate information about the things that might concern parents. The superintendent did not share this faculty member's view, however.

Given these problems, in the early 1990s Busby Tribal School attempted to improve its programs, work on student and teacher retention, and provide more opportunities for community support and participation in the life of the school. This was done under the supervision of another school superintendent and principal who appeared to work well together and agree on basic elements of a school philosophy and programs needed to address critical problems of the students and school. Several aspects of their approach included efforts to develop a better understanding of the changing needs of the student population, clarify their school policies so that school personnel, students, and parents would have more consistent expectations, coordinate more extensively with other resources and services for reservation children and youth, and strengthen both the academic and extracurricular activities of the school. As a result of these efforts, students on sports teams were required to maintain a certain grade point average (GPA) to be eligible for participation. The school principal reported that athletes generally met the new eligibility criteria. Although there were criticisms of the changes made at Busby, residents also indicated that community support for Busby School increased dramatically. Busby School administrators were also instrumental in 1991 in bringing to Busby a new residential chemical dependency treatment facility for adolescents.

Key Information Sources and Interviews

Important sources of information included members of the Northern Cheyenne Tribe who have lived all their lives on the reservation, although some left for brief periods of time. They range in age from young adults to tribal elders and include full-bloods as well persons of mixed ancestry. The schooling experiences of the key sources include attending Busby when it was a boarding school as well as when it became a tribal school, and St. Labre Mission School and Colstrip High School. Some of the sources not only attended these schools but also have worked for them, and several have children or grandchildren attending them. Most of the key sources have extensive knowledge of the reservation communities and a wide range of experiences with the schools by virtue of their work and social contacts. Several of the sources dropped out of high school and later received a high school diploma or GED. Others have attended college and received degrees. All were significant partners in this collaborative research effort.

In addition to the information received through ongoing contacts with key sources during the project and beyond (1987 through the present), I also interviewed a number of people who could tell me about crucial aspects of schools and reservation communities. These people included both Indian and non-Indian teachers and staff as well as students from the three local schools and community members. Students were both older and younger than the cohorts included in the study, and some were members of the three cohorts. Interviewees were selected for their ability to provide information that would offer multiple perspectives on relevant dimensions of the study.

Quantitative Analyses

The Northern Cheyenne Dropout Project

In spite of their efforts to improve understanding of both the problems faced by Indian students and the programmatic efforts of the schools, members of the Northern Cheyenne Education Commission continued to experience frustration regarding their lack of knowledge in two areas: (1) the nature and extent of the dropout problem, and (2) factors contributing to truancy and dropping out of school. To address the need for more information, I worked with the Education Commission in 1987 to develop a request for research funds concerning the dropout problem. In connection with this effort, the Northern Cheyenne Tribe appointed me to the position of education information coordinator. The grant application, submitted by Chief Dull Knife College, was funded in 1988–1989 by the Office of Educational Research and Improvement of the U.S. Department of Education. Additional funding was provided by the College of Family, Home and Social Science, Brigham Young University.

Definitions of Dropout and Data Sources

The Northern Cheyenne dropout project involved collecting data for three student cohorts—1987, 1988, and 1989—attending Colstrip Public High School, St. Labre Catholic Mission School, and Busby Tribal School. (Ashland School District was not included since it had no high school at that time, and Hardin High School had few Cheyenne students.) Information gathered from these schools relates specifically to the aspects of students' school experiences that previous research indicated as relevant to school completion. The data collection procedures used for this project strictly followed the guidelines established in the Family Educational Rights and Privacy Act, 1980, which protected the confidentiality of the students and their families. There were 228 students in the 1987 cohort, 218 in the 1988 cohort, and 252 in the 1989 cohort, for a total of 698 students. A cohort included graduating seniors as well as those students who would have graduated had they completed the regular sequence of courses normally taken to meet high school graduation requirements over a four-year period. Information for each student was collected by approved school personnel directly from the school records and staff at each high school: attendance records, transcripts, yearbooks, student files, guidance counselors, and other school staff who had direct contact with the students.

Graduation from high school is the schooling outcome of primary interest in this study. Thus, the operational definitions of *graduate*, *dropout*, and *out-of-region transfer* are of particular importance. While defining *graduate*, that is, a student who completed high school and received a diploma conferring this status, was not problematic, defining other terms presented more of a challenge. The term *dropout* had not been defined uniformly across either local school districts or by most states at that time. Consequently, calculations of dropout rates varied considerably for districts and states. According to Chris Pipho of the Education Commission of the States (1988, 30), "Currently, what constitutes a dropout rate in one district or in one state may be completely different in another district or state. Unless a state uses one uniform definition and one uniform system for reporting dropout students, it is likely that even state statistics will be unreliable." A summary of dropout definitions obtained from a survey of school districts by the Center for Policy Research in Education (Pipho 1988, 30) stated that "a dropout is an individual who leaves school either prior to high school graduation or before completing a program of study without transferring to a private or public school or other educational institution." However, definitions varied by such criteria as the grade levels for the baseline population, age range of students, accounting periods, time periods for the unexplained absences, and the educational alternatives counted as an equivalent course of study.

Because we were most interested in the completion or noncompletion of high school, and we did not want to overestimate the dropout population for this study, we used a definition that emphasized the noncompletion of high school. A dropout is defined as a high school student who was enrolled in one of the relevant cohorts in a participating high school who left and did not graduate at the expected time for any reason except death. The failure to graduate was confirmed by the participating schools. Because this definition does not put a limit on the number of

CHAPTER FOUR

days of unexplained absences before a student is classified as a dropout, it may undercount dropouts. That is, this definition does not include "school leavers," or students who missed more days than allowed and were officially dropped by the school, but who later returned to school. A student is classified as a dropout from a particular school by virtue of his or her attendance at that school just prior to dropping out and not receiving a diploma. Therefore, students who switched to another school, that is, left one school and enrolled in another, are not classified as dropouts unless they dropped out of the new school.

The definition of *out-of-region transfer* for this study refers to a specific category of students who left school and the region and whose graduation statuses could not be determined. Consequently, they were eliminated from the dropout analyses. If we were able to determine the graduation status of students who left one school and enrolled in another local school, they were included in either the graduate or dropout categories. Again, only students for whom we could not determine a graduation status are treated as out-of-region transfers. We established this convention specifically because we were interested in determining the graduation status of students in the study. We will use this definition of *transfer* in the descriptive data concerning graduation status of the student population. (Transfers among local schools, or switching, are designated as such in later analyses.)

The graduation status of Indian students that schools reported as dropouts was confirmed with a second source, Northern Cheyenne Adult Education. This source provided information about students' educational history and the reason(s) they left school. The Talent Search programs, funded by the State of Montana to provide educational advising and assistance to Indian junior high and high school students, also provided information about graduation status.

A source of socioeconomic background information on Indian students was the 1989 Northern Cheyenne Educational Census (Ward and Wilson 1989), which included about 75% of the households on the reservation. The educational census included information for each member of the household and socioeconomic data for adults in the household. We were able to merge the census data for students and their families with the student data set obtained from the schools. Comparable household information for Crow students at St. Labre School was provided by the Crow

CASE STUDY APPROACH AND DESCRIPTIVE DATA

Talent Search program staff who had direct contact with and knowledge of these students and their families. This gave us relatively complete information on family characteristics for students in the three cohorts.

Additional individual-level data were collected for Cheyenne students on cultural and social variables that indicate the students' familiarity with the Cheyenne language, students' problems and conflicts with authorities, their families' participation in cultural activities and knowledge of Cheyenne history and language, family involvement in recovery from substance abuse, and family support for schooling. These data items were created through assessments of each student and his or her family by three independent sources. The data were then triangulated to produce a single indicator for each variable.

Selection of Relevant Variables

As suggested by the statements of expected findings in chapter 2, this research examines the effects of several types of independent variables on school performance and completion. Choices of variables were based on their theoretical and empirical relevance to the Indian population in the study as well as practical considerations related to data availability. With regard to substantive interests, a variety of variables were selected that indicate individual, family, and school characteristics. Individual characteristics include gender and hometown residence. Although Indian education studies show mixed results for the role of gender in school outcomes, knowledge of the local school populations suggested the need to investigate the effects of gender on school performance and completion. Specifically, information received from the Adult Education Center as well as key sources indicated that girls often dropped out of school because they were pregnant and not because of poor school performance or other school-related reasons. This suggested that gender was likely to be an important influence on school completion.

Additionally, while national studies show that residence in urban or rural locations makes a difference in educational outcomes, Indian education studies indicate that residence in specific local communities may have an influence related to cultural and family ties. Students' residence in specific reservation communities is a rough indication of cultural factors related to family settlement patterns and social and cultural groups within

CHAPTER FOUR

the reservation social structure. The selection of this measure is based on local knowledge that communities differ, to some extent, in their cultural orientations, attachment to education, the work force, and groupings of extended family. Finally, in terms of individual attributes, a measure of reservation origin is included, since the student population includes both students from the Crow reservation who attended St. Labre and students from the Northern Cheyenne reservation.

Family background indicators are related to socioeconomic status (SES) and family structure. While the household census did not provide comprehensive SES data, it did collect information on the educational levels of adults in the students' homes as well as their employment status. The latter item was chosen rather than occupation since a large percentage of adults (49%) on the reservation were unemployed (Ward and Wilson 1989). Obviously, these two indicators do not provide a complete specification of individual positions within the social structure on the reservation. However, they do provide an indication of the attachment of adults in the home to education and to the labor market, two aspects of social life found to be important in studies of educational attainment. Another relevant aspect of family background suggested by recent research on minority schooling is family structure. Therefore, a family structure variable indicates whether or not a student's household includes only one adult.

School experiences of students are of particular concern in this research and are indicated by the extent to which students have had discipline problems as well as their school attendance and the number of times they switched schools. Additionally, involvement with extracurricular activities indicates students' participation in the social life of the school, while school performance measures indicate the degree of academic success. These indicators address different dimensions of the engagement of students with schooling, which has been found to be crucial in other studies of dropout behavior.

Given the expected relevance of school context, specifically, attending a Catholic private school, tribally controlled school, or public school, information is included on which school students last chose to attend. These variables provide a rough indication of differences in the organizational contexts of the three types of schools—resource levels, orientations toward Indian students, academic expectations, and so on—which were identified as relevant in chapter 2.

Understanding the relationship between the cultural experiences and resources of students and their families and schooling is an important aspect of this research. Therefore, new variables were created from student and family cultural data that provide for the analysis of this relationship. The cultural variables represent student and parental knowledge of their native language and culture, and parental knowledge of tribal history and participation in traditional activities. New variables were also created to represent the extent to which students and their parents were engaged with or distracted from schooling processes, as indicated by substance abuse and conflicts with school or legal authorities. Parents' support for schooling, which may be affected by involvement in recovery from substance abuse, is indicated by their efforts to monitor their children's schoolwork and interact with local schools.

Finally, whether a student drops out or completes high school is the primary educational outcome of interest. However, in several analyses, school performance is treated separately as a dependent variable in order to assess the influence of other school experiences on this school outcome.

Operational Definitions of Variables

Operational definitions of variables used in the analyses are shown in table 4.1. The first group of variables, all of which are categorical, includes individual attributes of students: hometown, reservation, and gender. The hometown variables indicate the effects of residence in Ashland, Busby, or Lame Deer, the largest communities, compared to other communities on the Northern Cheyenne reservation, and the reservation variable indicates the effects of being from the Crow reservation compared to Northern Cheyenne. The gender variable shows the effect of being female compared to male on outcome variables. The next group of variables is related to student family background: high school graduation of adults, full-time employment of at least one adult in the home, and the presence of only one adult.

Student and parental cultural variables are ordinal-level variables and include the following: student's language (an index based on whether students speak or understand Cheyenne) and family traditionality (an index created from the following items: whether parents speak or understand Cheyenne, parents' knowledge of Cheyenne history and

Table 4.1. Variable Definitions

Student Characteristics

Gender
- 0 = Male
- 1 = Female

Student's language[a]
(This measure is the mean of the combination of "native language spoken" and "native language understood" variables.)
- −1 = No
- 0 = Don't know
- 1 = Yes

Problem[a]
(This measure is the mean of the combination of the "conflict with authority" and "use of illegal substance" variables.)
- −1 = No
- 0 = Don't know
- 1 = Yes

Family Characteristics

Only one adult in the family
- 0 = No
- 1 = Yes

At least one adult with high school diploma
- 0 = No
- 1 = Yes

At least one adult employed full-time
- 0 = No
- 1 = Yes

Family school support[a]
(This measure is the mean of the combination of "parent's school support" and "parent's school participation" variables for both the mother and father.)
- −1 = No
- 0 = Don't know
- 1 = Yes

Family recovery[a]
(This measure is the mean of the combination of "recovery" and "still uses" variables for both the mother and the father.)
- −1 = No
- 0 = Don't know
- 1 = Yes

Family traditionality[a]
(This measure is the mean of the combination of "ceremony participation," "native language," and "knowledge of history" variables for both the mother and father.)
- −1 = No
- 0 = Don't know
- 1 = Yes

Community/School

Community/reservation residence
- 1 = Busby
- 2 = Ashland
- 3 = Lame Deer
- 4 = Crow
- 5 = Other

School attended
- 1 = Colstrip
- 2 = Busby
- 3 = St. Labre

School Experiences

Extracurricular activities
- Total number of extracurricular activities during the 9th and 10th grades

Ever been suspended from school
- 1 = Yes
- 0 = No

CASE STUDY APPROACH AND DESCRIPTIVE DATA

Table 4.1. *(continued)*

Absences	Total number of absences in the 9th and 10th grades
Local school transfers	Total number of local transfers in high school
Dropped out of high school	0 = No
	1 = Yes
School performance	Mean GPA

[a] This variable is an index created from the variables identified and coded −1 = No, 0 = Don't know, 1 = Yes. We assume that 0 falls between −1 and 1 categories.

culture, and participation in traditional ceremonies). Student and family relations to schooling are measured by the following variables: student problems (an index based on whether students had conflicts with authorities, and current drug/alcohol use), parents' school support (an index based on both mother's and father's support of schooling, and participation in local schools), and family recovery (an index based on both mother's and father's drug/alcohol use, and participation in recovery from drug and alcohol abuse).

School variables are primarily continuous and represent several aspects of students' experiences during the ninth and tenth grades, the years that most students remain in school. These include having one or more suspensions (a categorical variable), the total number of absences, the total number of school transfers (i.e., switching enrollment to other local schools), and the total number of extracurricular activities in which students participated.

Other school-related variables represent the effects of the school last chosen for enrollment prior to either dropping out or graduating: Busby (tribal school) or St. Labre (Catholic mission school) compared to Colstrip (public school). This variable does not indicate that this is the school in which the student was enrolled the longest, but only that it was the last school attended by the student. While not a comprehensive indication of the effect of the total high school context on students, this item is important for representing the influence of the school from which the student either graduated or dropped out, outcomes that are theorized to be influenced, at least in part, by the school context.

Additionally, the two school outcome variables include mean GPA, the average of annual GPAs for all years of high school attended, and

CHAPTER FOUR

graduation status, whether a student leaves high school without receiving a diploma or graduates.

Limitations of the Data

The data collected for this study are limited partially by the nature of the study itself. First, rather than collect information directly from students, we collected data primarily from school records, which are more reliable than student self-reports. Using school records meant that the data would be limited to the information contained in these records. This limitation was particularly important because it affects the outcome measures, performance and graduation status. For example, although we collected sufficient data on course grades, we also collected standardized test scores as a second measure of performance. However, the latter measure was especially affected by limitations of school records: if no test scores were available in the student's files, then we had no test data for that student. Schools administer tests several times a year, but if students miss the tests, they are not usually made up. Consequently, there were a lot of missing data for standardized tests. In fact, although standardized test scores were most likely to be available for students in the ninth and eleventh grades, more than half of the three cohorts (54–58%) did not have standardized test scores for these two grade levels.

Since we could not use test scores to adequately measure performance for all students in our study, we wanted to determine the relationship of this measure to course grades (as indicated by mean GPA) for the students having both measures. In an analysis (not shown) of the relationship between mean GPAs and standardized test scores in the one school in which both measures were available for a substantial number of students, test scores showed the same relationship to the independent variables as mean GPAs. (A correlation of .6 was found between the two school performance measures.) Although standardized tests are often used to measure school performance, this type of measure is inappropriate for this study for two reasons. First, standardized tests have been criticized as an appropriate measure of performance for Indian populations whose cultures differ from the cultural assumptions of the test instrument (Reyhner 1992b). More importantly, the substantial number of missing standardized test scores for Indian students required that another measure be used. Since all three schools in the study utilize GPA as an important indicator of scholastic performance, we believe that it represents an acceptable measure for an analysis of the relative influence of several independent variables on high school performance. Although grading practices may vary among schools, there are several factors that mitigate this possible problem. First, grading is as likely to vary within schools as between, since grading standards may differ among teachers and subjects and may change by cohort and semester. Without systematic research on grading practices, differences in school means on this performance measure cannot be attributed to this single aspect of school context. Rather, we suspect that school differences are likely to be the result of multiple dimensions of these three very different school contexts. The purpose of this research is to determine whether, relative to other variables, school contexts made a difference in students' school performance. A significant finding would suggest the need to investigate further the sources of such differences.[1] Important considerations include that the mean GPAs are distributed normally at all three schools, and differences among the means for the three schools are small (.3) but statistically significant.

Second, information on school completion is limited as well by the availability of records of requests for transcripts from schools outside the area to which students transferred. Schools often did not have follow-up data on students who transferred out of the area, which we needed to determine graduation status and other data items. This required that we use other sources, such as the Talent Search and Adult Education programs, to verify whether students dropped out. Students for whom we could not determine a graduation status were excluded from the analyses.

Third, schools varied in the records they kept on extracurricular activities. Much of the information on students' extracurricular activity participation was assembled from school yearbooks and similar sources as well as personal knowledge by the school staff.

Descriptive Data on Student Characteristics, School Performance, and Completion

Descriptive data are presented for the students in this study by school in the following areas: overall student characteristics, school completion

CHAPTER FOUR

results, and school performance levels. The first two sections provide overviews of some important student characteristics, such as their distribution by school, ethnic group, and gender, as well as the graduation status of these groups. The last section discusses the school performance patterns of students with different graduation statuses, overall as well as among the three schools, by gender and ethnicity.

Student Characteristics: Ethnic Group, Gender, and School Cohort

Descriptive data provide some insight into the school completion and performance levels of three cohorts of high school students in this study. Data were collected for 698 students, including 130 from St. Labre Catholic Mission School, 489 from Colstrip Public School, and 79 from Busby Tribal School. These numbers include students who graduated, dropped out, or transferred out of the school districts for the years 1987, 1988, and 1989. The largest cohort is 1989 with 252 students (36%) from all three schools, and the second largest is 1987 with 228 students or 33%. The decline in the number of students in the 1988 cohort can be traced to enrollment reductions at both Colstrip and Busby. St. Labre, however, had an increase in its high school enrollment of about 30% in 1988 as well as in 1989.

Indian students, numbering 366, composed 52% of the total student population from the three schools. At St. Labre and Busby, 95% and 99% of the students respectively are Indian, while about a third, or 34%, of the students attending Colstrip are Indian. Among the Indian students at St. Labre, about 54% are female, while at Busby only 33% of the Indian students are female. Among the Colstrip students, 51% of the Indian students are female and 49% are male, compared to 52% female and 48% male among non-Indians.

Table 4.2 shows descriptive statistics for the Indian students for whom we have graduation data. Of the total Indian student population, 51% are male and 49% are female. The majority of Indian students (46%) reside in Lame Deer, the largest of the reservation communities, followed by Ashland (16%), Busby (14%), Crow (12%), and other areas (12%).

School enrollments are as follows: 40% of Indian students attend Colstrip Public School, 24% attend Busby Tribal School, and 36% attend St. Labre Catholic School. Participation in extracurricular activities, an important means for engaging students with schooling, is relatively low;

Table 4.2. Distribution of Students' Background Characteristics and School Experiences (N = 319)

Variables	N	%	Overall Mean (SD)	Graduates	Dropouts
Student Characteristics					
Gender			.49 (.50)	.47	.51
Male	163	51			
Female	156	49			
Student speaks Cheyenne[a]			.23 (.63)	.51	.54
Speaks Cheyenne	120	43			
Doesn't speak Cheyenne	44	16			
Unknown	112	41			
Problem/conflict with authority[a]			.61 (.54)	.51	.54
Yes	195	71			
No	64	5			
Unknown	67	24			
Family Characteristics					
Only one adult present			.29 (.45)	.19	.40
No	227	71			
Yes	92	29			
At least one adult employed full-time			.48 (.50)	.56	.38
No	153	48			
Yes	118	37			
Unknown	48	15			
Family school support[a]			−.08 (.65)	.09	−.25
Supportive	70	25			
Nonsupportive	98	36			
Unknown	108	39			
Family recovery[a]			−.08 (.65)	.09	−.25
In recovery	115	42			
Not in recovery	42	15			
Unknown	119	43			
Family traditionality[a]			.21 (.42)	.15	.21
Traditional	159	58			
Nontraditional	65	23			
Unknown	52	19			
Community/School					
Community					
Lame Deer	148	46			
Busby	46	14			
Ashland	50	16			
Crow	37	12			
Other	38	1			
School					
Colstrip	128	40			
Busby	76	24			
St. Labre	115	36			

(continued)

Table 4.2. *(continued)*

Variables	N	%	Overall Mean (SD)	Graduates	Dropouts
School Experiences					
Number of extracurricular activities			1.00 (1.85)	1.70	.16
0	214				
1–3	69				
4–6	28				
7 or more	8				
Ever suspended			.13 (.33)	.10	.16
No	279				
Yes	40				
Number of absences			18.89 (21.20)	20.97	16.42
0	100				
1–20	97				
21–40	82				
41–60	26				
61 or more	14				
Number of transfers			1.18 (1.12)	1.17	1.20
0	100				
1	124				
2	43				
3	41				
4	11				
Dropout			.46 (.50)		
No	146				
Yes	173				
Mean GPA			2.20 (.61)	2.38	1.90
0.50–0.99	8	3			
1.00–1.55	29	9			
1.56–1.99	62	19			
2.00–2.55	95	30			
2.56–2.99	46	14			
3.00–3.55	21	7			
3.56–3.99	4	1			
4.00	0	0			
Unknown	54	17			

[a] Data on these variables available only for Northern Cheyenne students (N = 276).

less than half of the Indian students (33%) are involved in some type of extracurricular activity. Over two-thirds (69%) of the students have switched schools (enrolled in a different school in the area) during high school, while 13% have been suspended from school at least once. Seventy percent of the students have had conflicts with authorities or problems with substance abuse. Forty-three percent of the students speak or understand Cheyenne.

CASE STUDY APPROACH AND DESCRIPTIVE DATA

Family background variables of interest include family structure, parental education, and employment. About a third of the students (29%) are from single-parent homes. Over half (58%) of students' households are traditionally oriented. Sixty-five percent of the students have at least one parent who has completed high school, and almost half of the students are from homes with only one adult employed full-time. Twenty-five percent of students' parents actively support the schooling of their children, while almost half (42%) of students' families have experiences with recovery from alcohol or drug abuse.

School Completion: Graduation, Dropout, and Out-of-Region Transfers by Ethnic Group, Gender, and School

Analyses of the student data are primarily concerned with identifying the conditions associated with the specific educational outcomes of school performance and completion. The students are categorized as "graduates" and "dropouts" as well as "transfers" (students switching schools for whom we do not have graduation data). Findings from previous studies and fieldwork suggest the following expected results for school outcomes:

1. Indian students will have higher dropout rates and lower graduation rates than White students.

2. Females will have higher dropout and lower graduation rates than males.

3. The tribal and Catholic schools will show higher graduation rates and lower dropout rates than the public school among Indian students.

Addressing high school completion first, we distinguish graduates from nongraduates in order to determine the overall high school graduation rate for students from the three high schools. The results verify the magnitude of the dropout problem. For all students who were in the 1987, 1988, and 1989 cohorts, the total percentage of graduates is 55%. The dropout rate for the total student population is 25%, while the percentage of transfers out of area schools is 20%. The graduation rate for Indian students was 47% overall, with a dropout rate of 40% and a transfer rate of

CHAPTER FOUR

13%. By comparison, White students completed high school at a rate of 63%, dropped out at a rate of 8%, and transferred away from the area at a rate of 29%. (Since most White students attended Colstrip high school, this transfer rate refers primarily to this school.) Our findings support the expectation that Indian students would have a higher dropout rate than White students. In fact, when the transfers (out of area schools) are removed from the calculations, the dropout rate for Indians is 46%, and the graduation rate is 54%, compared to a dropout rate of 11% and a graduation rate of 89% for Whites.

As mentioned earlier, the transfers are students who left a school included in this study and did not return, and whose graduation status could not be determined. A note of explanation for this high rate of transfer out of the public high school should be mentioned. The two earlier cohorts (1987 and 1988) were among the last affected by a population change occurring in Colstrip, which was precipitated by employment changes at the local power plants. With the completion of construction of a new power plant and changes in the use of this new facility, many workers were laid off. Cohort data not shown indicate a decrease across the three years in the number of White students. Consequently, the school population changed as students left with their families. We have no reason to believe that the transfer students were substantially different from those who stayed with regard to relevant school characteristics. Indian students were less affected by the employment changes since there were far fewer Indian workers at the power plants. In fact, the number of Indian students increased with each cohort.

Comparisons of school completion data for males and females show that girls graduated at a slightly higher rate (56%) than boys (54%). However, girls also dropped out at a rate of 26% compared to 23% for boys. Overall, boys transferred out of area schools at the rate of 23%, which was 5% higher than the rate for girls (18%).

Comparatively, White students showed higher graduation rates: girls graduated at a rate of 66%, while 60% of the boys graduated. Dropout rates for White students are also lower than for Indian students: White boys had the lowest dropout rate at 5%, while girls dropped out at a rate of 10%. In contrast, high school completion among Indian students is quite different: boys graduated at a higher rate (49%) than girls (46%). However, similar to the pattern for all students, Indian females dropped out at a higher rate (42%) than males (38%).

The rates of transfer out of area schools are similar for Indian males (13%) and females (12%) and are much lower than for White students. White students had the highest rate of transfers away from area schools, with boys transferring at a rate of 36%, 12% higher than the rate for girls (24%). When transfers are excluded from the calculations, the dropout rate for Indian girls is 48% compared to 44% for the boys. The graduation data presented here support the expectation that females would have different dropout and graduation rates than males. These data show that, as with the White students, Indian females dropped out more often than males. However, while White females had the highest graduation rate of all, Indian females composed a lower proportion of graduates than Indian males.

High school graduation data for Indian students by school (shown in table 4.3) reveal that the percentages completing high school range from 45% at Busby and Colstrip to 52% at St. Labre. An important finding is that Busby Tribal School had the highest dropout rate at 54%. St. Labre Catholic School had the next highest dropout rate at 41%, while the public school had a dropout rate of 33%. However, when transfers are excluded, the dropout rates are as follows: Busby (55%), St. Labre (44%), and Colstrip (42%). Comparing the dropout rate for Colstrip Indian students to the dropout rate of 8% among White students shows that Indian students drop out five times more often. These findings contradict the expected magnitudes of dropout rates for the three types of schools. Analyses of school completion processes presented in chapter 6 will examine more closely the reasons for these differences. Comparing transfer rates by school, the smallest transfer rate was found at Busby with 1%, while St. Labre had a transfer rate of 7%, and Colstrip had a transfer rate of 22%.

Graduation and dropout data for the three schools also show some distinct differences by gender. For example, at two of the schools, dropouts were more likely to be girls: 56% at Colstrip and 55% at St. Labre. However, at Busby, boys were more likely to leave school; they composed 60% of the dropouts. Comparing the graduation rates for Indian girls by school, however, shows that more than half graduated at St. Labre (52%), while a smaller percentage of girls graduated at Colstrip (44%) and Busby (35%). Among boys, at least half graduated at Busby (50%) and St. Labre (52%), while 46% graduated at Colstrip. The highest transfer rate among both boys and girls occurred at Colstrip, where 25% of the boys and 20% of the girls transferred out of this school.

Table 4.3. Graduation Status for Indian Students by School Attended and Gender

Graduation Status	School Attended									
	Colstrip			St. Labre			Busby			
	Male	Female	Total	Male	Female	Total	Male	Female	Total
Graduate	.50 (37)	.50 (37)	.45 (74)	.45 (29)	.55 (35)	.52 (64)	.74 (26)	.26 (9)	.45 (35)
Dropout	.44 (24)	.56 (30)	.33 (54)	.45 (23)	.55 (28)	.41 (51)	.60 (25)	.40 (17)	.54 (42)
Transfer[a]	.54 (20)	.46 (17)	.22 (37)	.50 (4)	.50 (4)	.07 (8)	1.00 (1)	.00 (0)	.01 (1)
Total	.49 (81)	.51 (84)	1.00 (165)	.46 (56)	.54 (67)	1.00 (123)	.67 (52)	.33 (26)	1.00 (78)

[a] Transfer refers to student transfers to schools out of the region.

CASE STUDY APPROACH AND DESCRIPTIVE DATA

School Performance: Comparisons of Mean GPAs by Ethnic Group, Gender, School, and Graduation Status

School performance, an important school outcome as well as an intervening variable in the school completion process, is indicated by mean or average grade point average (GPA). Expected results for school performance include the following:

1. Indian students will have lower performance levels than White students.

2. Females of both ethnic groups will have higher performance levels than males.

3. Performance levels will be higher for graduates than dropouts.

4. Indian student performance levels will be higher at the tribal and Catholic schools than the public school.

Data on the performance levels by ethnic group indicate that the mean GPA overall among Indian students (2.16) is lower than that of the White students (2.66). Additionally, the mean GPA among Indian females (2.19) is higher than that of males (2.13). For White students, this pattern holds as well, except in the dropout category, in which the mean GPA for boys (2.22) is higher than that of girls (1.89) who dropped out. These findings generally support the expectations stated above.

Also as expected, the mean GPA of graduates is higher than that of dropouts. Among Indians, graduates have a mean GPA of 2.38 compared to 1.90 for dropouts. Among White students, graduates have a mean GPA of 2.71 compared to 2.01 for dropouts. Comparisons of all groups reveal that Indian boys who dropped out had the lowest mean GPA at 1.87. However, White females who dropped out had the mean GPA (1.89) closest to that of Indian male dropouts. Interestingly, White female graduates had the highest mean GPA (2.92) among all groups.

Comparison of GPA data for Indian students by school also indicates some important differences: students at Colstrip did not perform quite as well as students at St. Labre and Busby. St. Labre students had the highest overall mean GPA (2.30), followed by students at Busby (2.21) and Colstrip (2.04). Mean GPAs for students at the two Indian schools are

CHAPTER FOUR

Table 4.4. Mean GPA by School, Community, Gender, and Graduation Status

	Graduates		Dropouts		Total	
	Male	Female	Male	Female	Male	Female
Colstrip	2.26	2.26	1.74	1.85	2.04	2.05
Indians	2.26	2.26	1.74	1.84	2.13	2.19
Lame Deer	2.25	2.53	1.74	1.76	2.06	2.12
Ashland/Busby	2.17	2.54	1.97	2.50	2.21	2.38
Non-Indians	2.44	2.92	2.05	1.77	2.51	2.79
St. Labre	2.41	2.61	1.99	1.95	2.26	2.34
Cheyenne	2.17	2.24	2.15	2.12	2.17	2.24
Ashland	2.35	3.31	2.14	2.02	2.25	2.80
Lame Deer	2.55	2.41	2.21	2.03	2.42	2.32
Crow	2.42	2.33	1.77	1.66	2.20	2.02
Busby	2.26	2.59	1.95	2.03	2.16	2.29
Busby	2.46	3.09	1.96	2.75	2.30	2.79
Lame Deer	2.04	1.91	1.94	2.36	2.01	1.96

Note: Mean GPAs are shown for selected communities for each school population.

substantially higher than for students attending the public school; while the difference between mean GPAs of the two Indian schools is .09, the differences between these two schools and Colstrip are .17 for Busby and .26 for St. Labre. Again, expectations for school performance are supported by these data.

Comparing the differences in mean GPAs of Indian students by school, gender, and graduation status, we found the same overall pattern that females tended to outperform males. The only exception is for dropouts at St. Labre; the mean GPA for boys is slightly higher (1.99) than that of girls who dropped out (1.95). Additionally, graduates in each subgroup have higher mean GPAs than dropouts. This pattern holds true for each of the three schools. However, dropouts at Colstrip have a lower mean GPA than both St. Labre and Busby dropouts. On the other hand, comparing mean GPAs by school completion status in each school shows that St. Labre has the largest discrepancy between graduates and dropouts: the difference at St. Labre is .55, while Colstrip graduates and dropouts differ by .46 and Busby graduates and dropouts differ by .36 on mean GPA.

So far these data suggest that Indian students at Colstrip Public School do not perform quite as well as students at St. Labre and Busby Indian schools. However, performance levels also vary by community, as shown in table 4.4. For example, Colstrip Indian high school students from Busby and Ashland have performance levels that compare well with

CASE STUDY APPROACH AND DESCRIPTIVE DATA

Cheyenne students at St. Labre and Busby Tribal School. However, students from Lame Deer at St. Labre had the highest mean GPA. Lame Deer residents attending both Colstrip Public High School and Busby Tribal School have the lowest performance levels among Cheyenne students attending all three schools. However, Lame Deer males perform better than most other groups (except Ashland females) at St. Labre Catholic School.

Summary

This chapter presented some basic findings about school performance and completion among Indian and White students attending the three high schools serving the Northern Cheyenne reservation. Among the notable findings are the following:

1. Of the 698 students included in the study, 52% were Indian and 48% were White. The largest percentage of Indian students in the three cohorts identified for the study last attended or graduated from Colstrip Public High School (40%), while 36% attended St. Labre Catholic School, and 24% attended Busby Tribal School.

2. Indian students had a higher dropout rate than White students, and the dropout rate for students at the three high schools was very similar to the dropout rate identified nationally for Indian students at about 40%, compared to 8% for White students locally (based on total population). The dropout rate for Indian students was 46% compared to 11% for Whites (excluding transfers). Indian students dropped out of Busby Tribal School most often (55%), with St. Labre Catholic School next (44%) and Colstrip Public School last (42%).

3. Indian girls had a higher dropout rate than boys overall (48% and 44% respectively).

4. Information on academic performance as measured by mean GPAs shows that Indian students had lower performance levels than White students overall.

CHAPTER FOUR

5. Indian and White dropouts had poorer school performance than graduates.

6. Indian graduates had higher mean GPAs overall at St. Labre Catholic school and Busby Tribal School than at Colstrip Public School.

7. Indian students who dropped out of St. Labre and Busby had similar performance levels overall, but Colstrip dropouts showed somewhat lower levels of performance than dropouts from other schools.

These findings reveal some interesting similarities to, as well as departures from, the findings of other school completion studies of minority students, including American Indians. For example, our results also showed Indian students to have lower performance levels and higher dropout rates than White students. However, in contrast to some studies, higher overall dropout rates were found among Indian girls than among boys, and higher dropout rates were found for Indian students at the tribal and Catholic Indian schools compared to the public school. The analyses presented in the next three chapters will examine more closely school performance and school completion for Indian students overall, within the three schools, and finally, in comparison with White students. Additional descriptive information about the individual and family characteristics and school experiences of the Indian student population will be presented along with evaluations of models of school performance in chapter 5.

Note

1. The use of mean grade point average follows the precedent set in previous research regarding the effects of student background characteristics, family traits, community and school settings, and school experiences on school performance (Alwin and Thornton 1984); Dornbusch et al. 1987; Dornbusch, Ritter, and Steinberg 1991; Roderick 1993; Valenzuela and Dornbusch 1994; Rumberger 1995). While these studies use either self-reported grades or grades from school transcripts, all the studies measure school performance as grades reported on a four-point scale. In none of these studies was GPA standardized. Although other studies (e.g., Marsh 1987, and Elliott and Strenta 1988) standardize GPA, their

purposes were different from those of the other studies and this research; the studies were designed either to utilize GPA in testing models of other dependent variables (e.g., academic self-concept) or to test the reliability of GPA as a predictor of college success. In the latter study, standardizing GPA was designed to utilize information known about grading differences between college departments (Elliott and Strenta 1988), while the former study standardized GPA for the whole sample (not within each school), since students from eighty-seven schools were involved in the study (Marsh 1987). Since the purpose of the present study is to assess the effects of several influences, including school context, on school performance, standardizing GPAs within the schools would eliminate the effects of school contexts, therefore nullifying the purpose of including these variables in the regression equation. In analyses (not shown here) in which GPAs were standardized for the whole study population, the findings showed the same variables to be significant as the analyses in which GPAs were not standardized.

CHAPTER FIVE
EVALUATING ECOLOGICAL MODELS OF SCHOOL PERFORMANCE: THE RELATIVE EFFECTS OF INDIVIDUAL, FAMILY, SCHOOL, AND COMMUNITY INFLUENCES

In this chapter, models of students' school performance will be examined using multivariate techniques. This school outcome will be addressed first since school performance has been shown to have a significant influence on dropout behavior. The influences addressed in the first two models include variables found in previous studies to be relevant to performance levels: students' individual attributes, family background characteristics, type of school attended, and students' school experiences. In the final models, several new variables represent the effects of additional social and cultural influences on school performance. Expected findings for the school performance analyses are summarized at the beginning of each section. The analyses of the statistical models are followed by additional insights and interpretations that draw on ethnographic data.

Analyses will first examine the selection process affecting Indian students' choice of schools to attend. Several researchers have identified the selection process as a critical part of identifying important influences on student behaviors. For example, Blalock (1989) suggests that it is important to understand as much as possible about the selection process affecting the creation of student bodies of schools in order to determine the sources of differences in school populations. This point is especially relevant to research on public and private schools that attempts to distinguish between school outcome differences related to student characteristics (e.g., social class, ethnicity) and those produced by school contexts (e.g., orientation or organization of the school). Next, models of school performance are presented in three parts: the first analysis includes a general model for all Indian students; the second includes models for the three different school populations; and the third analysis incorporates new cultural and family variables into general models of Indian school performance.

Ordinary least squares (OLS) regression equations are used as a means of assessing the relative influence of multiple independent variables on school performance, an interval level measure. For example, the coefficient for an independent variable like school transfers would show the effect of that variable on school performance compared to all other variables in the model (see Hoffmann 2004, 9). Where the dependent variables are coded as discrete categories, as for the three schools attended or for school completion, logistic regressions for dichotomous and polytomous dependent variables are estimated (Hanushek and Jackson 1977). (For the school transfers variable, the coefficient represents the effect of school transfers on whether students dropped out or not [see Hoffmann 2004, chapter 5].) Specifically, maximum likelihood estimation methods are used to estimate the models of school attended and school completion. This method is appropriate since the logistic estimates tend to be less biased and more efficient for categorical dependent variables than OLS methods (Aldrich and Nelson 1984). For all regression models, unstandardized coefficients and standard errors (SE) are presented.

Missing data on variables used in several of the analyses are treated as follows: either students with missing data were assigned the mean for that variable or dummy variables were created for the missing data. Means were assigned to cases with missing data on school experience variables, transfers, absences, and suspensions, and to mean GPA (mean grade point average) in models in which this variable is an independent variable. Dummy variables were created to represent missing data on family background variables, adult employment status, adult completion of high school, and family structure. Additionally, a dummy variable was used for cases with data missing on the mean GPA variable in the dropout models (presented in chapter 6) in which mean GPA is an independent variable. This use of dummy variables allows the effects of the variables to be distinguished from the effects of missing data.

The population size for each analysis is shown in the tables presented below. The size of the population varies for several reasons. First, only students from the Northern Cheyenne reservation were included in the analysis of schools attended and later analyses including cultural

CHAPTER FIVE

variables. Additionally, cases that had missing data on the dependent variables were excluded.

Influences on Type of School Attended

The following analysis will address the effects of individual and family characteristics of students on the last school that students chose to attend prior to either leaving school or graduating. Since students in this study could select any high school to attend, this analysis will establish whether there are important differences among the three school populations that affect educational outcomes.

The distribution of students' hometown communities by school attended shows that the largest numbers of students from the towns of Busby and Ashland chose to attend the school located in their respective communities. However, most Lame Deer students attended Colstrip School. Looking at the distribution of students within each school, an important consideration is that large proportions of the students attending both Busby School and St. Labre were from Lame Deer: 47% at Busby School and 21% at St. Labre. All of the Crow students attended St. Labre. These data suggest that the community residence of students did affect which school they attended. The analysis presented below examines the influences on school choice in order to compare the effect of residence with other individual and family characteristics. Expected findings include:

1. Community residence will have more influence than gender on type of school attended.

2. Among family background characteristics, adult high school education and full-time employment will affect type of school attended; higher levels on these variables will negatively affect enrollment in the Indian schools.

Table 5.1 presents coefficients for regression equations that identify the effects on school attended of residence, gender, and three family background measures, family structure and parental high school education and employment status. The two models evaluate the influences on choosing Busby Tribal School and St. Labre Catholic Mission School over Colstrip Public School.

EVALUATING ECOLOGICAL MODELS OF SCHOOL PERFORMANCE

Table 5.1. Logistic Coefficients for the Effects of Community Residence, Gender, and Family Characteristics on School Attended

	Busby[a]		St. Labre[a]	
	Coef.	SE	Coef.	SE
Community Residence				
Ashland	−.78	(.51)	1.73***	(.31)
Busby	1.36***	(.33)	−1.14**	(.50)
Lame Deer	−.28	(.27)	−.72***	(.27)
Gender[b]				
Female	−.35**	(.16)	.08	(.16)
Family Characteristics				
Nonintact Family	−.03	(.36)	−.37	(.40)
At least 1 adult employed	−.43	(.37)	−.09	(.39)
Primary adult HS diploma	−.24	(.38)	.34	(.46)
Model chi-square			170.48	
N			307	

[a] Omitted "school attended" dependent variable is Colstrip.
[b] Omitted category is male.
* $p < .10$, ** $p < .05$, *** $p < .01$

In the first part of the table, the effects on school enrollment are shown for residence in Ashland, Busby, and Lame Deer compared to any other community. Coefficients indicate that residence in Ashland has no effect on choosing Busby Tribal School over Colstrip High School but does significantly affect choosing St. Labre, which is located in Ashland. Similarly, residence in Busby has a strong, positive influence on choosing to attend Busby High School over Colstrip, while it has a significant, negative influence on choosing St. Labre. Coefficients for residence in Lame Deer reveal that being from this town negatively influences choosing to attend St. Labre over Colstrip. However, Lame Deer residence has no effect on choosing Busby over Colstrip.

In relation to gender, the findings indicate that being female has a negative influence on choosing to attend Busby over Colstrip. In contrast, being female has no effect on choosing St. Labre rather than Colstrip. Similarly, the variables in the last set, related to family structure, parent education, and parent employment status, do not affect students' choice of either Busby or St. Labre Catholic School over Colstrip.

From these analyses we can conclude that residence close to a high school is, in fact, the major factor affecting school attended. That is, Busby residents tended to choose Busby High School over Colstrip, and Ashland residents tended to choose St. Labre over Colstrip. However, Lame Deer

CHAPTER FIVE

residents tended to choose Colstrip over the other two schools, although some Lame Deer students chose Busby and a smaller number attended St. Labre. Only in the case of Busby Tribal School was gender an important influence on school choice. Females tended to choose the other two schools over Busby. This analysis gives no indication that socioeconomic characteristics of students' families influenced their school enrollment choices. Thus, expectations about the effects of individual community residence and gender variables on the type of school attended were generally supported by the data. An exception is related to the effect of gender on choosing to attend Busby Tribal School over Colstrip.

General Model of School Performance: Individual, Family, School Type, and School Experiences

This analysis examines the effects of several groups of variables on Indian students' mean GPA: individual attributes, family characteristics, school type, and school experiences. In the first column presented in table 5.2, which represents model 1, regression coefficients show the effects of the first three groups of variables on mean GPA. The second column presents coefficients for a model that indicates the effects of all four sets of influences—individual, family background, school choice, and school experiences—on mean GPA. Expected findings for these models can be summarized as follows:

1. Students' residence or origins in more culturally homogeneous and/or traditional communities (Busby and Ashland vs. Lame Deer) or reservation (Crow) will negatively affect school performance, while being female will positively affect school performance.

2. Family background characteristics (the completion of high school by one adult and full-time employment of at least one adult in the home) will positively affect students' school performance, while having only one adult in the home will negatively affect performance.

3. Attendance at the tribally controlled school and the Catholic Indian school will more positively affect school performance compared to attendance at the non-Indian public school.

4. Absences from school, suspensions from school, and transfers to other schools will negatively affect school performance, while participation in extracurricular activities will positively affect school performance.
5. Residence, family SES, and school experience variables will have the greatest relative effects on school performance.

The analysis in table 5.2 addresses the relative importance for school performance levels of Indian students' individual and family background traits as well as the schools they attend. The first model reveals that only the community residence, reservation origins, and school attended variables

Table 5.2. OLS Coefficients for the Effects of Community and Reservation, Gender, Family Characteristics, School Attended, and School Experiences on Mean GPA

	Model 1		Model 2	
	Coef.	SE	Coef.	SE
Community/Reservation[a]				
Ashland	.15	(.12)	.10	(.11)
Busby	.21*	(.11)	.21*	(.11)
Crow	−.29**	(.14)	−.28**	(.13)
Gender[b]				
Female	.06	(.07)	.09	(.07)
Family Characteristics				
Nonintact family	−.09	(.09)	−.05	(.08)
At least 1 adult employed	.13	(.08)	.09	(.08)
Primary adult HS diploma	.12	(.10)	.08	(.10)
School Attended[c]				
Busby	.13	(.11)	.21*	(.10)
St. Labre	.35***	(.10)	.31***	(.09)
School Experiences				
Transfers			−.07**	(.03)
Absences			−.01***	(.002)
Ever suspended			−.18*	(.10)
Extracurricular activities			.09***	(.02)
R-square	.09		.22	
N		296		296

Note: Controls not shown are for variables with missing data on family characteristics.
[a] Omitted category for the community variable is Lame Deer and for the reservation variable is Northern Cheyenne.
[b] Omitted category is male.
[c] Omitted category is Colstrip Public School.
* p < .10, ** p < .05, *** p < .01

CHAPTER FIVE

have important effects on school performance levels. While the effect of the school attended variable was in the direction expected, the effects of the community and reservation variables were mixed. That is, the expected negative effect for Crow reservation origins was found, but the effect of Busby residence was slight, and Ashland residence had no effect compared to Lame Deer. The evidence presented does not indicate effects of either gender or family characteristics on Indian school performance levels.

The second model shows that controlling for the effects of community, reservation, gender, and school attended, school experiences have important effects on school performance. In particular, suspensions, absences, and school transfers negatively affect mean GPAs, while students' involvement with extracurricular activities positively affects mean GPA. These results support expectations about the effects of school experience variables on school performance. Similarly, the expected effects of attending the Indian schools were also supported with coefficients indicating Busby Tribal School's and St. Labre Catholic School's positive effects compared to Colstrip Public School. Again, slight positive effects were found for students' residence in the traditional community of Busby.

Since both community residence and the school attended have important influences on mean GPA in model 2, the effects of the interaction of these and other background variables warrant further investigation. The question is, does choosing to attend a school other than the one closest to home—that is, the typical school choice for the student's home community—have special influences on mean GPA? In the models shown in table 5.3, several interaction terms are included for community and school combinations: choosing to attend the school serving the student's hometown community (vs. another school), choosing to attend an Indian school in the hometown community (vs. the non-Indian public school), and the combination of being female with the two previous school and community interactions. The first two school and community interactions had no effects on school performance. A preliminary conclusion is that the results support the expected effects of the type of school attended and community residence.

Although analyses of the interaction of school and community residence variables did not produce significant findings generally, additional analyses regarding the effects of gender on this interaction show that the effects of school attended and community residence differ in important ways for girls and boys. Table 5.3 shows that when gender (female vs. male) is included in the interactions for school attended and community of residence, this combination of factors positively affects school performance. Thus, while previously Busby residence was seen to positively influence school performance, the new models show that attending an Indian school in one's home community (Busby or Ashland) is especially positive for girls' school performance. Also, absences have negative effects on performance, and extracurricular activity involvement improves school performance.

The findings of both of the general models of school performance indicate the importance of the school experience variables. However, they

Table 5.3. OLS Coefficients for the Effects of Community, Gender, Family Characteristics, School Attended, Interactions Terms, and School Experiences on Mean GPA

	Model 1		Model 2	
	Coef.	SE	Coef.	SE
Student Characteristics				
Community residence[a]				
Ashland or Busby	−.003	(.16)	.02	(.15)
Female[b]	.06	(.16)	.08	(.15)
Family Characteristics				
Nonintact family	−.16**	(.07)	−.11	(.07)
Primary adult HS diploma	.13	(.10)	.05	(.10)
School Attended[c]				
Busby or St. Labre Indian schools	.11	(.17)	.18	(.15)
School/Community/Female Interactions				
Attends home community school	−.03	(.18)	−.03	(.17)
Attends Indian home community school	.13	(.31)	.10	(.29)
Female/attends home community school	−.06	(.21)	−.02	(.19)
Female/attends Indian school	−.11	(.20)	−.13	(.19)
Female/attends Indian home community school	.62**	(.29)	.54**	(.27)
School Experiences				
Transfers			−.04	(.03)
Absences			−.01***	(.001)
Ever suspended			−.15	(.10)
Extracurricular activities			.09***	(.02)
R-square	.13		.26	
N		307		307

Note: Standard errors are shown in parentheses. Dummy variables for missing data on adult high school diploma and community are not shown; there were no significant effects for these variables.
[a] Omitted category for community residence is Lame Deer and other communities.
[b] Omitted category for gender is male.
[c] Omitted category for school attended is Colstrip Public School.
* p < .10, ** p < .05, *** p < .01

also indicate the lack of effect of the family characteristics. In only one model—the first model of table 5.3—was the effect of family structure significant. This finding indicates that having only one adult in the household negatively affects school performance. However, this effect disappears with the addition of school experience variables to the model, suggesting that family structure indirectly influences school performance level. These results contradict expectations based on other studies about the direct effects of family background traits on school performance and achievement. On the other hand, these findings provide support for analyses (e.g., Deyhle 1989) suggesting that students' traditional community ties do not necessarily correspond to poor school outcomes. This important departure from conventional expectations for the effects of traditional communities on American Indian schooling will be explored further in the school performance and dropout analyses in the next chapter.

To understand more about the patterns shown in this analysis of Indian students' school performance, it is useful to consider ethnographic data from the case study of the Northern Cheyenne reservation. Information about parents' education and involvement with their children's schooling provides particularly important clues about the transmission of related values and skills within the family. Additionally, the following section includes discussions of the effects of employment, family structure, and community residence patterns on school performance.

The Northern Cheyenne Context

Family Background Influences

Consideration of the influences of parents on children's socialization includes attention to both family values and practices concerning education. Regarding the value placed on education, a number of sources and interviewees indicated that their own view of education, as well as the prevailing view in the community, is that education is very important for their children. The Northern Cheyenne Educational Census (Ward and Wilson 1989) and other surveys support this finding. In fact, Cheyenne leaders, including Chief Dull Knife, advocated for education, and knowledge and learning were highly valued (Rowland 1994). However, there is also a certain ambivalence as well regarding book learning that represents "White man's knowledge and ways" and use of this knowledge to become superior to other members of the community. For example, high levels of education are better tolerated if community members do not feel that the person has changed or become snobbish.

Ethnographic sources also indicated two other conditions that affect general support for educational achievement: adults' incomplete or negative experiences with education, and the minimal role of parents in supervision of children's schoolwork. Regarding the educational experiences of the adults in the home, one important structural factor is the generational differences in educational experiences; some older generation members had negative experiences with boarding schools, but others attended the public high school and had somewhat better experiences. While some graduated, many others never finished high school because of pregnancy, marriage, work, or a variety of other reasons. For example, one source (who was in school in the 1950s and 1960s) reflected on support for schooling at that time on the reservation: "When I think back to grade school, there was a lot of parents who didn't see the importance of having a productive home for their kids. A lot of the kids had to baby-sit instead of coming to school . . . so a lot of the girls in the eighth grade quit; they didn't go on to high school. A lot of boys quit just because of no encouragement." Another younger source indicated some differences in schooling patterns for her generation: "Some of them stuck through it through high school, but I'd say about 15% of them just went to school, transferred to different schools, got kicked out and had problems with drinking and at home, and they were like two grades short from graduating" (Ward 1993).

These experiences have affected adults' views of education; some see it as important while others wonder what education credentials are worth. This is not to say that parents do not want their children to attend school or finish but rather that they don't have the knowledge to help their children get good grades in school. Additionally, students' grandparents did not participate in their children's schooling because, at that time, Indian parents were not encouraged to do so, and they were generally not well educated. It is only within the last two generations that more than 50% of adults have finished high school. Therefore, the parents of recent high school students had few childhood role models who taught them about how adults support their children's schooling, such as helping with homework, attending parent–teacher meetings, and so forth. Thus, while some adults now support education either as role models or by helping their children, others may take actions only when graduation becomes problematic. Closely monitoring and assisting with homework are not typical behaviors for parents who utilize a more traditional, noninterference parenting style. Other parents do not intervene because of competing personal problems or family needs. These approaches represent the diversity of cultural norms and divergent views among Cheyenne parents.

As described by one Cheyenne educator, traditional parents typically provided guidance to their children: "They did not tell the child everything to do. They encouraged the child to develop independence in making decisions, and they rewarded good behavior rather than punish bad" (Sooktis 1988). These practices can still be seen today. For example, one mother, a Head Start teacher, said that she and her husband did not monitor their high school son's school performance; they left it up to him to do his homework and pass his courses in high school. This noninterference approach is typical of some traditional Northern Cheyenne parents who allow adolescents more freedom in making decisions than is characteristic of American middle-class culture. However, some community members now see this approach as too permissive and problematic, especially when they believe that parents do not adequately discipline their children.

Criticisms of permissive parenting are based on the belief that Cheyenne traditional parenting (that involved extensive mentoring of children by adults in the extended family) as well as current non-Indian norms prescribe closer contact between adults and children and therefore provide for better socialization. Additionally, critics contend that in the absence of family members' close guidance of children, others external to the family, such as law enforcement agencies, social services, and schools, often must assume more responsibility for adolescent behavior. For many families, involvement with children, including discipline, is affected by substance abuse.

Substance abuse among adults and children is a major reason for the lack of direct support for schooling in some homes. When adults abuse alcohol or drugs, children often lack sufficient supervision and may even have to get themselves up in the morning and get ready for school. In such situations, parents' education levels and educational values may have little positive effect, since they rarely translate into behaviors that guide students' school efforts. Additionally, substance abuse may result in family violence and emotional trauma that have negative effects on students' attention to their schooling. For example, some teachers and school administrators described the seriousness of problems related to substance abuse that students bring to school with them; they often have such an impact that students are incapable of concentrating on schoolwork. Thus, to the extent that adults (and children) in the home are involved with substance abuse and belong to groups that support these behaviors, it is much more likely that children will not receive the support they need for schooling and that their performance will suffer.

Other family variables of interest in the analysis are family structure and employment status. Again, ethnographic information is useful in shedding some light on these dimensions of students' families. First, students live in a variety of family structures: single parents, two biological parents, stepparents, grandparents, aunts and uncles, and so on. Thus, to understand the effects of family life and the presence of adults we must consider the fact that adults in many students' homes may not be their parents but other adult members of their extended family, and that these adults may not have the same authority or influence on the child.

Of particular interest are the reasons that children on the Northern Cheyenne reservation live with members of their extended family. One reason is related to the employment status and income of adults on the reservation. Since a large percentage of persons on the reservation are unemployed (about 50%), financial need is common. Rather than rely on welfare payments, many adults depend on extended family for support or assistance. Therefore, when someone is financially unable to care for his or her children, other family members may help by taking the children into their homes. This is often an informal arrangement that may be either temporary or permanent. Other reasons are related to problems with substance abuse. Many children are formally placed in foster care with grandparents or aunts and uncles by the Tribe's social service agency when their parents go to treatment or exhibit a long-term incapacity to raise their children due to such problems as drug or alcohol addiction or violence.

While there is no systematic evidence indicating how living with extended family members affects students' school performance, information from community sources suggests two types of effects. One is that the generational effects discussed above may become more important as disproportionately more students are raised by grandparents or older members of

CHAPTER FIVE

the family, and concrete, practical support for school performance is lacking. An important aspect of this situation is that older members of the community are much more likely to speak Cheyenne and, in many cases, have limited English skills. For some students, this may provide the opportunity to become bilingual, while for others, it may limit their language development. Another effect is that students who live in formal foster care situations may be especially affected by the influences of having been in a dysfunctional home and having to adjust to a new home environment with non–family members or extended family members. However, although adjustment to a foster home placement may be difficult and negatively affect some students' school involvement and performance, for others it provides security and the chance to give more attention to schooling.

The effect of family structure is complicated by the type of household in which the student lives. Information from community sources suggests that the effects of various types of family structures are mediated by such factors as the education of the adults, their attitudes and skills relevant to schooling, health conditions, and the time and attention provided to the child and supporting schoolwork.

In summary, although other studies suggest that family background variables should have an important effect on school performance of children, the findings so far do not indicate the effects expected from these variables. Such measures typically have been used with assumptions about the mechanisms by which the human capital of parents or adults in the home influences children. In this study, however, several social and cultural conditions that affect Indian households modify these mechanisms such that, regardless of educational attainment levels, adult characteristics do not significantly affect school performance. A primary reason for the lack of effect of parental education level is the lack of adult involvement with students' schooling, for example, practical support, help, and monitoring. Even in cases in which parents are educated, they may not help their children with schoolwork. This is related to a variety of conditions, including the lack of role models for students' parents or guardians regarding involvement with schoolwork as well as lower educational attainment among parents or other guardians; values regarding schooling and parenting styles that result in lower levels of direct intervention in children's activities; and the prevalence of substance abuse, which detracts from attention to schooling. Thus, family structure effects are complicated by adult attitudes toward and attention to children's schooling. The result is that living in a two-parent family does not always have the expected positive effects for school performance, nor does living in a single-parent household have negative effects. This suggests the relevance of the concept of "native capital," the cultural knowledge and social relations among extended family and community members, which is a significant mediating influence on human capital formation and labor market processes. Specifically, the meanings of schooling and the ways in which students' families relate to and show support for schooling are unique among the Cheyenne and therefore have particular effects on students' school performance. (The lack of effects of parental employment status will be discussed in greater detail in relation to the dropout models discussed in chapter 6.)

Family, Peer, Reservation, and Community Effects

In spite of the absence of family background effects on school performance, the statistical evidence does point to the importance of students' community residence and reservation origin. In particular, residence in Busby (and both Busby and Ashland for girls) has a positive effect compared to Lame Deer, while being from the Crow reservation has a negative effect on school performance. Although these findings suggest that community residence affects schooling outcomes, caution must be taken in interpreting the results: at this point, it is unclear exactly what the community effect represents. What dimension of community life is responsible for the positive effect? How is it related to the process by which individuals attain social status? Ethnographic data suggest that social status within the reservation is achieved via both individual status and family relations. Individual status may be related to personal achievements, such as educational or occupational accomplishments, skills, or traditional knowledge, or it may be linked to drinking or recovery. However, an individual's social prestige is also affected by membership within his or her extended family, the traditionality or honor of the family, and the resources at their disposal. These considerations suggest the types of family social and cultural resources, or aspects of native capital, that are important to understand in this reservation population.

Family groups are located within general geographic areas of the reservation based on the original settlement patterns of the reservation,

CHAPTER FIVE

the allotment of lands, and efforts to consolidate land holdings among family members. While there is certainly diversity in the appraisal of the honor or status of reservation family groups, a pattern of general recognition of the families within the reservation social structure can also be discerned. Since everyone knows the extended families of students, they are affected by this pattern of recognition in their interaction with their peers and their families. In the same way, the drinking/recovery status of students and their family members is also fairly well known. This also contributes to their social status, perhaps more now than before recovery from substance abuse became as prevalent as it is today. Additionally, family groups may have particular orientations toward education that affect students' school outcomes. Because family groups may still occupy specific areas and influence community dynamics, communities are also likely to shape schooling.

As a case in point, reasons for the positive effect of Busby community residence on school performance compared to Lame Deer are suggested by cultural and historical data. First, Busby was established primarily by the White River Cheyenne band of the Northern Cheyenne Tribe. Today many families in Busby can still trace their lineage to the earliest settlement of this band. As suggested above, these residents still control the land in the area and have strong cultural and family ties to the other residents. Although ties to family and land provide the main reasons for living there, Busby Tribal School offers important employment, social, and cultural resources. Another consideration is the relative educational attainment of residents of Busby. In 1989 Busby had one of the highest percentages (76%) of high school and GED graduates among adults on the reservation. It also had one of the largest percentages of Cheyenne speakers on the reservation (45%). In contrast, Lame Deer had a much more diverse population than Busby: about a third of the adults did not have high school diplomas or GED certificates, and a smaller percentage of residents were Cheyenne speakers (38%). (The characteristics of Lame Deer will be discussed further in the next section.) More importantly, Busby is also the home of the tribal school, a source of pride to Busby residents. Busby residents work in all levels of the school, from maintenance to administrative positions. As the largest employer in the community and one of the most important Cheyenne organizations, Busby Tribal School is central to the life of the community, and Busby residents provide important feedback in the development of school policies and decisions.

In sum, the relatively more positive influence of Busby residence compared with that of Lame Deer may be related to, first, students' enrollment in an Indian, community-based school and, second, Busby students' locations within households, family groups, and community networks that are relatively more traditional as well as generally supportive of education. While some parents may use traditional, noninterference parenting styles, students may receive support from many sources in the community. Ethnographic data suggest that traditional community location generally affects students' schooling positively, but girls' school performance may benefit more than boys'.

According to Bonvillain (1988), family residence patterns may also indicate important aspects of gender relations. Although families are currently more widely dispersed than in previous eras when the Cheyenne were characterized as matrilocal (Moore 1987), the older pattern still exists in some areas. More importantly, the gender-related behavior and relations associated with matrilocality, which often include central roles and statuses for women within family groups and communities, have persisted to the present (Sawyer 1993). Evidence of the current strength of Cheyenne women's roles is found in their increased postsecondary education, higher-paying jobs, and active involvement in community life in terms of tribal business as well as the public sector (Ward 1993). Women in traditional communities are no exception to this pattern in relation to the strength of their roles within home and community life.

In contrast to the more positive effect of residence in Busby, residence in Lame Deer has a negative effect on school performance compared to other communities. One explanation suggested for these community effects involves being an "outsider" at these schools; that is, being from Lame Deer rather than the community in which the high school is located (i.e., Colstrip, Ashland, or Busby) sets these students apart. At Colstrip, this represents being Indian rather than White. However, at St. Labre, Lame Deer residence may represent reservation (or tribal affiliation) differences from Crow students or differences from Cheyenne residents of other communities. At Busby Tribal School, Lame Deer residence also means that the outsider status is related to being from a different reservation community.

CHAPTER FIVE

An alternative contextual explanation suggests that students from Lame Deer have socioeconomic or other disadvantages that negatively affect their educational performance. This is due to the fact that Lame Deer is much larger than the other two communities; is more diverse in terms of both socioeconomic and cultural groups; includes a large proportion of people who are unemployed, poor, and likely to be receiving social services; and has a lower overall level of schooling than the other two communities (about a third have no high school diploma or GED [Ward and Wilson 1989]). Lame Deer includes a number of different residential areas; for example, there are neighborhoods north and east of the main "downtown" that are distinguished from the neighborhoods to the south and west, some of which are known to be particularly poor. To the extent that Lame Deer youth come from economically stressed households and neighborhoods, or are isolated from support for schooling from family, peers, and other social networks, they may face greater obstacles to success in school.

Lame Deer also has a relatively higher incidence of activities (often illegal) that provide alternatives to school goals. For example, gang activities and crime involving juveniles and young adults have increased during the 1980s and early 1990s, especially crimes involving drug and alcohol use (Northern Cheyenne Tribal Action Plan 1994). Additionally, parents may be less involved with the schools their children attend, since they are located from sixteen to thirty miles away. Thus, despite the fact that Lame Deer is the site of tribal social services and agencies that offer resources to the community, the greater poverty and diversity of social circumstances among students as well as the distance from both the Indian schools and the public non-Indian school create important barriers to school participation for these students.

Finally, some sources have suggested that a combination of these views may actually provide the best explanation for the effects of Lame Deer residence. In other words, being from a relatively disadvantaged home situation as well as from a different community than the majority of students at St. Labre and Busby schools may serve to isolate Lame Deer students. Such isolation, often in combination with less adult support for education, may negatively affect students' performance levels.

Ethnographic data suggest that Ashland students may experience some similar effects as a result of the relatively low level of education and per capita income in this community. However, Ashland has some unique qualities as a Northern Cheyenne border community. For example, this town is largely segregated; Indian residents typically live in housing near the St. Labre Mission School as well as within a development within the reservation boundaries just across the Tongue River from Ashland. Other Cheyennes live on ranches along the road going north to Colstrip or south from Ashland toward Birney. Since Ashland is largely non-Indian, the Indian community has little, if any, control over town resources, such as land, businesses, and organizations. Because Ashland has bars and taverns, Indian residents have the opportunity to purchase alcohol legally, something that the reservation communities do not have. On the other hand, counteracting this influence are the resources of the Catholic Indian mission school, which offer a range of opportunities for students and parents to participate. Additionally, the small size of the Indian community and its traditional leadership as well as family and community networks often provide the close interaction among community residents that can encourage students.

In contrast to those living in Busby, relatively fewer Ashland community residents have high school diplomas or GEDs. Similarly, fewer Cheyennes work for local organizations that can provide graduates with jobs. Although over the last twenty years an increasing number of Cheyennes have been employed at St. Labre Catholic School in staff, counseling, and administrative positions, the majority of teaching jobs are held by non-Indians. Cheyennes also make up a substantial proportion of the workforce of St. Labre enterprises, which help to support the school. Nevertheless, Cheyenne workers compose a small part of Ashland's total labor force and have little direct influence on decisions in the community or the schools. On the other hand, many Cheyenne residents of Ashland support the education of students at St. Labre and Colstrip. These adults, many of whom are St. Labre alumni, are important role models who support St. Labre's recent efforts to provide greater recognition of the Cheyenne and Crow cultural heritages of its students. However, others in the local community continue to see St. Labre as an agent of assimilation that, at crucial times in the past, exercised strict, if not harsh, policies toward its students. Some adults who experienced these earlier periods of St. Labre's history remember the school's requirements to attend mass and its strict dress and behavior codes, which they perceive as intended to make

CHAPTER FIVE

them "White." One St. Labre alumna described the cultural conflict she experienced at St. Labre (Ward 1998a):

> And so I was subjected to the Catholic religion. . . . We were told that if we did something bad, we'd go to hell and that any little thing . . . any little wrong move we would go to hell, and I always thought that it was a really scary religion, and I was scared and I had never been hit in my whole life until I went to that Catholic boarding school where a nun slapped me straight across the face for throwing spit wads on the bus. I was a little tom boy, and so we were playing spit wads on the bus, and I was reported, and she slapped me . . . just smacked me across the face, and that . . . that memory stayed with me for the rest of my life, 'cuz nobody had ever hit me. . . . I don't believe in it. You know, the Catholics might believe in it, but I didn't believe in it because I felt it was a real cruel . . . form of religion because we had to kneel down for hours upon hours and pray all the time. They taught us how to pray in their way, but it was empty because it was in English. And it didn't mean anything to me. And I felt like we were praying to a non-Indian god. I never accepted it.

Despite its efforts to accommodate the cultural communities it serves, St. Labre continues to experience tensions with students, parents, and community members. While Cheyenne family and community networks often provide support for education, their influence on students must compete with peers' and other influences that distract students from schooling. The Indian community's influence on the meaning and value students place on schooling is also mediated by the Catholic school's culture and resources.

The statistical analyses presented above on the effects of reservation origins reveal that the school performance levels of St. Labre Indian students are negatively affected by being from the Crow reservation. Because they reside at St. Labre Catholic School during the school year, Crow students may not have the same level of contact with their reservation communities as Cheyenne students. For Crow students, attending St. Labre, where instruction is in English, involves an important transition in their schooling, not just because it is a new school, but because they no longer speak Crow in the classroom. Thus, Crow reservation affiliation indicates a greater chance of language problems in the classroom, a situation that school counselors report often negatively affects grades. Additionally,

Crow and Cheyenne students form somewhat distinctive social groups around which tensions and conflicts sometimes develop. Such tensions erupt from time to time, producing some negative experiences for the students involved, particularly the Crow students, who are in the minority. In some ways, these tensions reflect very old tribal rivalries (Stands In Timber and Liberty 1967). However, over time, the conflicts between Cheyenne and Crow students have diminished, as evidenced by intertribal dating and some marriages. Additional discussion of the effect of reservation origins will be presented in the next section, in which the effects of school climate and context on school performance levels will be examined.

Peer pressure is another significant dimension of the social context influencing students' choices, often resulting in the use of drugs and alcohol. A study of chemical abuse among minors by the National Institute on Drug Abuse (1987), which included schools serving the Northern Cheyenne reservation, found that the majority of students used drugs and alcohol often enough to jeopardize their physical and emotional health (see chapter 3).

Ethnographic data also indicate that community and peer influences support particular gender orientations to school performance and future goals. There is a great deal of continuity across generations in women's aspirations to be mothers and homemakers. In a study of three generations of Cheyenne women (Sawyer 1993), most young women (ages 18–25) reported marriage and family as primary goals. Among the younger high school–age girls, peer culture affirms and supports the goals for marriage and family by encouraging romantic relationships. One mother expressed a typical concern about her teenage daughter's preoccupation with romantic relationships: "I see her doing exactly what I did in high school. She is totally preoccupied with romance. [A friend] calls it 'warrior love.' I really don't want her to go through what I did [divorce], but I don't know what to do about it." This mother's concerns are supported by the increasing number of Cheyenne girls having children.

The data presented above suggest that many high school students experience pressures pulling them away from school involvement and graduation, including substance abuse, social groups, and assumption of adult roles. Given the relatively low level of parental intervention in children's schooling, most parents' lack of experience with college, and the widely held perceptions of limited opportunities, many students do not see schooling as particularly relevant. Thus, attention to school performance is not a priority. An interesting paradox is that girls often do better than boys in school while at the same time experiencing contradictory influences that often distract them from school performance. Support for assuming the adult roles of wife and mother is particularly strong in some traditional groups as well as among some peer groups. Cheyenne high school–age girls must often negotiate among these different interests and find appropriate roles in school, friend, family, and community groups. Regardless of their ultimate choices, girls' mean GPAs typically show that they are quite capable of high performance levels.

Each of the communities and groups discussed above provides different levels of social and cultural resources and specific orientations to schooling. In particular, the effects of community residence and reservation origins indicate the importance of students' integration into both cultural groups and geographic communities. Within these social contexts, students experience different levels and types of social capital that affect perceptions of the meaning of schooling and shape their attitudes and actions, including school participation and performance. While Busby appears to be the most homogeneous and potentially supportive of schooling, both Lame Deer and Ashland have sources of support for schooling. However, overall they seem to be more diffuse than Busby. This means that students experience more diverse messages about schooling and therefore respond with somewhat more ambivalence. The effects of specific school contexts and the relationship of communities to schools, then, become important mediators of these influences.

School Performance Models by School Type: Individual, Family, and School Influences

In the following analysis, models are presented for each of the three school populations that show the effects of the independent variables discussed above on school performance. Thus, this analysis is intended to assess whether there was a difference in the influences on school performance in the three school populations. Descriptive data on student experiences for the three school populations suggest several important differences. First, Busby and Colstrip students had larger mean absences (19.4 and 21, respectively) in the first two years of high school than St. Labre students

(15.6). On the other hand, St. Labre Catholic School had the largest percentage of students with suspensions (18%), followed by Colstrip Public School (13%) and Busby Tribal School (11%). However, a larger percentage of Colstrip students transferred to other local schools (89%) than students at the other two schools (58%). Finally, the percentage of students involved in extracurricular activities was highest at Colstrip (38%), with St. Labre (35%) following closely behind. The percentage of students involved in extracurricular activities at Busby Tribal School (10%) was less than a third of the percentages at Colstrip and St. Labre. Given these data showing the wide variation in students' school experiences across the three schools, the following analysis evaluates their impact relative to other variables.

In table 5.4, regression coefficients are presented for three school models that include the same variables as shown in model 2 of table 5.3. Differences in student population size among the schools may affect the significance of the statistics presented for the smaller schools. These models can be interpreted to show the effects of the independent variables when controlling for the school attended variable.

Table 5.4. OLS Coefficients by School for the Effects of Community, Gender, Family Characteristics, and School Experiences on Mean GPA

	Busby		St. Labre		Colstrip	
	Coef.	SE	Coef.	SE	Coef.	SE
Community/Reservation[a]						
Lame Deer	−.40*	(.22)	−.27*	(.16)	−.02	(.003)
Crow			−.50***	(.14)		
Female[b]	.26	(.19)	.07	(.11)	.08	(.10)
Family Characteristics						
Nonintact family	−.08	(.23)	−.10	(.13)	−.17	(.13)
At least 1 adult employed	.22	(.22)	.10	(.13)	−.06	(.12)
Primary adult HS diploma	.02	(.23)	.33	(.21)	.08	(.13)
School Experiences						
Transfers	−.07	(.09)	.01	(.05)	−.10***	(.05)
Absences	.003	(.004)	.04	(.004)	−.01***	(.003)
Ever suspended	−.17	(.42)	−.30	(.19)	−.19	(.13)
Extracurricular activities	.05	(.14)	.13***	(.04)	.08***	(.03)
N	52		107		137	
R-square	.05		.24		.22	
F	1.24		3.54***		4.15***	

[a] Omitted categories for community are Busby and Ashland, and omitted category for reservation is Northern Cheyenne.
[b] Omitted category is male.
* $p < .10$, ** $p < .05$, *** $p < .01$

CHAPTER FIVE

Only in the Colstrip model do a variety of school experiences significantly affect Indian students' school performance. Specifically, school transfers and absences, indicators of less engagement of students with schooling, have negative effects on mean GPAs. Involvement in extracurricular activities, however, has a positive, significant effect on mean GPAs. These findings are consistent with studies indicating that, generally, lower engagement with school negatively affects school performance while greater involvement has a positive effect. In contrast, the lack of effects by individual and family characteristics contradicts studies that show these variables to be important. One possible explanation of the absence of effects of parental education is related to the noninterference parenting style of many Indian parents. Parents who do closely monitor their children's schoolwork have less effect on school performance even when these parents have relevant educational experiences and credentials. Additionally, since unemployment is so high, many families rely on assistance from extended family, the informal economy, and other forms of assistance. Thus, the employment status of parents is more diffuse and does not have the expected relationship to schooling. In essence, the lack of effect of parental employment on school outcomes may be related both to the poor opportunity structure and to Cheyenne cultural norms favoring extended family support that mediates parents' effects on children's schooling.

Although school experience variables are not significant in the models for St. Labre and Busby (with the exception of extracurricular activities at St. Labre), the signs of the coefficients suggest some similarity in the operation of these variables in the two Indian school contexts. Nevertheless, the lack of effects of these school experience variables is more difficult to interpret. While one possibility is that an unmeasured aspect of the school environments reduces the impact of negative school experiences on school performance, another possibility is that community residence and reservation origin may have particularly important effects on school performance relative to school experiences. The mixed results for the extracurricular activity involvement variable also indicate differences in the contexts of the three schools. In this case, the Catholic school and the public school are different from the tribal school, where, contrary to expectations, extracurricular activity involvement has no effect on cumulative GPAs.

In sum, the variation among the three school populations indicates support for expectations that traditional community residence would more positively influence school performance than residence in other communities. However, the results do not support expectations concerning the positive effects of being female or those regarding the effects of family structure, adult employment, and adult educational attainment. On the other hand, findings do indicate the importance of school experiences within the public school and for extracurricular activities within both the public school and Catholic school. Such mixed results for the school and background variables require additional investigation.

Importantly, these results show the relevance of students' community residence and reservation origins as well as their location in specific school contexts. For Indian students at the two Indian schools, community and reservation origins had relatively more influence on school performance than school experiences, while the opposite was true for Indian students attending the public school. To clarify the effects of variables included in these models, the following discussion draws on ethnographic case study data concerning the school contexts, the three communities, their resources and orientations to Indian students and schooling, and the relations between schools and communities. In the sections that follow, the focus will be on dimensions of the different community social contexts as well as relations between schools and communities that influence school performance.

The Northern Cheyenne Context

School Experiences and School Climate

Qualitative information, received from a variety of community and school sources, is especially useful in suggesting a reason for the lack of effects by school experience variables on student performance in the two Indian schools. Several sources suggested that Indian students attending Colstrip and St. Labre are often prevented from playing sports, especially basketball, because of their poor academic performance. In such cases, athletes chose to leave those schools and attend Busby, where there were far fewer restrictions on eligibility to play on sports teams. In this situation, extracurricular activity involvement did not have the expected effect of motivating students to keep up their grades to meet scholastic standards set for athletes. Similarly, many Busby students had academic problems, and the poor attendance rate at Busby has been legendary. Because the

CHAPTER FIVE

tribal school was committed to helping students who couldn't "make it" anywhere else, some sources suggested that even excessive absences among Busby students were not often penalized. Given the greater possibility as well for "grade inflation" and social promotions, performance expectations only minimally affected students' grades.

Important aspects of school experiences, then, are the way students are treated and the academic expectations of teachers and administrators. Ethnographic data indicate that regarding these areas, the schools varied considerably. St. Labre and Busby schools are located in primarily Indian communities, while Colstrip Public High School is not. As suggested in chapter 3, few teachers at the Indian schools are Indian or understand the culture, history, and language of this population. Despite the lack of cultural continuity between faculty and students, however, both schools attempt to help Indian students succeed and to serve the interests of the Indian communities in which they are located.

However, success is not easy to accomplish. Administrators commented on the difficulties of serving populations plagued with social and economic problems. Indian school personnel emphasized the need for more parental support for education and for their schools. While this view does not differ from that of Colstrip administrators, the primary difference is in the actions that the Indian schools took to build support in the Indian communities they serve. Busby Tribal School and St. Labre Catholic School both had more extensive efforts in place to involve Indian parents, such as through their boards or advisory committees, school activities, and regular contact between Indian school personnel and members of the community. Since the schools are located in Indian communities, distance from the school was not a barrier to interaction. Activities were planned for regular exchanges on schooling issues. Colstrip School's communication with Indian parents also included parent–teacher meetings, other regular school activities, and the parent advisory committee meetings in Lame Deer. However, interaction between Colstrip School personnel and Indian parents was constrained by parents' unfamiliarity with Colstrip School personnel and lack of transportation to get to meetings.

Busby's and St. Labre's orientations to Indian students and parents resulted in accommodation to parents' and students' interests and needs when school-related issues were raised. Responses to problems took such forms as administrative solutions designed to meet the particular needs of the student and family; pressure on teachers to accommodate students; and a general view of schooling for Indians that assumes that problems with learning should be addressed by the schools. Although school personnel responded to such pressures in a variety of ways, some responded by lowering the standards and expectations for these students. Thus, the academic curriculum and extracurricular activities were more often perceived as areas that could be negotiated by Indian students and their parents. While this may have had positive results in terms of meeting individual student needs, the more negative aspects included Busby teachers' perceptions that the school's policies were unclear, and that there were no rules or guidelines that everyone agreed on. In such a politicized situation, teachers felt compelled to comply with parental and community wishes often despite their own feelings or beliefs.

While on the face of it, the two Indian schools appear similar in their negotiation of parents' and students' demands, the missions and policies of the schools provided different reasons for and approaches to the schools' relations with the Indian communities. These different approaches also resulted in somewhat different academic and behavioral expectations of students. For example, because St. Labre had resources for recruitment of personnel with administrative expertise and relevant teaching experience, the school could select faculty and staff that were at least highly supportive of the school's goals even if they were not familiar with the community they served. In spite of, or in response to, requests for help by Indian community members with their children's school-related problems, recent mission school policies have become stricter, but also more inclusive of parents. Specifically, the school now requires Indian parents whose children have school-related problems (truancy, discipline problems, etc.) to work closely with the school to remedy the situation. Otherwise, the school will expel these children so that others on the school's waiting list can attend.

However, the school and mission continue to be viewed as generally friendly to the Indian community, although their early history of antipathy to Indian culture also continues to create a barrier for many reservation community members. Most importantly, the mission is seen as a potential source of support in times of need. In response to numerous requests from the Northern Cheyenne community for assistance for a wide

CHAPTER FIVE

variety of needs, St. Labre Mission has often provided help. The extensive church resources are generally used to provide assistance with institutionally based self-help projects, and for educational improvements including funds for scholarships and special school programs.

In contrast, Busby School's accommodating orientation was more culturally and politically based in the Cheyenne community. While St. Labre and Colstrip could turn students away or suspend them, Busby Tribal School was mandated to take all Cheyennes who wanted to attend the school. Demands from parents regarding the school's responses to their children's needs were based on the fact that the school is a Cheyenne institution. They saw the job of the school as serving the unique needs of Cheyenne students. Consequently, parents felt freer to make demands on the school than they would otherwise. School officials tried to resolve the problems of their constituents and were highly motivated to avoid political struggles with other tribal institutions such as the Tribal Council or court.

Unlike St. Labre and Busby schools, Colstrip's staff reactions to parents' inquiries about and requests for assistance with Indian students' school-related problems were less responsive and flexible. Indian parents' perceptions were that there was not only a lack of understanding of their children but also a lack of willingness to help. For example, parents' requests for special help were met with statements that school policy was to treat all students equally. This resulted in Indian parents' belief that school personnel did not care about their children since they appeared to have greater respect for the rules and standards than the needs of the Indian students. School personnel did not realize that "equal treatment," which distanced them from the problems of Indian students, was perceived as discrimination by Indian community members. Thus, while Colstrip School generally made higher demands of students and parents, it was not perceived as highly responsive to the needs of Indian parents and students. On the other hand, Colstrip administrators were also quite aware of the different views parents held about how to handle specific students' problem situations. Consequently, there was a shift toward referring Indian students with school-related problems to Indian home-school counselors who could sometimes negotiate solutions among students, parents, and school personnel. This led to some relaxation of the stricter sanctions on Indian student behavior and more solutions to discipline problems that might otherwise have led to suspensions from school.

Another aspect of the situation involved the resources and opportunities offered by each school. As suggested by the information on types and levels of resources outlined in chapter 3, parents, students, and teachers all confirmed the extensiveness of the social opportunities provided by Colstrip Public Schools. However, Indian students also described the difficulties in taking advantage of these activities as well as the limitations on the roles they could play in student clubs and groups. (These are explored in greater detail in chapter 7.) In terms of academic opportunities, Colstrip offered the widest range of courses and remedial programs. Although its remedial assistance was more limited, St. Labre offered a wide variety of school activities in which Indian students held leadership positions. One mother explained why her daughter chose to attend St. Labre (Ward 1998a): "I told her she could choose which school to attend, but whatever school she chose, she had to stay. So she visited all three schools and decided on St. Labre. She said it was more open and friendlier to Indians, and there were more things for students to do." A former St. Labre student explained why she believes many Cheyennes choose St. Labre:

> Some of the girls don't want to have to deal with White students at Colstrip. They would rather just be with other Indians and not have to worry about what the White kids think. Some of the boys go to St. Labre because they think they have a better chance of playing on the football team and the basketball team than at Colstrip. Even though they know it's stricter at Labre, they still want to go there because of what they have for the students.

Busby Tribal School had the least to offer in relation to school activities. Sports and schoolwide social events were the primary extracurricular activities offered. Academic and remedial programs were limited by the meager resources available. As mentioned above, participation in school activities generally was not restricted by academic requirements at Busby as much as it was at the other two schools. Both teachers and community members explained this practice as a result of the need to encourage student participation in school activities.

These different school orientations in terms of treatment of students and parents as well as expectations and opportunities have important implications for understanding the levels of absences, suspensions, local school transfers, extracurricular activity involvement, and performance in the three schools. Tolerance for absences was highest at the tribal school, although Colstrip students also experienced high levels of absences. Similarly, the tribal school and public school were the least inclined to resort to suspensions for discipline problems. While the Catholic school was generally supportive of Indian students, it was stricter in its discipline policies. Information on school transfers and extracurricular activities for the three schools also indicates that the public school students were the most involved and seemed to have shopped around for a high school. The wider range of course offerings and remedial programs as well as social activities appealed to many students. This motivated some students to switch from the Indian schools to the public school, while other Indian students who moved to Lame Deer wanted to attend the school that most other students in Lame Deer attended.

Reservation Origins and Community Residence

In contrast to the absence of effects of school variables at the Indian schools, significant results for two of the individual variables have particularly interesting implications. First, school performance levels of St. Labre Indian students were negatively affected by being from the Crow reservation. Two possible explanations of the difference between Crow and Northern Cheyenne students in terms of their performance levels were offered by community and school sources. As suggested previously, one explanation is that many Crow students attending St. Labre attended elementary schools on the Crow reservation in which instruction was conducted in the Crow language. When these students transferred to high school at St. Labre where instruction is in English, many students faced language difficulties that negatively affected their grades.

Additionally, the Northern Cheyenne and Crow tribes have a long history of competition dating back to the Battle of the Little Big Horn and earlier. While some sources suggest that competition between members of the two tribes may affect the social climate of St. Labre Catholic School, others contend that such competition has diminished so much in recent generations that it would be very unlikely to affect these cohorts of students. Whatever the explanation, our analyses indicate a clear difference in performance levels of the two groups.

Additionally, the findings indicate a strong difference in performance levels of students residing in Lame Deer, compared to students from other communities, at both St. Labre and Busby schools. As suggested earlier, one explanation is that there may be negative effects of being an outsider, specifically, being from Lame Deer rather than the communities in which the high schools are located. Alternatively, Lame Deer residence may disadvantage students by offering more diffuse support for schooling.

Cultural Influences on Cheyenne School Performance

This section presents a final analysis of the school performance of Indian students in this study that includes additional cultural and social influences on students' school performance levels: cultural participation and distractions from schooling, parents' cultural orientations, and their involvement in and support of schooling. Descriptive statistics show how these cultural and school support variables are distributed across the communities in which students reside. For example, family traditionality (an index including parents' understanding and use of Cheyenne, knowledge of history and culture, and participation in social and cultural activities) varies as follows by community: Busby has the highest mean value (.38), followed by Lame Deer (.23) and Ashland (.12). Means for students' knowledge and use of Cheyenne follow the same pattern, with Busby (.41) having the highest level, Lame Deer (.26) next, and Ashland the lowest (.0). Mean values for student problems (an index including substance abuse as well as conflicts with authorities) are also highest in Busby (.71) and Lame Deer (.68) and lowest in Ashland (.53). On the other hand, mean values for family experience with recovery from substance abuse are highest in Ashland (.16) and Busby (.11) and lowest in Lame Deer (.09). Finally, means for family support for and involvement with students' schools are relatively low across all three communities.

This pattern appears to contradict the ethnographic information presented earlier about the relatively greater participation of parents in Busby Tribal School. However, it must be kept in mind that many traditional

CHAPTER FIVE

Cheyenne parents prefer not to participate extensively or may intervene only if problems arise. Thus, the greater traditionality of Busby parents may mediate how and when school support is shown. For Ashland parents and students, the effects of living in a border community and attending a Catholic school must also be taken into account when considering several of these variables. For example, characteristics of Ashland parents of St. Labre students (their education, their involvement with St. Labre School or enterprises) may correlate with a decline in traditional orientations among these families. Additionally, St. Labre's stricter atmosphere but greater opportunities for counseling and extracurricular activities may have diminished both alcohol use and conflicts with authorities among St. Labre High School students. Although Ashland residents have had more immediate access to alcohol, many families have turned to recovery programs for assistance. By comparison, Lame Deer is in the middle of the range of the communities on all measures. Lame Deer students and parents have relatively greater traditional culture and language use but also have high levels of student problems and lower levels of family recovery participation. However, family support for schooling is somewhat higher than in Busby.

These figures suggest that the additional cultural and school support variables included in the following analysis are likely to show some effects on school performance relative to the other variables. Two of the models presented below include terms representing the effects of specific community–school combinations that previous analyses suggested would be important. Contrast coding procedures were used to create variables showing the expected differences in community–school groups based on previous analyses and case study data.[1]

The results shown in table 5.5 indicate that while student use of Cheyenne has a negative effect on mean GPA in the first model, this effect disappears when family characteristics are included. Interestingly, the traditionality of families negatively influences performance levels, as does the presence of only one adult in model 2. However, family school support has a modest but positive influence on mean GPA. When community–school combinations are included in model 3, these family characteristics remain significant. Of particular interest in this model are the positive effects on school performance of living in Busby and Ashland while attending the local Indian schools, as well as the positive effect of living in Lame Deer and attending St. Labre. Also, in this model, gender (female vs. male) positively affects school performance. In the final model, the effect of gender increases in significance when school experiences are included. The negative effects of one adult in the household and family traditionality, and the positive effects of Busby community residence and attending Busby Tribal School, remain significant. As indicated in previous analyses, school experiences have important effects on school performance; extracurricular activity involvement is positive, while suspensions, absences, and school transfers are negative. In fact, several community-school combination variables indirectly affect school performance through school experiences, suggesting the importance of both school and community contexts.

These findings suggest that attention to cultural orientations and engagement with schools among both students and their parents can contribute to a better explanation of school performance. Of particular importance is the fact that cultural orientations are multidimensional: while students' use of Cheyenne and family traditionality may not directly support school performance, family support for schooling may still be positive. Additionally, the traditional environment of Busby, combined with attending the Busby Tribal School, also supports higher school performance. Thus, we must understand in what ways and for what reasons traditional orientations relate to schooling outcomes. For example, traditional parents may have had more negative experiences themselves with schooling, or they may prefer not to support schooling as overtly as other parents. Nevertheless, an analysis (not shown) of the distribution of family traditionality by parental high school graduation shows that many parents with higher levels of traditionality also have high school diplomas. Parents with higher levels of schooling also exhibit higher levels of school support. Therefore, it would be incorrect to conclude that a family's traditional cultural orientations and participation contribute negatively to schooling. In fact, analyses of the interactions of these variables show a far more complex picture in which parents' education, support for school, and cultural traits affect their children's school performance. However, the nature and direction of these effects are most likely shaped by the community in which families are located and the relation of the community to the school their children attend.

Table 5.5. OLS Coefficients for the Effects of Student and Family Characteristics, Culture, Community, School Attended, and School Experiences on Mean GPA

	Model 1		Model 2		Model 3		Model 4	
	Coef.	SE	Coef.	SE	Coef.	SE	Coef.	SE
Student Characteristics								
Female[a]	.064	.084	.082	.085	.118*	.079	.141**	.075
Student's language	−.112*	.066	.076	.081	.081	.085	.093	.081
Problem/conflict with authority	−.096	.077	−.100	.078	−.092	.076	−.025	.073
Family Characteristics								
Only one adult present			−.193***	.093	−.166**	.092	−.132**	.089
At least one adult with high school diploma			.049	.070	.051	.069	.065	.065
Family school support			.131*	.067	.134*	.065	.095	.062
Family recovery			.080	.123	.091	.123	.062	.116
Family traditionality			−.235***	.132	−.271***	.128	−.237***	.122
Community/School Combinations								
Living in Busby/attending Busby vs. Colstrip					.207***	.097	.213***	.093
Living in Busby/attending Busby or Colstrip vs. all other schools and communities					.056	.015	.075	.015

Predictor	β	SE	β	SE
Living in Ashland/attending St. Labre or Colstrip vs. living in Lame Deer/attending St. Labre or Colstrip	.042	.024	.031	.023
Living in Ashland/attending St. Labre vs. Colstrip	.128*	.101	.099	.096
Living in Lame Deer/attending St. Labre vs. attending Colstrip or Busby	.133**	.046	.101	.044
Living in Lame Deer/attending Colstrip vs. Busby	.030	.073	-.022	.070
School Experiences				
Extracurricular activities			.240***	.020
Suspensions			-.117*	.106
Absences			-.140**	.002
Transfers			-.094	.034
R-square	.034	.129	.219	.317
F	2.602	4.069	4.268	5.392
N	276	276	276	276

[a] Omitted category is male.

⁺ p < .10, * p < .05, *** p < .01

CHAPTER FIVE

Summary

The school performance models presented in this chapter reveal the importance of individual characteristics, specifically, community residence and reservation origins. Students' fluency in Cheyenne and their family traditionality negatively influenced school performance. However, traditional communities as well as family support for schooling continued to have positive influences on school outcomes. Statistical findings also show the relevance of the role of students' integration into family networks, cultural groups, and residential communities that provide the basis for different social groups within each school context. Social distinctions among Northern Cheyenne community and family groups were relevant at Busby Tribal School, while intertribal group distinctions (Northern Cheyenne and Crow) as well as intratribal differences were relevant among students at St. Labre. Students' residence in Busby and Ashland while attending local Indian schools had the most positive effects on mean GPAs, particularly for girls. In contrast, while Lame Deer residence was more problematic when students attended Busby and St. Labre, at Colstrip, school experiences were more important than Lame Deer residence for school performance.

Additionally, findings show that such school experiences as absences, school transfers, and extracurricular activities indicated how well students were integrated into groups and activities that supported their school participation; they had important influences on the level of school performance of students overall and, generally, within the different schools. The type of school attended also was important for Indian students' school performance levels. Specifically, students attending the two Indian schools had higher performance levels compared to Indian students attending the public, non-Indian school.

Family background characteristics had no influence on school performance in the analyses of all Indian students. However, among Cheyenne students, family structure had an important influence: the presence of only one adult negatively affects school performance. Qualitative data suggest that this is related, at least in part, to the absence of strong parental involvement with students' schooling. A second factor is that extended family support and other forms of assistance to families level the influence of parental employment, a socioeconomic variable found in other studies to influence children's schooling outcomes.

EVALUATING ECOLOGICAL MODELS OF SCHOOL PERFORMANCE

Given these findings, the analysis will now examine models of dropout behavior. Analyses in chapter 6 will assess the relative influence of school performance compared to the other background and school experience variables.

Note

1. Contrast coding for community residence and school attended combinations include the following: Hypothesis 1: Busby residence and Busby Tribal School + Ashland residence and St. Labre Catholic School = 1. Busby or Ashland residence and Colstrip Public School = −1. Else = 0. Hypothesis 2: Busby residence and Busby Tribal School or Colstrip Public School = 1. Ashland residence and Colstrip Public School = −1. Else = 0. Hypothesis 3: Busby residence and Busby Tribal School + Ashland residence and Colstrip Public School = 1. Busby residence and Colstrip Public School + Ashland residence and St. Labre Catholic School = −1. Else = 0. Hypothesis 4: Lame Deer residence and St. Labre Catholic School or Colstrip Public School = 1. Lame Deer residence and Busby Tribal School = −2. Else = 0. Hypothesis 5: Lame Deer residence and St. Labre Catholic School = 1. Lame Deer residence and Colstrip Public School = −1. Else = 0. Hypothesis 6: Lame Deer residence and St. Labre Catholic School = 1. Crow reservation communities and St. Labre Catholic School = −1. Else = 0. Hypothesis 7: Busby residence and Busby Tribal School or Colstrip Public School + Ashland residence and St. Labre Catholic School or Colstrip Public School = 1. Lame Deer residence and Busby Tribal School or St. Labre Catholic School or Colstrip Public School + Crow reservation communities and St. Labre Catholic School = −1. Else = 0.

CHAPTER SIX
EVALUATION OF SCHOOL DROPOUT MODELS

In this chapter, information from analyses of school performance in chapter 5 informs the analysis of dropout behavior. The analysis follows the same organization as the previous chapter, starting with general models of dropout behavior for the study population and proceeding to the comparison of school populations and then returning to the general models to evaluate the usefulness of additional cultural and school support variables. Each statistical analysis is followed by a discussion of ethnographic data that offer additional insights into these findings.

General Dropout Model: The Effects of Individual, Community, Family, School Type, School Experiences, and School Performance

The next analysis addresses the influence of individual and family background, type of school attended, school experiences, and school performance on graduation from high school for all Indian students. The first model examines the effects of individual and family characteristics as well as school attended on dropping out of high school. The second model adds into the analysis the effects of school experiences, that is, local school transfers, absences, suspensions, and extracurricular activity involvement, and the third model identifies the relative effect of school performance on dropping out given the effects of all the other variables. Expected findings for this analysis can be summarized as follows:

EVALUATION OF SCHOOL DROPOUT MODELS

1. Students' residence in more traditional communities (Busby and Ashland compared to Lame Deer) or reservation (Crow) will decrease the chances of dropping out, while gender (female) will increase the chances of dropping out.

2. Family background characteristics (the completion of high school by one adult, and full-time employment of at least one adult in the home) will reduce the probability of dropping out, while having only one adult in the home will increase the students' chances of dropping out.

3. Attendance at the tribal school and the Catholic school will more negatively affect dropping out than attendance at the non-Indian public school.

4. Absences from school, suspensions from school, and transfers to other local schools will increase the chances of dropping out, while participation in extracurricular activities will decrease the chances of dropping out.

5. Higher mean GPA levels will reduce the probability of dropping out.

6. Although community residence and family background characteristics will have important effects on school completion, school experiences will have the greatest effects.

Table 6.1 displays three models that show how dropout behavior is affected by individual student attributes and community residence compared to family and school variables. The coefficients in model 1 of table 6.1 show some very interesting changes compared to their effects on performance levels. For example, earlier we saw that residence in Busby positively affected school performance. In the analysis of dropout behavior, residence in Busby negatively influences dropping out of high school. However, unlike the earlier analyses, the effect of being from the Crow reservation and gender are no longer statistically significant.

An important development in this analysis concerns changes in the effects of family characteristics on dropping out of high school. While family structure had limited effects on school performance levels, family

Table 6.1. Logistic Regression Coefficients for the Effects of Community Residence, Gender, Family Characteristics, School Attended, School Experiences, and School Performance on Dropping Out

	Model 1		Model 2		Model 3	
	Coef.	SE	Coef.	SE	Coef.	SE
Community Residence[a]						
Ashland	.19	.40	.10	.47	.23	.51
Busby	-1.62***	.46	-1.73***	.49	-1.23***	.54
Reservation[b]						
Crow	.25	.47	-.06	.53	-.36	.58
Gender[c]						
Female	.24	.25	.08	.28	.27	.31
Family Characteristics						
One adult present	.74***	.29	.62*	.32	.63*	.35
At least one adult employed	.03	.29	.21	.33	.24	.36
At least one adult high school diploma	-.93***	.35	-1.28***	.43	-1.21***	.46
School Attended[d]						
Busby	.96***	.36	.43	.40	.21	.45
St. Labre	-.04	.36	.09	.41	.43	.44
School Experiences/Performance						
Transfers			.02	.13	.04	.14
Absences			.00	.01	.00	.01
Ever suspended			.91***	.44	.71	.46
Extracurricular activities			-1.00***	.19	-.82***	.18
Cumulative GPA					-1.38***	.33
Model chi-square	53.05		120.82		163.88	
d.f.	12		16		18	
N	317		317		317	

[a] Omitted category is Lame Deer.
[b] Omitted category is Northern Cheyenne.
[c] Omitted category is male.
[d] Omitted category is Colstrip Public School.
* p < .10, ** p < .05, *** p < .01

characteristics are very influential in relation to the completion of schooling. For example, having a family with only one adult present has a very significant effect on dropping out: Indian students with only one adult at home are much more likely to drop out of high school. Although having an adult at home who works full-time has no effect on dropping out, the education of adults in the home (a high school diploma or GED) has a very significant effect—Indian students are more likely to finish high school than drop out. These effects of family structure and parents' education suggest the relevance of structural features of the students' home environment to school completion.

The final part of model 1 addresses the effects of the type of school attended on dropping out. The coefficients for Busby and St. Labre show that only enrollment in Busby School has a very strong influence on students' dropout behavior compared to Colstrip. The effect of this variable is consistent with the high dropout rate at Busby School (shown in chapter 4). In contrast, attending St. Labre has no effect on dropping out compared to Colstrip.

Model 2 coefficients show some similarity to model 1 in terms of the effects of community residence and family variables. However, the addition of school experiences to the model has eliminated the effect of both the school attended and the family structure variables. Importantly, the effects of attending Busby School are now represented by two school experience variables—suspensions and extracurricular activity involvement; while being suspended from school increases the chances of dropping out, greater student involvement in extracurricular activities works in the opposite direction, to decrease dropout behavior.

Finally, model 3 adds the effect of mean GPA to the analysis. The addition of this variable to the model is important because it eliminates the influence of one school experience variable—suspensions—although extracurricular activity involvement remains significant. The school performance variable—mean GPA—is also significant and negatively affects dropping out. Thus, the lower the mean GPA, the more likely students are to drop out. Changes in the effects of school experience variables with the addition of mean GPA to the model suggest that school performance is an important intervening variable: school type and experiences affect school performance, which, in turn, affects dropping out.

CHAPTER SIX

The final model for Indian students suggests that the following variables are important for explaining dropout behavior: community residence (Busby compared to Lame Deer), having only one adult present in the home, having an adult in the home with a high school diploma or a GED, the level of extracurricular activity involvement, and mean GPA. These results do not support the expectation that gender would affect dropping out. However, the expectation that community residence, specifically, residence in the more traditional town of Busby, would increase school completion is supported. Conversely, Crow reservation origin had no effect. While expectations concerning the effects of family background are supported, expectations for school type are not. Additionally, student transfers, absences, and suspensions from school had indirect rather than direct effects on dropping out. However, the evidence strongly supports the importance of school performance levels for school completion.

These analyses show that individual, community, and family characteristics and school experiences all play a role—some direct and others indirect—in explaining dropout behavior for this population. Such findings, which partially support previous work on dropouts, suggest some new questions regarding how community location and family background affect Indian students. These influences will be explored using ethnographic data in the following section.

The Northern Cheyenne Context

Family Background Related to Education

The findings of the first analysis suggest a need to further explore the effects of family background variables with assistance from qualitative case study data. The question is, why do family characteristics have a greater effect on dropout behavior than school performance? An answer to this question must reconsider the influence of adults in the home concerning school performance compared to high school graduation. The analysis in chapter 5 indicates that the graduation status of adults in the home did not influence students' school performance. Qualitative data show that neither parents who are high school graduates nor parents who are dropouts provide concrete support for education for their children. However, when it comes to graduation from high school, ethnographic data suggest that the nature and level of parents' activity is quite different. In fact, the mother quoted (in chapter 5) who did not monitor her son's schoolwork responded very differently when the school notified her that because of failing grades and misconduct, her son would not graduate on schedule. She then became actively involved with the school to negotiate a solution to her son's problems that would allow him to graduate. When asked about these actions, she responded that she felt the school was wrong in preventing her son from graduating, and that it was up to her to correct the situation. Although her son had gotten into trouble with drug use and had some poor grades, she felt that because he had gone to treatment for his drug problem and had improved his academic performance, he should not be penalized. According to her, as well as many other parents, not graduating from high school is a mistake.

Thus, while parents did not closely monitor their children's studies or provide special help so they would succeed in school, they felt compelled to act on their children's behalf when schools threatened to hold them back. Many parents have experienced firsthand or have seen the effects of failing to graduate: dropouts are not eligible for the few jobs that are available on the reservation or elsewhere. Because higher-paying jobs on the reservation are largely with federal agencies, schools, and the tribal government, a high school diploma is a minimum requirement. While high school students may not consider the consequences of dropping out, their parents, relatives, or guardians usually do. One young woman who dropped out of high school explained her change in attitude about finishing high school:

> I was bored with school, and I did not see how graduating was going to do anything for me. I got married and had two children, and I was very happy. But when my husband died in a car accident a few years after we got married, I had to get a job to support us, and I couldn't get one. I realized then how important a high school diploma was. After I got my GED, I got a good job with the BIA. Now I tell my nephew that he should graduate, but he feels just like I did, and he doesn't listen to me (Ward and Wilson 1985).

Adults who had received their diplomas or GEDs were especially willing to take actions to ensure that high school students graduated so that they would not be excluded from job opportunities. The presence of two adults in the home strengthens this type of support for graduation. The pattern,

CHAPTER SIX

which is established by both the statistical data and ethnographic information, indicates the importance of social capital within households and extended families.

Family Characteristics and Economic Strategies

In contrast to graduation status, employment status of adults in the home has no effect on either this school outcome or school performance. In other words, there is no consistent pattern of variation indicating that adults' employment status affects students' performance or graduation. Reasons for this may be related to students' negative perceptions of the jobs available as well as the connection between schooling and employment or gainful activity. An important element of this situation is the value placed on support from family members when someone is unemployed and in financial need. Such assistance provides security as well as an alternative to working that allows an individual or family to survive. Additionally, there are other income-producing alternatives to holding a regular job. These include general assistance, seasonal work, subsistence activities, going to college and receiving a stipend, participation in job training programs, and illegal activities. Each of these elements of the situation is related to native capital. Before discussing the strategies by which individuals survive and support families, it is important to consider the effects of specific structural and cultural features of Northern Cheyenne reservation life that affect labor force participation.

Social conditions and cultural influences shape the perception of economic opportunities as well as the types of economic activities chosen by women and men. Specifically, the prevailing perception on the reservation is that jobs are scarce; most people know how high the unemployment rate is and how many of their neighbors and family members are unemployed. This fact has a depressing effect on aspirations for work and education. As one mother said (Ward 1992), "I encourage my son to leave the reservation to get an education after high school and to find a good job. It breaks my heart when I say it to him, but I know it's better for him than to stay here and be unemployed."

And yet, most people stay on the reservation or return after leaving for a period of time. The reasons are related to two factors. First, of course, are the social and cultural reasons for staying, including attachment to family and friends who are important for sentimental reasons as well as for gaining access to scarce opportunities—which alludes to the second factor: many realize that access to jobs is just as important as their availability. In other words, the chances of getting work may actually be better in the reservation community than elsewhere because of friendship and kinship ties. For example, a common belief is that while educational qualifications can help in the competition for jobs, being hired is affected as well by the relationship of the applicant to the person doing the hiring. Individuals often act as "sponsors" of family or friends when new opportunities become available in organizations in which they work. Most believe, also, that non-Indians are more likely to be hired for some jobs, especially teaching or managerial positions. Although this may seem contradictory given the majority of Indians on the reservation, the fact is that there are a substantial number of non-Indians on the reservation, some of whom are married to tribal members, who have been hired when there have been no "qualified" Cheyenne applicants. Hiring non-Indians and outsiders has been prevalent among local employers, even though the Tribe has an "Indian preference" ordinance. To some employers, this is an attractive alternative specifically because it prevents problems related to nepotism. Also, there are a number of higher-paying and highly visible jobs on the reservation that are occupied by so-called breeds, or half-breeds, who are part Indian. Consequently, one perception is that part Indians will be selected over full-bloods. There is some truth to the perception since, generally, "breeds" have received more education because of their upbringing in families in which schooling was a higher priority. Additionally, they may have had more experience interacting with non-Indians and may have felt comfortable in jobs that required contacts with non-Indians, federal agencies, the public, and so forth.

Thus, while educational credentials are needed to meet basic job requirements, kinship and friendship have often been the most important means for improving access to jobs (despite specific rules in government-funded organizations against nepotism and favoritism) (Ward 1992). On the other hand, individuals have also found that their access to jobs was more limited if they lacked friends or family who could act as sponsors. In sum, a person's position in the labor market represents not only his or her human capital but also the effects of native capital, which can facilitate access to particular niches in the local economy.

CHAPTER SIX

A related perception is that the chances for Indians of being hired off the reservation are much lower. Generally, reservation residents doubt that Indians will be seriously considered, much less hired, over Whites for off-reservation work, even at the mining operations and power plants where special considerations are given to the Cheyenne (Ward 1992). Thus, perceptions of the opportunity structure and efforts to access jobs have been influenced by beliefs about prejudice and discrimination against Indians. Because most potential employers off the reservation are located relatively long distances away, such as in Forsyth (sixty miles away), Hardin (forty-five miles away), or Sheridan (ninety miles away), the lack of access to reliable transportation, or the cost and the motivation to travel long distances, creates additional obstacles.

Such circumstances influence both attitudes toward unemployment and the perceived relationship between employment status and educational attainment. In particular, reservation residents often conclude, first, that having a job is not absolutely necessary in order to have an acceptable lifestyle since there are other resources that they can use to help support themselves and their families. Second, acquiring education has become less relevant for some people since other criteria (e.g., kinship) enter into the hiring process—higher educational credentials do not necessarily make a difference in getting a job. Third, jobs that require educational credentials may not be preferred since they usually require long hours and time away from other valued social and cultural activities. Given these considerations, being unemployed on the reservation is a status that has different meanings than it may have in other communities where regular employment has a higher status and is considered to be more beneficial than remaining unemployed or accepting part-time or temporary work. Thus, while having a job and supporting one's family is valued, being unemployed does not necessarily result in desperate circumstances for a person or his or her family.

In fact, even those who are unemployed do not lose social status and often contribute to the household economy. Family members may contribute to the income of the household through receiving general assistance or some other welfare benefit, a strategy that has become the norm for many reservation residents. While some persons avoid such a situation, for many others it is a necessity. However, this does not mean that they do not work; many women who receive some type of assistance (e.g., food stamps, housing assistance, etc.) have low-paying jobs that do not adequately support their families. One single mother of five explained, "Our family simply can't make it unless we get food stamps and other assistance. My salary is just not enough to support all of us. My [White] boss at work thinks it is terrible that I get assistance, but I would like to see him try to make ends meet on what I make. We just barely get by; we don't have a car, or buy a lot of clothes or any luxuries" (Ward 1992).

Women are much more likely than in earlier times to work in regular full-time and part-time jobs. Such jobs primarily include clerical and other service sector jobs (such as teacher aides at the schools, cashiers at local stores, waitresses, cooks, and cleaning and janitorial staff) but more recently have expanded to include management positions in tribal, state, and federal agencies as well as schools. These types of jobs are important for women, who typically also have family responsibilities. In contrast, men have become less likely to have regular full-time or part-time jobs. Those who have full-time work are generally federal, state, school, or tribal government employees, or they work for the few local businesses. A small percentage of them work for the large energy companies just north of the reservation. The rest generally have work that is seasonal, such as firefighting, forestry work, ranch or farm work, and construction or highway work, all of which can contribute substantially—although not consistently—to the household income.

One important aspect of native capital involves its relation to income-producing alternatives to holding a regular job; that is, native capital provides knowledge of and access to reservation-based social services, college and job training programs, the military, subsistence activities, and informal economic opportunities. Although little quantitative data exist regarding the extent of informal activities, current research efforts are addressing questions concerning the size of the informal economy and the nature of the activities prevalent in the reservation community. Among the informal activities in which Northern Cheyenne reservation residents participate are hunting, gardening, and other subsistence activities, as well as the production and sale of beadwork and other arts and crafts (such as paintings and other decorative items, quilts, jewelry, flutes, and traditional powwow outfits) and audiotapes and CDs of flute music and powwow, peyote, and sweat lodge songs. Production of these items is often intended entirely for local residents, who purchase them for personal use and for gifts. However, a small number of arts and crafts producers sell both locally and to buyers for a much larger market. The production of arts and crafts seems to have increased over the last decade both because of the demand from local and outside markets and also because this source of income has become increasingly necessary for many to meet their personal and family income needs (Ward 1992, 1998b).

Besides sales to individuals, another outlet for artists and community members is the monthly flea market or street sale in the small downtown area of Lame Deer during the first two days of each month. Setting up booths and tables, local vendors sell homemade foods such as "Indian tacos"; local artists sell their art and crafts; pawnbrokers sell pawned items; and local residents sell used clothing and household items. This not only brings some additional income into reservation households but also provides opportunities for people to acquire needed consumer items at reduced prices (Ward 1998b).

Among young adults, an increasingly popular avenue to obtain income is by enrolling in the tribal college. Since almost half of the reservation high school students drop out, many potential college students must first obtain a general education development (GED) diploma. From about a fourth to a third of the tribal college students enter with GEDs. Most students have incomes below the poverty level and are first-generation college students. Therefore, they are eligible for many services and benefits, including educational grants and stipends available to minority, low-income college students. Additionally, there are part-time jobs available on campus for a small number of students, such as library assistants, janitorial staff, day-care workers, and clerical staff. The college is one of the major employers on the reservation for young adults. Similarly, adults can get training through federally funded training programs that provide classroom and on-the-job training with stipends. Military service is pursued by an increasing number of young adults searching for avenues for personal achievement that bring income and honor to their families.

One important aspect of the employment situation concerns work aspirations and expectations about jobs. In a survey of adults on the reservation in the mid-1980s, aspirations for work identified by respondents were often general or vague (Ward and Wilson 1985). Work goals frequently included "working in an office," which was believed to represent a lucrative job, or "a job outdoors," which represented work that was seen as productive and well paid but not bureaucratic. For some, the nature of the work is less significant than the level of income it provides for supporting their families and desired social and cultural activities. Income is not typically spent on conspicuous consumption; whether individuals have large or small incomes, they generally have similar lifestyles in terms of clothes, houses, cars, and so on. A central value is that people do not try to exhibit superiority over other community members through their spending patterns. Whether it is because there is so much poverty or because of cultural reasons, community members who have larger incomes typically do not try to create the appearance of having more. Thus, while some may afford more expensive consumer items, their choices usually fall within a range that is acceptable within the community. One example is housing. Most tribal members take advantage of a U.S. Department of Housing and Urban Development (HUD) program that provides low-interest loans on houses built by HUD contractors. These houses are not very expensive, and many claim they are of poor quality. However, even those who can afford more generally choose to purchase HUD houses. Such constraints on spending choices result in a relatively comparable lifestyle and standard of living for most people in the reservation community.

Another important aspect of the current economy involves the Northern Cheyenne Area Chamber of Commerce, which was established about fifteen years ago to promote local business development. Members, including both local business owners and representatives of other organizations, have been pursuing plans for attracting businesses to the reservation and for assisting reservation residents in starting small businesses. Technical assistance provided by this organization and its members has typically involved developing business plans and acquiring the capital needed for business start-up in the reservation environment. These efforts have resulted in several new small businesses in recent years, primarily in construction, retail, and services, which have begun to expand work opportunities for local residents (Ward 1998b).

An informal economic activity that appears to have increased is the sale of bootleg alcohol and drugs. During the 1980s and continuing in the 1990s, law enforcement agencies reported that drug traffic increased dramatically in Rosebud County (Northern Cheyenne Tribe 1994). Although the reservation is dry, bars and saloons located just off the reservation have contributed to the availability of alcohol. However, many reservation residents currently believe that not only has the number of drug dealers and

CHAPTER SIX

alcohol bootleggers on the reservation increased substantially, but also that they are currently targeting a younger market. Evidence cited for this trend includes larger numbers of arrests of children and teenagers, and more youth in treatment for substance abuse (Northern Cheyenne Tribe 1994). Additionally, the number of youth involved in accidental killings and homicides is on the rise, and gang activity has become a source of concern to parents. Local law enforcement efforts have been unable to curtail these activities, due largely to the lack of resources, especially personnel.

Except for the last avenue, the economic and work alternatives discussed above are seen as reasonable. General assistance (or welfare) is most widely accepted for women, especially if they are single mothers, have large families, are married to someone who is an alcoholic, or have substance abuse problems themselves. Even for some men, it is seen as an acceptable alternative to working for pay. This is true, however, primarily for those who are older (55 years or older) but not old enough to collect social security, and who have little possibility of securing employment. Additionally, receiving general assistance is acceptable if the person is a respected "elder" who spends time on traditional activities such as healing, sweats, powwows, or rodeos or participates in tribal government affairs, such as committee work. It is also acceptable if someone is an alcoholic and can't support him- or herself any other way. In the case of seasonal work, because it is often a particularly demanding activity, and even dangerous, as in the case of firefighting, there is a certain amount of respect that is commanded. For those who do fire jumping, in particular, and who travel throughout the West fighting fires during the summer and early fall, there is a special feeling of respect. Tribal members are proud of the Northern Cheyennes who fight fires and of their good reputation in the West. In fact, this has been such an important avenue for young adults, primarily men, to earn an income that, during the period of this study, the tribal college adjusted its schedule to accommodate the firefighters.

Native Capital and Economic Status

Since most people are not spending their incomes on expensive consumer items, a logical question is, where does disposable income go? First, it hardly needs to be stated that most people spend their entire incomes on necessities. However, any extra they have is saved, although typically not for investments or other profitable activities. Rather, this money is largely used for activities important within the social and cultural structure of the community: support for family members in times of emergency, "giveaways," and participating in powwows and other social or ceremonial events of the Northern Cheyenne or other tribes in Indian country. For a small segment of the population, savings also go toward college education for their children or toward retirement, and for still fewer, toward starting small businesses. Among the activities that require cash expenditures, giveaways and other ceremonial activities such as fasts and the "sun dance" are traditional cultural forms that persist on the Northern Cheyenne reservation today. Powwows and other social activities (e.g., hand games, rodeos) are modern forms of traditional social gatherings that require preparation of traditional outfits or equipment, travel, and so on, but do not contribute to the redistribution of wealth like giveaways.

The persistence of such practices as giveaways, the use of family support, and other income-producing options within the Cheyenne community indicate not only that economic roles within this community are defined differently than in others but also that there is a different orientation to the accumulation of wealth; this orientation de-emphasizes personal accumulation and emphasizes redistribution of wealth and production of use values. Thus, conceptualizations of the local economy and social class structure must take such practices into account. With this in mind, we can interpret the absence of the effect of employment status on students' school completion in a particular light: it is an indication that the system of economic supports, fashioned by this community from its own cultural institutions as well as from the various resources provided by government programs, reduces, to some extent, the apparent differences among individuals and families within the Cheyenne tribal community. That is, the economic strategies and practices of the Cheyenne, which draw on various locally defined support systems, may reduce the inequalities related to different types and levels of attachment to the labor market, ranging from unemployment and underemployment to full-time work. This tendency toward status equalization has the result of eliminating the effects typically seen for parental employment on schooling, that is, the positive effect of adult labor force participation on school outcomes, primarily high school graduation. This observation is not meant to suggest that reservation work conditions are adequate in terms of their effect on the quality of life or the

CHAPTER SIX

life chances of the Northern Cheyenne. Rather, it is intended to emphasize the importance of existing economic practices for the meaning of employment and its relationship to school completion.

In this reservation context, the norm is for individuals and families to have low levels of income (due to low wages or work hours, or the small number of workers in a household), which is supplemented when needed with financial and other types of support from extended family and other social resources. Combining work with other sources of support makes it possible for many Cheyennes to continue to live in their reservation communities, a choice that is strongly valued for both the proximity to family and for cultural reasons. Perceptions of obstacles to obtaining work off the reservation provide another reason for remaining on the reservation despite scarce opportunities. Importantly, employment and financial struggles among adults are understood well by their children, who often conclude that there is little reward for schooling, especially compared to drug trafficking, which offers a more lucrative alternative. Thus, the need for multiple sources of support for family survival often has the unintended consequence of reinforcing children's perceptions that schooling (human capital development) has little value. However, this contradicts families' efforts to develop skills and obtain the jobs needed to escape poverty.

In contrast to families that struggle to support themselves with wage work, more serious isolation from the labor market occurs for a smaller proportion of Cheyennes. This group, which experiences chronic unemployment and extreme poverty, very likely represents three social situations. In the first case, adults lack family or social networks that can help them gain access to jobs or financial support. Second, lack of labor force attachment may represent a very traditional cultural orientation: adults choose not to take jobs that detract from other more culturally valued pursuits (traditional healing, rodeos, powwows, informal economic activities, etc.). In the third case, adults may participate in the drug or alcohol subcultures, which tend to alienate them from most groups and opportunities, especially if substance abuse (or drug trafficking) results in sustained problems for family and friends.

This information suggests that adaptations to structural deficiencies in the local economy (such as low wages and lack of jobs) are influenced not only by the social resources available to individuals and families but also by cultural orientations and norms that differ from the dominant society and surrounding population's values and norms for work. These unique adaptations show that native capital translates into economic value, sometimes at higher rates than education credentials and other forms of human capital. Additionally, the use of a variety of strategies to support families ensures that all will survive, albeit many in poverty. These localized adaptations also provide the flexibility for some reservation community members to pursue traditional activities valued by the larger community. Finally, those lacking native capital are also likely to experience the most economic vulnerability.

Revised Dropout Model: Adding the Effects of Student and Family Cultural Resources and Community–School Relations

Given the preliminary findings that community residence influences school enrollment and that Busby residence influences dropout behavior, the next analyses will ascertain whether or how residence in a particular community and enrollment in a specific school affects students' dropout behavior. The three models presented include seven terms that represent hypotheses about the effects of specific community–school combinations. Contrast coding procedures are used to create variables that represent expected differences in community–school groups based on previous analyses and case study data.[1]

Hypotheses include the following:

1. Dropout behavior will be decreased by residence in a traditional Cheyenne community (Busby, Ashland) and attending the nearest community school compared to residence in a less traditional community (Lame Deer) or Crow community and attending a school outside the community.

    a. Residence in Busby or Ashland and attending the local Indian school will decrease dropping out compared to attending the public school outside the community.

    b. Busby residence will decrease dropping out compared to Ashland residence regardless of the school attended.

    c. Residence in Busby or Ashland and attending either the tribal school or public school will decrease dropping out compared to attending St. Labre.

CHAPTER SIX

    d. Residence in the Lame Deer community and attending either Colstrip Public School or St. Labre will decrease dropping out compared to being from Lame Deer and attending Busby Tribal School.

    e. Residence in Lame Deer and attending St. Labre will decrease dropping out compared to residence in Lame Deer and attending Colstrip.

    f. Residence in Lame Deer and attending St. Labre will increase dropping out compared to being from Crow communities and attending St. Labre.

    g. Residence in Busby and Ashland will decrease dropping out regardless of school attended compared to the effects of being from Lame Deer and Crow communities.

2. The combination of community residence and school attended will have greater effects than the other variables, gender, family characteristics, and school experiences.

The coefficients in the first model of table 6.2 include only the community–school combinations and gender (female compared to male). Three of the community–school combinations are significant. First, as suggested by the previous analysis, residence in Busby (compared to Ashland) negatively affects dropping out, regardless of whether students attend Busby Tribal School or Colstrip Public School. Second, the significance of the fourth term indicates that students from Lame Deer are less likely to drop out if they attend St. Labre or Colstrip than if they attend Busby Tribal School. Again, this is consistent with the data showing that more Lame Deer students drop out at Busby School. The significance of the last term also supports the hypothesized importance of community residence: students residing in Busby and Ashland are less likely to drop out than students residing in Lame Deer or Crow communities. These findings confirm that it is insufficient to know only which school students attend or the community in which they reside; rather, it is also important to know the specific combination of community residence and school attended. In this context, residence in the more traditional community of Busby (and

Table 6.2. Logistic Regression Coefficients for the Effects of Community, School Attended, Gender, Family Characteristics, School Experiences, and Performance on Dropping Out

	Model 1		Model 2		Model 3	
	Coef.	SE	Coef.	SE	Coef.	SE
Community Residence and School Attended Contrasts						
Busby and Ashland residence/attends Busby or St. Labre	.45	.30	.34	.34	.54	.37
Busby residence/attends Busby or Colstrip vs. Ashland residence/attends St. Labre or Colstrip	-.71**	.30	-.85**	.36	-.91**	.37
Busby and Ashland residence/attends Busby or Colstrip	.35	.30	.17	.34	.26	.36
Lame Deer residence/attends St. Labre or Colstrip vs. Busby	-.53***	.16	-.20	.18	-.07	.20
Lame Deer residence/attends St. Labre vs. Colstrip	-.24	.24	-.08	.29	.08	.32
Lame Deer vs. Crow residence/attends St. Labre	.19	.28	.11	.32	.11	.36
Busby or Ashland vs. Lame Deer or Crow residence	-.41**	.17	-.50***	.20	-.36*	.21
Gender[a]						
Female	.28	.24	.13	.28	.38	.31
Family Characteristics						
One adult present			.59*	.32	.64	.35
At least one adult employed			.20	.33	.19	.36
At least one adult high school diploma			-1.25***	.43	-1.18***	.46
School Experiences/Performance						
Transfers			.00	.13	.04	.14
Absences			-.00	.01	-.00	.01
Ever suspended			.91*	.44	.72	.46
Extracurricular activities			-.99***	.19	-.79***	.18
Cumulative GPA					-1.40***	.33
Model chi-square	24.03		123.62		166.91	
d.f.	18		18		20	
N	319		319		319	

[a] Omitted category is male.
* $p < .10$, ** $p < .05$, *** $p < .01$

CHAPTER SIX

attending either Busby or Colstrip schools) is the most advantageous for graduating from high school. However, living in Ashland may also have more positive effects on graduation than residence in other communities. Finally, if students live in Lame Deer, it is more advantageous to attend either the Catholic or public school than the tribal school.

In the second model, the community–school terms are included along with the gender, family characteristics, and school experience variables to determine their significance relative to these other influences. This analysis shows that among variables representing student attributes (gender and the combination of community residence and school attended), only two community–school combinations are important for dropout behavior. The first shows that residence in Busby (compared to Ashland) negatively affects dropping out of both Busby Tribal School and Colstrip Public School. The other significant term indicates that residence in Busby and Ashland negatively affects dropping out compared to Lame Deer and Crow communities.

Other findings show the importance of one family background characteristic, high school/GED completion of the primary adult at home. While having only one adult in the home modestly increases the chances of dropping out, the parental education variable significantly decreases the chances of dropping out. The coefficients for school experience variables reveal that having been suspended from high school increases the chances of dropping out, while greater involvement with extracurricular activities reduces the chances of dropping out.

Finally, model 3 coefficients show the effects of adding mean GPA into the model. In this complete model, the second community–school combination, the effects of Busby (compared to Ashland) residence, continues to significantly decrease the chances of dropping out, although the effects of the sixth term, residence in Busby or Ashland compared to Lame Deer and Crow communities, have declined. Parent high school/GED completion continues to be a significant deterrent to dropping out, as is greater extracurricular activity involvement. Finally, mean GPA also has a crucial negative effect on dropout behavior.

These results suggest answers—albeit limited—to questions concerning the nature of the influences on dropout behavior, in particular, the effects of community–school combinations. First, residence in the more traditional community of Busby (and Ashland to a moderate degree) negatively affects dropping out compared to other communities. However, the most advantageous community effect, overall, for reservation students is Busby residence, whether they attend Busby Tribal School or Colstrip Public School. Regardless of the effects of community and school, school experience variables are particularly meaningful within this reservation population. In fact, the coefficients suggest that when gender, community residence, and school attended are taken into account, school performance reduces the chances of dropping out. Additionally, student involvement in extracurricular activities is crucial. The only important family factor for dropout behavior is the high school/GED completion of adults in the student's home. Thus, in the complete model, the effects of community residence and school attended are somewhat diminished, revealing that the effects of community–school combinations also indirectly affect dropout behavior through school experiences. The last column of the complete model summarizes the relative effects of the community–school, family, and school experience variables: students' residence in Busby and Ashland combined with attendance at Busby Tribal and Colstrip Public schools, the high school/GED completion of their parents, students' involvement in extracurricular activities, and a higher mean GPA reduce the risk of dropping out relative to the other variables.

Overall, these dropout analyses provide the basis for some new insights into the process of school completion that can be related to previous research. For example, the findings for school experiences, extracurricular activity involvement, and school performance, in particular, support previous research findings. On the other hand, while findings for parental education effects on dropout behavior support results of other studies, the absence of effects of other family variables (employment and family structure) contradicts research that indicates relatively strong relationships between family socioeconomic characteristics and school outcomes.

Of particular interest are findings related to community residence. Although not definitive, the results suggest that students' community residence is an important factor for school completion. However, the community effect varies with school context. Thus, these findings support the hypothesis that specific community–school combinations have important effects on dropout behavior relative to family and school experiences. Although the specific connections between community and school effects

CHAPTER SIX

remain unclear within each school population, these analyses suggest that they provide fruitful avenues for further investigation.

Influences on Dropping Out, by School: Individual and Family Characteristics, School Experiences, and School Performance

Before we turn to models of dropout behavior by school, the possible effect of community residence on dropout and graduation behavior will be considered. Since we know that some of the students at all three schools are from Lame Deer, and that Lame Deer residence has a negative effect on mean GPA, we will discuss the proportion of dropouts and graduates from each of the communities within each school. The distributions presented in table 6.3 indicate that dropouts within Busby and Colstrip schools are typically from Lame Deer. However, at St. Labre the dropouts are primarily from Ashland and elsewhere (usually Crow); there are few Busby residents who attend St. Labre. These figures show that while the residence factor is likely to be important, it needs to be considered in combination with the effects of the schools on dropout behavior. The marginal percentages for the three schools indicate that dropout rates for St. Labre

Table 6.3. Students' Graduation Status by School Attended and Community

	Busby		St. Labre		Colstrip		Total	
	%	N	%	N	%	N	%	N
Ashland								
Graduate	0.0	(0)	51.4	(18)	58.3	(7)	50.0	(25)
Dropout	100.0	(3)	48.6	(17)	41.7	(5)	50.0	(25)
Busby								
Graduate	70.0	(21)	50.0	(1)	92.9	(13)	76.1	(35)
Dropout	30.0	(9)	50.0	(1)	7.1	(1)	23.9	(11)
Lame Deer								
Graduate	27.8	(10)	65.4	(17)	58.1	(50)	52.0	(77)
Dropout	72.2	(26)	34.6	(9)	41.6	(36)	48.0	(71)
Other/NA								
Graduate	57.1	(4)	53.8	(28)	25.0	(4)	48.0	(36)
Dropout	42.9	(3)	46.2	(24)	75.0	(12)	52.0	(39)
Total								
Graduate	46.1	(35)	55.7	(64)	57.8	(74)		
Dropout	53.9	(41)	44.3	(51)	42.2	(54)		

(44%) and Colstrip (42%) are similar and less than the dropout rate for Busby Tribal School.

We also must consider the role of family background characteristics that were found to be important influences in the dropout process for all Indian students. Distributions of the family characteristics for the three school populations reveal some important patterns of socioeconomic attributes. For example, smaller proportions of the families of Busby (27%) and St. Labre (26%) students are single-parent households than families of Colstrip students (31%). Conversely, somewhat larger proportions of Colstrip (50%) and St. Labre (48%) students are from households with at least one adult working full-time than Busby (40%) students. St. Labre (55%) has a slightly larger proportion of parents with a high school diploma or GED than Busby (52%) and Colstrip (51%). Given that the effects of students' community residence vary by school, these variations in family characteristics by school also suggest the importance of examining the intersection of individual, family, and school factors in shaping students' school experiences and outcomes.

School Models of Dropping Out: The Effects of Community–School Combinations, Gender, Family Characteristics, and School Experiences

Coefficients presented in table 6.4 show the relative effects of community–school combinations within each school population. In each model, relevant community contrast terms were created that allow for testing the effects of the pertinent community locations of students within that school.[2] The first model for each school shows the effects of community residence, gender, and family characteristics, while the second model adds the school experiences and school performance variables to the dropout model.

In the first Busby model, the relevant community term shows that the effect of living in Busby compared to Lame Deer is significant and deters dropping out. Among the other variables, two family characteristics, the presence of one adult in the home and the adults' high school education, have only moderate effects. Interestingly, in the second model, the effects of Busby residence disappear, but gender (female) uniquely increases the chances of dropping out. The family characteristics remain modest in effect, while a school experience variable (absences) and mean GPA show modest

Table 6.4. Logistic Regression Coefficients by School for the Effects of Community, Gender, Family Characteristics, School Experiences, and Performance on Dropping Out

	Busby Tribal School				St. Labre Catholic School				Colstrip Public School			
	Model 1		Model 2		Model 1		Model 2		Model 1		Model 2	
	Coef.	SE	Coef.	SE	Coef.	SE	Coef.	SE	Coef.	SE	Coef.	SE
Community Residence												
Busby vs. Lame Deer	-.89**	.31	-.31	.40								
Ashland/Lame Deer vs. Crow					-.15	.23	.01	.34				
Busby/Ashland vs. Lame Deer									-.37**	.19	-.41*	.23
Gender[a]												
Female	.77	.58	1.70**	.82	.04	.40	-.22	.61	.16	.41	.09	.50
Family Characteristics												
One adult present	1.09*	.64	1.33*	.80	.33	.47	.40	.64	.76	.50	.33	.62
At least one adult employed	-.14	.66	-.86	.85	.06	.48	1.36*	.78	.00	.48	.00	.60
At least one adult high school diploma	-1.08*	.67	-1.67*	.96	-.88	.72	-4.14**	1.95	-.74	.51	-.44	.66
School Experiences/Performance												
Transfers			.21	.36			-.25	.24			.00	.26
Absences			-.03*	.02			.00	.20			.02	.01
Ever suspended			1.14	1.50			.51	1.00			.97	.67
Extracurricular activities			.14	.63			-1.34***	.42			-.96***	.28
Cumulative GPA			-1.17*	.71			-1.67***	.64			-1.30**	.56
Model Chi square	20.66		43.77		10.68		78.37		25.26		70.17	
d.f.	8		14		8		14		8		14	
N	76		76		115		115		128		128	

[a] Omitted category is male.
* $p < .10$, ** $p < .05$, *** $p < .01$

negative effects on dropout behavior. The minimal effects of the family, school experience, and performance variables may be related to the small population size relative to the number of variables. However, the findings suggest the potential importance of these factors as well as the indirect positive effects of Busby compared to Lame Deer residence.

Although none of the variables are significant in the first St. Labre model, the second model shows that parental high school completion, extracurricular activity involvement, and mean GPA all significantly decrease the chances of students dropping out of school. While modest in its effect on dropping out, parental employment status increases the chances of dropping out. In this school population, the community residence variable, which shows the influence of being from Ashland and Lame Deer compared to Crow communities, has no effect.

Finally, the effects of community residence are seen again in the models for the Colstrip School population. In the first model, the community variable (the effects of living in Busby and Ashland compared to Lame Deer) indicates that Busby and Ashland residence negatively affects dropout behavior compared to residence in Lame Deer. In the second Colstrip model, these community effects are attenuated by the addition of school experience and performance variables; extracurricular activity involvement and mean GPA significantly decrease the chances of dropping out. This model shows that community residence indirectly influences dropping out.

Further considerations of the effect of community residence include the fact that the dropouts from Busby Tribal School were largely from Lame Deer. Thus, it appears contradictory that Lame Deer residence had no effect on dropping out at Busby School in the second Busby model of table 6.4. However, the effect of living in Busby compared to Lame Deer was significant in the first model. Thus, it has an indirect effect through the school experiences of students. This suggests that although community residence patterns do affect school performance, students' school experiences and performance levels are most important in determining who drops out and graduates.

The complete dropout models for these three school populations add partial support to the previous findings that community and school variables are important for dropping out. When school context is held constant, Busby and/or Ashland community residence indirectly deters

CHAPTER SIX

dropping out in two of the three schools. In each of these schools, community effects are mediated by the school experiences of the students. Additionally, while community residence indirectly affects dropout behavior among both Busby and Colstrip students, Busby students' dropout behavior is directly influenced by gender, while Colstrip students' dropout behavior is influenced primarily by school experiences. In contrast, St. Labre students' dropout behavior is affected by a family characteristic (parental education), extracurricular activity involvement, and school performance.

These results provide answers to questions concerning the nature of the influences on dropout behavior and similarities and differences among the three school populations. First, these analyses indicate that the previously observed influences on dropping out are generally upheld in the three new school models. That is, with a few exceptions, variables important for the Indian student population as a whole are also meaningful for the three school contexts. For example, the coefficients suggest that there are some overall similarities of the three schools with respect to the effects of school experiences and school performance on dropping out. Within each of the three schools, school performance strongly affects whether a student drops out. The better the performance, the less likely it is that students will drop out. Additionally, students' involvement in extracurricular activities is also crucial, although it is more important at St. Labre and Colstrip. The only other factor that has a somewhat consistent effect on dropout behavior at the Indian schools is the high school completion of adults in the student's home, which decreases the likelihood of dropping out.

We can identify some interesting differences among the schools as well. For example, Colstrip and Busby are the only schools to show effects of students' community residence. Concerning other individual variables, only at Busby does the effect of gender increase dropout behavior. Additionally, being from a single-parent family is an important influence on dropping out for students only at Busby Tribal School. And finally, absences at Busby school negatively affect dropping out. In other words, excessive absences from school do not necessarily keep a student from graduating, nor do they automatically result in a student's termination. Although this may be an artifact of the small number of Busby students, absences appear to even forestall dropping out. At the other two schools, absences do not affect dropping out relative to the other variables.

As suggested in the analysis of school performance, the tribal school context appears to reduce the expected effects of school experience variables on dropping out. However, the lack of effect of family characteristics for public school students contradicts previous research findings. Again, interpretation of these findings requires that we turn to ethnographic data that may help to explain these patterns. In the following section, qualitative data are presented concerning individual and family characteristics as well as school contexts.

The Northern Cheyenne Context

The Role of Gender and Community Residence

Qualitative case study data are useful in understanding something about the differences among the three schools. For example, we have noted the absence of the effect of gender on school performance in all three schools, and the dropout analysis by school shows gender to be important only in Busby High School. Explanations of the role of gender at Busby School may be related both to the reasons why students attend Busby and to other personal experiences. While girls at Busby may have academic problems due to frequent school switching and other school-related problems, the general patterns of school performance show that girls at all three schools have higher performance levels than boys. The explicit reason for girls dropping out of Busby School is personal; in many situations girls drop out due to pregnancy. While this is true for the other schools as well, it is more prominent at Busby.

Data from the Adult Education Center for the 1990–1991 school year (Ward and Wilson 1991), for example, indicate that the majority of GED applicants are young women, most of whom dropped out because of pregnancy or marriage. The majority of the female GED students live in Lame Deer, but the last school they attended was Busby Tribal School. This suggests the validity of our previous findings that although the dropout rate is highest at Busby, Lame Deer students attending Busby School are more likely to drop out than the Busby residents. It also indicates an important element of the dropout experience for girls. Girls at Busby School who live in Lame Deer may come from family situations that are disadvantaged in a number of ways: drug or alcohol problems, unemployment, mental health or health problems, and so on. According to local Indian Health

CHAPTER SIX

Service counselors, these young women attempt to create their own families in order to have something that is positive in their lives. Pregnancy gives them a reason to stop drug and alcohol use, and to get attention and caring from others. Within the Northern Cheyenne community, generally a pregnant woman is to be nurtured, and children are valued regardless of the situation of their birth.

Many young single mothers who drop out of high school get their GEDs and attend the tribal college in Lame Deer. The majority of women GED students state that their reasons for getting a GED include establishing eligibility for college and qualifying for jobs. In discussions with these women, many remarked that they did not know what to do with their lives when they were nearing the end of high school (the majority dropped out in the eleventh grade). They saw no positive alternative to drinking. Being a mother was the only adult role they felt they could assume successfully, and motherhood would meet some emotional needs that they could not address in their own families. Although these young mothers often said they found it very difficult to raise a child (often without a spouse), they generally had support from friends or extended family members, if not from their immediate families. Despite its frustrations, the role of mother gave these young women a feeling of self-worth and accomplishment and provided them the courage and incentive to do more. In fact, many gave their reason for going back to school as the need to obtain credentials that would help them get a job to support their children. As GED students, at that time, they were eligible for general assistance and could get by for a time on this income if they could find low-income housing. When they entered college, they could often get a combination of resources such as stipends, Pell Grants, and part-time jobs on campus. They could also take advantage of the college's day-care facility and get meals in the school cafeteria. All in all, they found the drug-free, college environment supportive of both their sobriety and their roles as student and parent since many of the tribal college students also had families to support.

The Effects of Family Characteristics and Community Residence

A similarity between St. Labre and Busby schools is the effect of education of the adults in the home. It is interesting to note that this effect is seen only at the two Indian schools and not at the primarily non-Indian public high school. Why would parents' education play a more important role at these schools? Qualitative information based on firsthand observations as well as from school and community sources indicates that working against the many factors that push Indian students to drop out are the crucial efforts of adults within the home who have graduated. As suggested above, when it comes to the issue of graduating, parents who have diplomas or GEDs are more likely to step in and make their wishes known as well as take actions to ensure their children's completion of school. Furthermore, Indian parents are more likely to take action within the context of an Indian school than a non-Indian school. Parents know that the tribal school is there to provide secondary education for Cheyenne students, while St. Labre serves two reservation populations. Within such apparently benevolent environments, parents' actions to ensure graduation are perceived to be more acceptable. Additionally, parents often know school personnel at Busby or have political leverage that can be used to influence the situation. On the other hand, parents are suspicious about the reception of Colstrip schools to their intervention as well as about Colstrip's interest in helping Indian students to graduate.

An important family characteristic that influences dropout behavior for Busby students is family structure. A part of the reason for this pattern within the Busby School population is related to the large number of students from Lame Deer. As noted above, the high incidence of poverty, unemployment, and single-parent households in Lame Deer is likely to affect students from Lame Deer attending Busby School. While this may explain the effect of family structure on dropping out at Busby, where there is a fairly large group of Lame Deer students, it also raises the question of why family structure is not important for dropping out among Lame Deer students attending Colstrip Public School.

A closer look at the family structure variable for these two schools reveals that they have similar proportions of students from single-parent families, about 30%. So again, we must ask what makes the family structure variable more important for Busby than Colstrip Indian students? Ethnographic information suggests that the answer lies in further consideration of the Busby and Colstrip students with respect to their family network attachments and parental resources. The Busby School student population is split such that a large proportion of the students come from the relatively closer family networks of Busby, and another group is from

CHAPTER SIX

the more heterogeneous Lame Deer population. One possibility, then, is that there are sufficient differences in family structure between these two groups of Busby students to create the statistical effect found in our analyses. On the other hand, the Colstrip Indian population, which is largely from Lame Deer, may not benefit as much from family networks. This suggests that the family structure variable may also reflect the extent to which parents can draw on family members for support or action when it comes to issues of dropping out or graduating. The Lame Deer student population may be handicapped both by less access to supportive family networks and by the reluctance of parents, many of whom may be single, to intervene on students' behalf in the Colstrip Public School. This pattern suggests that different levels of social capital in the reservation communities can affect school outcomes as social networks and family resources either support schooling and graduation or fail to intervene when graduation becomes problematic. A more detailed treatment of Indian students at Colstrip and their school experiences is the subject of the next chapter.

School Contexts

School completion processes were similar in the Indian schools in terms of the influences of family, school experience, and performance variables. The finding that parents' education and the presence of two adults decreased the likelihood of dropping out suggests that there is greater support for graduation among adults and families than for school performance in general. Although the two Indian schools differed in the role of extracurricular activity involvement, higher school performance increased school completion in both schools. Given the impact of the school performance variables on dropping out, as well as the effects of the family characteristics within the two Indian schools, the question remains, why do larger proportions of Indian students drop out of these two schools? Qualitative data suggest that the relationship of school context to the local social contexts helps to clarify the higher dropout rates.

The two Indian schools were weaker than the public school in terms of their academic demands due to the level of instructional resources and lower academic expectations, and, therefore, they did not challenge Indian students to perform quite as much as Colstrip. Student performance levels indicate that many Indian students were only marginally involved with school. Getting a GED certificate was a viable alternative to high school graduation for many students. Consequently, students who were bored, dissatisfied with school, or involved in other activities (e.g., drugs and alcohol) that detracted from their school performance and made graduation unlikely could choose dropping out over completing high school. In the Indian schools, where accommodation to Indian students' resistance to school and negotiation of school requirements was more prevalent, even intervention of parents in the eleventh hour could not prevent some students from choosing to exit school.

This suggests that an important aspect of school context is the orientations of the schools toward Indian students and communities. Since the schools that served primarily Indian students had greater contact with and interest in Indian families, parents concerned with the graduation of their children were more likely to take action in support of this outcome within these two schools. However, for many students, such intervention came too late or not at all. In contrast, within the context of the public school, which was primarily oriented to the non-Indian students, the responsibility for graduation, therefore, rested essentially on the students, many of whom made the choice to attend Colstrip Public School after trying the two Indian schools. In this school context, peer pressure supporting school and consideration of the consequences of dropping out were much higher overall. However, in this non-Indian school context, being from Lame Deer was the only individual/family characteristic that influenced graduation status. The fact that most Indian students attending Colstrip were Lame Deer residents suggests that the school completion process for Indian students at Colstrip differed from that of the other two schools. (A more in-depth examination of the school completion process at Colstrip is the subject of the next chapter.) An analysis of the effects of school and community contexts as well as school participation and cultural orientations of Cheyenne students and their parents is presented in the final section of this chapter.

Cheyenne Dropout Model: The Role of Cultural Variables

The influence of student and parent cultural orientations on dropping out is addressed in the following analysis, which includes only Cheyenne

CHAPTER SIX

students. First, school comparisons of mean values on the school problems, support, and cultural variables reveal some important patterns. The cultural variables indicate a general level of students' Cheyenne language skill as well as the level of family traditional cultural resources. Regarding Cheyenne language use, students at Busby (.46) were considerably more likely to speak Cheyenne than students at Colstrip (.16) and St. Labre (.10). Interestingly, the mean value on Cheyenne language skill is even higher for Busby School students than for students from the town of Busby (discussed in the community comparisons on this variable in chapter 5); this suggests that some of the Cheyenne speakers at Busby School were from Lame Deer. Similarly, parents of Busby School students (.34) were more likely to have traditional cultural knowledge, such as speaking Cheyenne, and participate in cultural activities. However, on the family traditionality variable, the presence of Lame Deer students at Busby School reduced the mean value (compared to the community mean shown in chapter 5), suggesting that these students' families had somewhat fewer traditional cultural resources. Interestingly, families of Colstrip (.16) and St. Labre (.16) students had the same mean value on this measure that, at a much lower level, suggests fewer cultural resources for these students as well. Regarding student problems (substance abuse and conflicts with authorities), Busby students (.70) were more likely to experience these than Colstrip (.62) and St. Labre (.50) students. Additionally, families of Busby (.13) and St. Labre (.13) students were more likely to have participated in recovery from substance abuse than families of students at Colstrip (.07). Finally, family support for schooling, while low overall, was much lower among students at Busby School (−.21) than students at St. Labre (−.03) and Colstrip (−.02) schools. Importantly, compared to the very low level of family school support in Busby (discussed in the chapter 5 community comparisons), these figures suggest that the overall level of family school support benefits from the presence of Lame Deer students and families at Busby School.

These mean values provide some important clues about the possible roles of cultural resources and distractions from schooling in the school completion process. For example, the high level of student problems at Busby School indicates the high incidence not only among students from the Busby community but also among Lame Deer students attending Busby School, while the somewhat lower level at St. Labre may reflect the stricter policies at this school. Higher values on family recovery experiences at Busby and St. Labre may be related to higher levels of student problems at these schools. However, at St. Labre, this may reflect the counseling services and special programs offered to students and their families. Importantly, the level of traditionality seems to vary inversely with parental involvement in and support for schooling; higher traditionality is accompanied by lower family school support at Busby, while greater school support is accompanied by fewer traditional cultural resources at St. Labre and Colstrip. Additionally, although distance may affect Lame Deer parents' participation in school activities, family school support is higher at Colstrip and St. Labre. Finally, although all three schools have negative mean values on family school support, the fact that Colstrip and St. Labre schools offered more sports activities and extracurricular activities than Busby may have encouraged parents' participation in these schools as well as helped to reduce student conflicts with authorities.

Logistic regression models shown in table 6.5 evaluate the effects on dropping out of individual characteristics (Cheyenne language skill, problems with authorities, and gender), family characteristics (family structure, parental education, family school support, family recovery, and traditionality), community–school combinations, and school experiences. The purpose is to determine how the new variables, concerning student and parental school participation and cultural practices, influence dropping out relative to the other variables analyzed previously. This analysis presents four models that evaluate the relative influence of several sets of variables. Model 1, which includes gender, students' Cheyenne language skill, and problems or conflicts with authorities, however, shows that these variables have little effect.

The second model adds the effect of family characteristics. Coefficients in this model, similar to the previous dropout model for all students, show that having single-parent households increases the likelihood of students dropping out. On the other hand, students are somewhat less likely to drop out of school if at least one parent graduated from high school. In addition, the new family school support variable has a significant negative influence on dropping out.

Model 3 includes community–school combinations (using the terms created with contrast coding shown above). Coefficients indicate important effects of residence in Busby and attending either Busby or Colstrip

Table 6.5. Logistic Regression Coefficients for the Effects of Student, Family, and Cultural Characteristics, Community, School Attended, and School Experiences on Dropping Out

	Model 1		Model 2		Model 3		Model 4	
	Coef.	SE	Coef.	SE	Coef.	SE	Coef.	SE
Student Characteristics								
Female[a]	.191	.247	.256	.280	.325	.298	.223	.338
Student's language	.093	.196	−.382	.288	−.491	.307	−.607*	.349
Problem/conflict with authority	.109	.234	.239	.292	.300	.312	.343	.371
Family Characteristics								
Only one adult present			1.216***	.325	1.123***	.338	.621*	.381
At least one adult with high school diploma			−.535*	.300	−.488	.301	−.874**	.346
Family school support			−1.198***	.293	−1.23***	.309	−.884**	.349
Family recovery			−.233	.443	−.352	.470	−.566	.563
Family traditionality			.0552	.516	.274	.531	−.047	.604
Family traditionality by adult high school			.933*	.543	.926*	.551	1.209*	.629
Family traditionality by adult high school by school support			.932*	.537	1.054*	.569	.527	.631
Community/School Combinations								
Living in Busby/attending Busby vs. Colstrip					.546	.514	.534	.555
Living in Busby/attending Busby or Colstrip vs. all other schools and communities					−.225***	.076	−.243***	.083

	Model 1		Model 2		Model 3		Model 4	
Living in Ashland/attending St. Labre or Colstrip vs. living in Lame Deer/attending St. Labre or Colstrip					.045	.085	.015	.098
Living in Ashland/attending St. Labre vs. Colstrip					.059	.372	.171	.430
Living in Lame Deer/attending St. Labre vs. Colstrip or Busby					-.351*	.173	-.088	.201
Living in Lame Deer/attending Colstrip vs. Busby					-.553**	.244	-.322	.264
School Experiences								
Extracurricular activities							-.908***	.209
Suspensions							.628	.494
Absences							-.003	.008
Transfers							.080	.151
Mean GPA							-.859**	.364
Model Chi square	1.03		52.28		73.76		134.21	
d.f.	2		10		16		21	
N	276		276		276		276	

[a] Omitted category is male.
* $p < .10$, ** $p < .05$, *** $p < .01$

CHAPTER SIX

schools; these combinations significantly reduce the likelihood of leaving school before graduation. Living in Lame Deer and attending St. Labre has a modest negative effect on dropping out, while Lame Deer residence and attending Colstrip (rather than Busby) also reduces the chances of dropping out. In this model, the family structure and family school support variables continue to play an important role in the dropout process. Although there is no effect of family traditionality in the model, the interaction terms for traditionality and parental education as well as traditionality, parental education, and family school support show positive relationships to dropout behavior. These results indicate that the relationships of parents' cultural practices, education, and school support to dropping out are not simple. The findings suggest that higher levels of family traditionality increase the chances that students will drop out even when parents have higher levels of education and support for schools.

The final model incorporates the effects of school experiences into the analysis. Only two measures of school experience have significant influences on dropping out. Similar to previous analyses, higher levels of participation in extracurricular activities and academic performance continue to reduce the likelihood of dropping out. Only one community–school combination, Busby residence and attending Busby or Colstrip school, continues to have a significant independent effect on dropping out. On the other hand, the single-parent family structure increases dropout behavior, while family school support and parental education reduce the chances of dropping out. Additionally, in this model, being female has a modest negative effect on dropping out and Cheyenne language skill shows a tendency toward reducing dropout behavior.

The results of this analysis represent important new findings concerning the dropout behavior of Cheyenne students. The finding that both traditional community residence and family school support reduce the chances that students will drop out not only shows the relevance of community context for the analysis of school outcomes, but it also indicates that family–school relations are an important factor to consider. Cultural variables are important as well since the school performance analyses suggest that they may indirectly influence the dropout processes through the school performance variable. The negative effects on school completion of family cultural practices mediated by parental education and school support suggest the complexity of these influences. However, students'

Cheyenne language skill may support a positive school experience. The concept of native capital, indicating the potential for overlap as well as conflict between Cheyenne cultural and educational institutions, helps to interpret these findings. The results suggest that conventional assumptions about the uniformly negative effects of Indian communities and cultural practices on schooling should be questioned.

Summary

The dropout analyses presented in this chapter added the effects of school performance as an independent variable into the models. These findings departed from previous models in the importance of several of the family background variables. Unlike some of the school performance models, family structure and parental education strongly influenced dropout behavior, but only within the two Indian schools. The effects of the community residence variables also changed when the dropout processes were examined for the different school populations. For example, Busby residence negatively affected dropping out in the overall model, although community residence effects generally declined within the specific school analyses. However, Busby residence had a negative effect on dropping out at both Busby School and Colstrip. School experiences and performance also had important effects on dropping out; extracurricular activity involvement and a higher mean GPA both reduced the chances of dropping out. However, these are influenced indirectly by the specific combination of school attended and the students' community residence.

Qualitative data suggested several possible explanations for these findings on dropout behavior. First, parents' behavior was different regarding the completion of high school than regarding school performance. While many parents had a traditional, noninterference parenting style, especially concerning school performance, parents with a high school diploma or GED had more influence on their children's graduation. This may be related to the general belief that a high school diploma is important as well as to a greater tendency to take action to ensure their children's graduation than to affect their school performance. The presence of two adults in the home amplified the effects of support for graduation. The fact that effects of the family variables were present only in the two Indian schools was interpreted in light of qualitative data to suggest that parents feel more empowered to act on behalf of

CHAPTER SIX

their children within these more familiar, Indian-oriented school settings. Even so, somewhat larger percentages of students dropped out of these schools. Reasons suggested for these higher dropout rates include the weaker instructional programs and demands or expectations (both school and peer) placed on students in the two Indian schools. In the dropout models, school performance levels directly affected dropping out. This variable also absorbed the effects of school experiences that previous analyses showed were important influences on mean GPAs. Extracurricular activity involvement was particularly important in the two larger schools (Colstrip public and St. Labre Catholic), but not the tribal school, where eligibility for participation was not as closely tied to academic performance.

The lack of effect of parental employment status was attributed to the local system of financial supports, alternatives to full-time work, and kinship-based employment practices for reservation residents. The effect of these factors was a general equalization of status as well as a leveling of the importance of educational attainment for participation in the local economy. In this way, cultural and social aspects of the reservation economy and society reduced the effects of adult employment differences on school outcomes of children.

These findings also showed the importance of the cultural and social influences on the school completion process. Importantly, the traditional cultural resources of their families negatively affected Cheyenne students' school completion. However, students' residence in more traditional, homogeneous communities strongly supported school completion, while Cheyenne language skill modestly supported graduation. These findings suggest the complexity of the roles of cultural influences in dropping out. We can also point to the need to consider the nature of the social distinctions that affect students' school performance and dropout behavior within specific school contexts. Thus, not only are the nature and effects of students' ties to their home communities important, but the values, practices, and relations within the family that provide different levels of support and relations to specific school contexts are influential as well.

The ethnographic data suggested that sociocultural practices and their relations to institutions such as schooling (as represented by the notion of "native capital") are central to the development and allocation of human capital in the reservation area labor market. Because unemployment and low incomes are increasingly common, and many people rely on a variety of strategies to support themselves and their families, work has a particular meaning in Northern Cheyenne communities. It is seen not only as a resource for a single individual or household, but it is also an indication of a person's location within an extended family and community. In other words, because hiring criteria often include friendship and kinship, having a job may signal not only that a person was able to meet educational or skill requirements but also that he or she was able to draw on social resources (e.g., kinship and friendship networks) to land the position. Thus, school credentials may be equal to or even less important than kinship and social relations for accessing local opportunities.

Ethnographic data also confirmed the importance of school context in the school completion process. While an important element of the school environment was the cultural and social distinctions among students, other aspects included the nature of the school's resources, expectations, and support for academic achievement and school involvement. Within the context of the non-Indian public school, attention must be given to the nature of support for Indian compared to non-Indian involvement. At all three schools, an important contextual factor was the extent to which the school could compete with alternative activities and peer pressures on students. The quality of students' experiences, as indicated by absences, suspensions, transfers, and extracurricular involvement, affected their performance levels and was an important indication of the pull of the different school contexts to keep students engaged. Additionally, qualitative data suggested the importance of the schools' receptivity to both Indian parents and students for explaining school completion. The relationship of these findings to relevant theoretical and empirical work will be discussed in chapter 8.

Notes

1. Contrast coding for community residence and school attended combinations include the following: Hypothesis 1: Busby residence and Busby Tribal School + Ashland residence and St. Labre School = 1. Busby or Ashland residence and Colstrip Public School = −1. Else = 0. Hypothesis 2: Busby residence and Busby Tribal School or Colstrip Public School = 1. Ashland residence and Colstrip Public School = −1. Else = 0. Hypothesis 3: Busby residence and Busby Tribal School + Ashland residence and Colstrip Public School = 1. Busby residence and Colstrip

CHAPTER SIX

Public School + Ashland residence and St. Labre School = −1. Else = 0. Hypothesis 4: Lame Deer residence and St. Labre School or Colstrip Public School = 1. Lame Deer residence and Busby Tribal School = −2. Else = 0. Hypothesis 5: Lame Deer residence and St. Labre School = 1. Lame Deer residence and Colstrip Public School = −1. Else = 0. Hypothesis 6: Lame Deer residence and St. Labre School = 1. Crow reservation communities and St. Labre School = −1. Else = 0. Hypothesis 7: Busby residence and Busby Tribal School or Colstrip Public School + Ashland residence and St. Labre School or Colstrip Public School = 1. Lame Deer residence and Busby Tribal School or St. Labre School or Colstrip Public School + Crow reservation communities and St. Labre School = −1. Else = 0.

2. Contrast coding for relevant community locations for each school include the following:

Busby Tribal School: Busby residence = 1. Lame Deer residence = −1. Else = 0. St. Labre School: Ashland residence = 2. Lame Deer and Crow community residence = −1. Else = 0. Colstrip Public School: Busby residence = 1. Ashland residence = 1. Lame Deer residence = −2. Else = 0.

CHAPTER SEVEN
EVALUATING MODELS OF SCHOOL PERFORMANCE AND COMPLETION FOR INDIAN AND WHITE STUDENTS AT COLSTRIP HIGH SCHOOL

The purpose of this chapter is to compare school performance and dropout processes for Indian and White students. This analysis is based on the premise that inter–ethnic group comparisons are useful for analyzing the influences on school outcomes for this population. In particular, analyses of Indian and White students' school completion processes at Colstrip High School benefit from holding the school context constant. This provides the opportunity to identify aspects of this desegregated school environment that may be important for understanding ethnic group school performance and dropout levels. Such an analysis is not possible for the other two schools, in which there are few, if any, White students.

Questions were raised in the previous chapter concerning the effects of individual characteristics, such as community residence, on school performance and dropping out at Colstrip High School. Since the analyses including only Indian students showed significant effects for residence in Lame Deer, the community on the reservation in which most Colstrip Indian students reside, the primary question of interest is what community represents within this school setting. In other words, what are the effects of community context, or of being Indian? Although this student body includes the largest number of Indian students among the three schools, Indian students compose only about a third of the total number of students in the high school. The majority of students are White. An important part of such an analysis is evaluation of the effects of ethnic minority versus majority status on school outcomes. Of particular concern is the persistence of

CHAPTER SEVEN

the effects of such individual characteristics when school experiences are taken into account, as suggested by the findings presented in chapter 6. Thus, in addition to questions concerning the effects of individual attributes, the analyses will examine the effects of school variables for all Colstrip students. Although the previous analyses of dropout behavior indicated the relevance of family characteristics for understanding dropping out, the lack of data for White students on family variables prevents further testing of these variables with the Colstrip student population.

Multivariate Analyses: School Performance and Completion

Table 7.1 presents the means and standard deviations for the variables included in the analyses for Colstrip students. The means and standard deviations for White students can be compared to those for the whole student body. These figures show that White students have higher mean GPAs and a higher average number of extracurricular activities. However, means on transfers between schools, absences, and suspensions are lower for White students compared to the total school population.

In table 7.2 coefficients are presented that indicate the effects of the two categories of influences—individual characteristics and school experiences—on school performance or mean GPA for all students at Colstrip High School. The intent of this analysis is to examine the effect of ethnicity on educational outcomes relative to the other independent variables of interest. Expected findings include:

1. Gender (female) will positively affect school performance for both Indian and White students.

2. Being Indian will negatively affect school performance.

3. Absences, suspensions, and school transfers will negatively affect school performance for all students.

4. Ethnic status and school experiences will have the greatest effects on school performance.

In this analysis residence is excluded since previous analyses showed that most of the Indian students attending Colstrip live in Lame Deer,

Table 7.1. Means and Standard Deviations for Colstrip Students

	All		White	
	Mean	SD	Mean	SD
Female	.54	.50	.55	.50
Indian	.36	.48		
School Experiences				
Transfers	.73	.91	.39	.63
Absences	18.35	16.02	16.96	13.67
Ever suspended	.10	.31	.07	.25
Extracurricular activities	2.54	2.82	3.17	2.94
Mean GPA	2.45	.70	2.64	.70

and the effect of Lame Deer residence did not have a significant effect on mean GPA. Additionally, reservation origin is excluded, since the vast majority of Indian students are from the Northern Cheyenne reservation. Findings are presented for separate models for all students and for White students. Because the models for Indian students were presented previously, we will avoid the duplication of showing additional models for Colstrip Indian students. However, results for Indian students will be compared with the two new models shown.

Coefficients presented in table 7.2 show that individual characteristics have significant effects on school performance. Among all students, being female has a strong, positive influence, while being Indian has a strong, negative influence on school performance. Comparing the model for White students with the previous analysis of Indian students, we find that being female is more important for White student performance levels.

All of the school experience variables are significant, indicating that they have strong effects on school performance in the model for all students. Suspensions from school, absences, and school transfers have negative effects on mean GPA, while involvement in extracurricular activities has a strong, positive effect on school performance. The White student model is quite similar, with the only exception being the lack of effect for school transfers.

These findings indicate that some of the influences on school performance observed in previous analyses also hold true for the entire Colstrip student population. In particular, school experiences have crucial effects on how well all Colstrip students perform, and their influence is similar to that observed for Indian students at Colstrip. However, new

CHAPTER SEVEN

Table 7.2. OLS Coefficients for the Effects of Individual Characteristics and School Experiences on Mean GPA for all Students at Colstrip

	All		White	
	Coef.	SE	Coef.	SE
Female[a]	.12**	(.57)	.14*	(.07)
Indian[b]	−.32***	(.07)		
School Experiences				
Transfers	−.07**	(.04)	−.08	(.05)
Absences	−.01***	(.002)	−.01***	(.003)
Ever suspended	−.35***	(.09)	−.58***	(.14)
Extracurricular activities	.09***	(.01)	.09***	(.01)
R-square	.37		.28	
N	454		306	

[a] Omitted category is male.
[b] Omitted category is White.
* $p < .10$, ** $p < .05$, *** $p < .01$

findings in this analysis include that gender and ethnicity both have important influences within the context of a public school with a mixed student body. Unlike our previous findings, the ascribed attributes of students have important effects: being female has a positive effect on both White and Indian students' school performance. However, being Indian has a negative impact on student performance. The expected results are supported by these findings.

In table 7.3, coefficients are presented for the effects of individual characteristics, school experiences, and school performance on dropout behavior for all students. As in the previous analysis, we will examine the effects of all the independent variables on dropping out, focusing on the relative effect of ethnicity, given the effects of the other variables. Expected findings include the following:

1. Gender (female) will negatively affect dropping out.

2. Being Indian will increase the chances of dropping out.

3. Suspensions, school transfers, and absences will increase the chances of dropping out, while extracurricular activity involvement and better school performance will negatively affect dropping out.

4. Ethnic status and school experiences will have the greatest effects on dropping out.

Table 7.3. Logistic Coefficients for the Effects of Individual Characteristics, School Experiences, and School Performance on Dropping Out for Students at Colstrip

	All		White	
	Coef.	SE	Coef.	SE
Female[a]	.62*	(.35)	1.55**	(.62)
Indian[b]	1.05***	(.38)		
School Experiences				
Transfers	.19	(.20)	.77**	(.39)
Absences	−.0004	(.01)	−.002	(.02)
Ever suspended	.57	(.49)	.73***	(.88)
Extracurricular activities	−.71***	(.16)	−.44**	(.22)
Mean GPA	−1.28***	(.36)	−1.35**	(.59)
Model chi-square	154.50		59.12	
d.f.	8		7	
N	356		228	

Note: Models include a dummy variable for missing data on mean GPA that is significant at the .01 level.
[a] Omitted category is male.
[b] Omitted category is White.
* $p < .10$, ** $p < .05$, *** $p < .01$

Coefficients presented in table 7.3 show some similarities in the two dropout models for Indian students and for all students at Colstrip. Two of the most important influences on dropping out, mean GPA and involvement in extracurricular activities, are statistically significant and negatively affect dropping out. However, this analysis also shows that ascribed traits, that is, being female or Indian, increase the likelihood of dropping out. Similar to the pattern observed for Colstrip Indian students previously, school experiences (suspensions, school transfers, and absences) do not affect dropping out in the model for all students. Again, these school experiences are intervening variables between school performance and dropout behavior. An important difference between this model and the model for White students is that transfers and suspensions have significant effects for White students, increasing the chances of dropping out. Consequently, these findings indicate that negative school experiences are more important for White students' dropout behavior.

The two analyses presented in tables 7.2 and 7.3 indicate, first, that both personal characteristics and school experiences are strongly correlated with how well students perform academically at Colstrip. Second, personal characteristics, school performance, and school experiences are crucial to dropout behavior. These analyses indicate that Indian and White students at Colstrip experience schooling differently in terms of their levels of academic success.

CHAPTER SEVEN

Additionally, females and males have different levels of school performance overall, with girls outperforming boys. To the extent that students experience problems that lead to transfers, suspensions, and absences, they have less academic success in terms of performance. However, extracurricular activity involvement increases the probability of higher levels of school performance. Even taking this into account, Indian students are still more likely to have lower levels of school performance. In relation to dropping out, gender (female) and ethnicity (Indian) negatively affect completing school. Overall, students are much more likely to make the decision to leave school if they are less involved in extracurricular activities and have lower levels of school performance; White students are also affected by behavioral problems (e.g., suspensions).

These findings do not support the predicted negative effect of being female and the direct effects of school transfers, suspensions, and absences on dropping out for this student population. Only in the model for White students were the expectations for these school experience variables supported. However, in both models the negative effects of greater involvement in extracurricular activities and higher school performance on dropping out were supported. Finally, expectations concerning the relative effects of ethnicity and school experiences were not supported, since in the general model these influences were equally important in their effects on dropping out. While the model for White students is more typical of the expectations based on the literature, there are several surprising results for both of these models. Among these are the positive relationship of gender (female) to dropping out and the lack of direct effects of several school experience variables in the model for all students. Additional qualitative data will help to explain the effects of ethnic status and school variables that differentiate school outcomes of Indian and White students at Colstrip.

Qualitative Analyses

Interpretation of the Colstrip student analyses will utilize several sources of qualitative data that can shed light on school processes at Colstrip. In addition to the information provided by key informants and interviewees, another source is the testimony given at hearings held by Rosebud and Big Horn counties in response to a petition for a new public high school on the Northern Cheyenne reservation. In February 1991, hearings were held to gather information relevant to the Northern Cheyenne Tribe's request for a new high school that would serve the entire Northern Cheyenne reservation as well as certain communities to the south of the reservation (which are currently served by very small, independent schools or by Sheridan, Wyoming). The petition was based on conclusions of the Northern Cheyenne Tribal Council that the educational needs of the Northern Cheyenne high school students were not adequately being met by the schools that Cheyenne students attended.

In hearings before the county superintendents, both advocates and opponents of the new public high school presented testimony. This testimony is important because it illuminates the experiences of students, parents, teachers, and administrators associated with the three schools included in this study. In particular, details are provided on the experiences of Indian students concerning their treatment by the schools, their achievement patterns, and any barriers they faced or special assistance they received for schooling. Similarly, the experiences of parents and members of the educational community show prevalent perceptions and patterns of interaction between Indian families and the school personnel. Additionally, information presented by opponents to the petition emphasized the advantages of each school as an enrollment option for Indian students, focusing on different resources available in these school settings. Moreover, the information provided for each school revealed how school personnel understood and addressed Indian student needs. Therefore, the information characterizes each school's treatment of Indian students and parents as well as its assessment of Indian students' academic and social achievement within that school environment. The views of students, parents, and school personnel concerning Colstrip High School are presented in the sections that follow.

Students

Northern Cheyenne student views about attending Colstrip High School are varied. On the one hand, some students believed that Colstrip was the best high school in the state, and their experiences at Colstrip were nothing but positive. These students pointed to the variety of school activities, clubs, sports teams, courses, and social events as well as the high-quality academic programs that the school offers. Other Indian students

CHAPTER SEVEN

countered such statements, contending that despite the programs offered, being Indian limited their involvement. First, being bused from the reservation meant bus rides of one to two hours each way. Colstrip had an "activity bus" (paid for by special BIA program funds) that took students from outlying areas home after they attended school activities, but for those who lived at the farthest points, this was still a hardship. With their school day starting at six in the morning, students who stayed for activities in the evening arrived home anywhere from eight to ten at night. This kind of transportation situation precluded participation in extracurricular activities for a number of Indian students.

A second feature of Indian students' school experiences was also related to their limited access to extracurricular activities. Students reported that since Indian students were in the minority, they were rarely elected to positions such as officers in school clubs or other honors. While Indian students said they had White friends and socialized with White students, this did not routinely result in the election of Indian students to offices. Consequently, Indian students felt they had little real input in the decisions about activities; their voice in school activities was minimal. Additionally, students who wanted to participate on sports teams, particularly basketball, indicated that they did not get the playing time they wanted. One mother explained her daughter's reaction to this situation (Ward 1998a): "My daughter finally got fed up with the little time she got to play. So she decided to transfer to [one of the Indian schools] where she will probably get a lot more recognition and playing time. Even though she really wanted to graduate from Colstrip, she feels that this move will be better for her [sports] career." Students in other sports, such as track, had more positive experiences, suggesting that Indian students' experiences varied by type of sport, with more dissatisfaction expressed about more visible sports. Finally, others suggested that Indian students with problems related to drug and alcohol abuse or family problems did not have adequate resources at school to help them.

For these reasons, some Indian students believed that a new high school on the reservation was a good idea, since it would provide more opportunities for school involvement. Additionally, problems related to truancy might be improved. Excessive absences among Indian students were often attributed to transportation problems; for instance, if students missed the bus, they stayed home from school. Other reasons included drugs and alcohol abuse and uninvolved parents who did not make sure that they got up and went to school. It was suggested that a more accessible local high school better equipped to deal with these types of problems could better meet the needs of students and parents.

Indian students' observations about Colstrip suggested the relevance of prejudice and discrimination to their school experiences. Students' accounts of such experiences range from few, if any, problems to frequent and overt prejudice and discrimination. Despite this range of responses, students generally agreed that Indian students at Colstrip had different experiences resulting from busing, living in different communities than the majority of White Colstrip students, and experiencing negative perceptions of their culture, history, and social circumstances. Until recently, Colstrip High School had no Indian club, special activities, or efforts to involve Indian students more actively in the social life of the high school. Consequently, Indian students expressed the need to try to fit in with the White student groups; for example, to meet the approval of their White peers, they emulated their style of dress, interests, and social activities. Sometimes this paid off in social acceptance, but sometimes it did not. While high school students generally struggle to belong to peer groups, for these Indian students the struggle involved overcoming barriers that were based on perceived ethnic differences, in particular, negative stereotypes of Indians from the reservation.

Comparisons of remarks by Colstrip students with those of students from St. Labre provide additional evidence of these types of concerns. One young woman who attended St. Labre said that she started high school at Colstrip but switched to St. Labre because she did not want to deal with meeting the expectations or social standards set by the White Colstrip students. Another young woman visited all three high schools and chose St. Labre because she liked the social climate there; the school personnel appeared friendly, and she was not afraid to interact with the other students.

Such comments are instructive for what they reveal about the social climate at Colstrip. Both of these young women were good students, from relatively well-educated, middle-class families. Their concerns were not related to fears of academic failure; rather, both young women were very aware of, and intimidated by, what they perceived as the distinctive (and generally more negative) social status of Indians, a prominent element of the social environment at Colstrip.

CHAPTER SEVEN

Other students' experiences also reflect the pressures to fit in with both their Indian friends from the reservation and White students with whom they attended classes and school activities. This often led to very divergent behaviors. For example, even the "good" students felt compelled to meet the expectations of Indian friends to drink and "party" on the reservation, where such activities were common (although illegal), but would try to keep up their grades and fit in with the expectations of non-Indian social groups and teachers at school. Many students ended up choosing between such groups rather than trying to be accepted in both.

An important indication of the tensions and pressures felt by Indian high school students at that time was the number of suicides and attempts reported by reservation mental health agencies: there was one suicide as well as nine suicide attempts by Indian students in the middle school and high school during the last two months of school in the spring of 1991. An Indian senior at Colstrip committed suicide. Observations about these tragedies included two important points. First, sources who had specific knowledge of the suicide observed that it could probably have been prevented if the student's mental health problems had been identified earlier and taken seriously. Second, the reasons for the suicide attempts were varied; some involved drug and alcohol abuse, and others were related to different mental health problems.

When asked about these incidents, mental health workers on the reservation indicated that a central concern in most of their interactions with reservation youth was self-esteem. Many students struggled to come to terms with their identity, being Indian and coming from homes with a number of social and emotional problems. The social status of the family within the reservation community most likely suffers due to such problems. For example, students might have seen their parents snubbed by other community members because of their drinking or drug problems, that their parents couldn't cash checks in Billings or other towns because they were Indian, or that they wouldn't be served in stores or restaurants off the reservation. Such students were faced with the need to find an identity that allowed them to be proud of themselves in circumstances where they couldn't see many sources of pride. For a substantial group of reservation youth, coping with such dilemmas involved substance abuse or other such behaviors.

Responses from Indian students about the reasons for such behaviors as suicide attempts, alcohol and drug use, and dropping out of school were that, although most knew Indian students who did these things, not many knew of the specific reasons. However, they did report that boredom, frustration, problems at home, and drug and alcohol use were common problems of their Indian peers.

A final observation about the school environment of Colstrip High School involves information about the composition of the Indian student population itself. In chapter 4, the discussion of social status on the reservation identified one of the important distinctions as whether a person is full-blood or of mixed parentage (i.e., part Indian). This aspect of status within the Northern Cheyenne social structure may help explain the lower dropout rate of Colstrip Indians compared to students in the other two schools. Most of the Indian students enrolled in Colstrip come from Lame Deer, the most heterogeneous community on the reservation. Therefore, it is likely that many of the Indian students attending Colstrip are part Indian, or from families in which there is a White parent and other extended family members. One possibility is that, in spite of the generally negative attitude toward Indians suggested earlier, part Indian students had a relatively easier adjustment to Colstrip High School than full-blood students, who were more likely to have physical traits and language problems that created additional barriers to their integration into the school. Thus, the lower dropout rate for Colstrip Indian students may have been related to their blood quantum, which created a unique social status for these students. This status, in turn, provided for a greater facility in relating to White students and relatively greater involvement and success within a school environment with a majority of White students. However, whether a student's blood quantum actually affected the choice of school to attend and subsequent performance and attainment is not clear at this point but rather provides an important area for future investigation.

Indian Parents

Indian parents' descriptions of the experiences of their children attending Colstrip High School are as diverse as the students' accounts. Some parents who had attended Colstrip themselves thought highly enough of the school based on their own experiences to send their children there. However, few, if any, parents contended that there was no prejudice or discrimination toward Indian students at Colstrip. Some said that they wanted their children to go to a school that included Whites so that they would not be sheltered from discrimination and prejudice. One mother specifically wanted her children to learn how to handle such realities so that when they left the reservation they would not be afraid to interact with Whites. Other parents were very resentful of the prejudice and discrimination experienced by their children.

Interestingly, not many parents reported favorable interactions with school personnel. This did not necessarily mean that their children did not like their teachers or that the teachers showed overt prejudice toward Indians. Instead, it became apparent from the testimony that parents (mostly mothers) did not have much contact with the teachers at Colstrip, usually because they could not leave work to meet with teachers, they had transportation problems, or they felt too intimidated to go to parent–teacher meetings. On the other hand, some parents reported that when they did go to the school to discuss a problem with teachers or administrators, Colstrip School personnel were not particularly receptive to working out solutions. These types of experiences left many parents concerned about their children's education, but reluctant or confused about how to take action.

The chairwoman of the Indian Parent Advisory Committee (Bixby 1990) for Colstrip schools reported that poor parent participation in the advisory group could be attributed to the fact that they felt helpless about school-related problems. They did not feel that any problems or solutions they identified would be taken seriously by the Colstrip school administration. While the chairwoman had been made aware of many incidents of prejudice and discrimination at Colstrip, committee efforts to get parents to approach the schools or take actions to correct the problems had met with little interest among Indian community members.

School Personnel

Colstrip teacher responses to Indian students ranged from apathy to intense interest and support. However, the majority of teachers were reported to fit into the category of having some understanding of Indian students' educational needs but little knowledge or support for addressing them. Consequently, the typical reaction to an Indian student's problem was to send him or her to one of the two Indian home-school coordinators for the school district. In general, teachers made minimal efforts to incorporate Northern Cheyenne or any American Indian cultural material into their courses. There were a few teachers, however, who worked closely with Indian students, taught cultural sensitivity to all their students, and incorporated information into their classes about Northern Cheyenne and other Indian cultures, history, and social conditions.

This information suggests that an important aspect of the school's social environment was the attitudes of Colstrip teachers toward Indian students. Because the teachers generally had not gone to Colstrip specifically to teach Indian students, as is the case with St. Labre and Busby schools, they did not exhibit the paternalistic attitudes that often resulted in passing Indian students who would not pass otherwise. Colstrip's somewhat stricter grading and evaluation of student performance may explain, in part, why grades of Colstrip Indian students were relatively lower than grades of students attending the two Indian schools. Higher teacher expectations may have had positive effects as well. While teachers did not often go out of their way to help Indian students succeed academically, Indian students did experience a school environment that was generally more challenging. As indicated in chapter 4, Indian graduates had lower grades overall than White students. However, this was true up to the twelfth grade, at which point seniors were closer to parity. This suggests that the Colstrip context, which provides greater demands and offers greater opportunities, was one to which a relatively large proportion of Indian students responded positively. Nevertheless, a relatively large proportion of Indian students also chose to transfer to other schools or drop out, leaving those at Colstrip who were more likely to succeed.

Administrators at Colstrip pointed to several teachers as examples of how the school district was making efforts to adapt its curricula to meet the needs of Indian students and parents. The administrators' testimony at the hearings (Montana Public Hearings on Northern Cheyenne Petition for Public High School 1991), for example, included references to in-service meetings at which cultural sensitivity to Indian students was discussed and related materials were offered to teachers. However, when asked how many of their teachers actually followed up on the development of new curricula or materials that addressed such issues, the administrators could not say. Although the high school principal said she frequently asked teachers about such matters in face-to-face evaluations, their responses were not quantified or evaluated overall. Consequently,

CHAPTER SEVEN

the school's progress in going beyond "token" gestures toward its Indian students could not be assessed.

Similarly, information presented by school personnel on the Indian student dropout rate at Colstrip High School was based on an "event" rate, or the proportion of students who leave school anytime during the school year and do not return during that year. This type of calculation resulted in a dropout rate of about 15% on average across several years. Although the "event" rate has been shown to inherently underestimate the phenomenon of dropping out because it only estimates single events of leaving school and does not address noncompletion of high school, Colstrip administrators preferred not to address this issue. Moreover, they could not explain the fact that over a third of their Indian students from three cohorts (1987–1989) did not graduate. Explanations of the poorer school performance of Indian students included such generalizations as, "Indian students were not as well prepared entering Colstrip schools as other students," and the suggestion that many Indian students were negatively affected by problems at home. However, as far as school personnel were concerned, Colstrip schools were doing a good job of helping Indian students succeed in high school.

Colstrip administrators asserted that a new school was not needed to serve Indian high school students. Alternatively, they emphasized the effects a new school would have on their district. If virtually all of the Indian students were to leave, Colstrip's enrollment and budget would be dramatically reduced, causing the elimination of both facilities and school personnel. This was seen as devastating to the school district. Thus, the administrators' discussion of the school's ability to serve Indian students effectively was closely connected to an assessment of the financial plight of the school district should the Indian students (and the federal payments for the education of Indian students) leave.

Reactions from Indian parents to the school administrators' testimony were somewhat mixed but revealed the level of trust between many Indian community members and Colstrip school personnel. Some believed that Colstrip administrators only wanted the Indian students so that they would not lose this source of financing. Others were less pessimistic. Still other parents did not think that a new school offering Indian cultural programs was the answer to Indian education problems; others said they did not want the schools to teach students to "be Indian." However, still others suggested that, after two generations of Indian students attending Colstrip, the schools needed to go beyond a minimal understanding of Indian students, do a better job of including Indian materials in the curriculum, and more effectively address prejudice and discrimination.

Criticisms of Colstrip schools (expressed at the hearings and elsewhere) met with a great deal of animosity among the Colstrip administrative personnel. These school personnel expressed the belief that they should not be blamed for the problems Indian students and parents perceived; they did not condone discrimination, and they felt they had done as much as they could to change their schools over the last few years. From their viewpoint, it was the lack of cooperation from the Indian community that was the primary obstacle to improving conditions for Colstrip Indian students.

These Colstrip school personnel did not understand why Indian parents were reluctant to voice their problems with the schools through ordinary channels. Since Indian parents "voted with their feet" (i.e., stayed away from Colstrip schools), the administrators concluded that the parents either had no concerns or were unwilling to help solve the problems. Since the school administrators knew of no specific demands of Indian parents for the improvement of their schools, they were shocked and frustrated at the outpouring of accusations from some of the Indian community members.

Colstrip Community Members

The views of Colstrip school personnel toward Indian students were generally representative of the community of Colstrip. White parents at the hearings supported both sides of the issue, representing the general ambivalence of Colstrip residents about the association of their children with Indians from the reservation. While some parents allowed their high school–age children to date Indian classmates, others opposed such social interaction. Most Colstrip residents lived in this small town because of their employment at the energy plants, and long-term residents had generally lived in Colstrip for twenty to thirty years; however, most had lived there considerably shorter periods of time. Few had made efforts to interact with the Northern Cheyenne or to gain an understanding of their culture, history, and circumstances. Their information about

CHAPTER SEVEN

Indian people came from seeing them in Colstrip stores and bars, and from White neighbors. Colstrip residents typically felt that Indians were very different from them, not only in lifestyle, but also in basic values and orientations, particularly toward education and work. They did not understand, for example, that Indians did not receive monthly per capita payments. Because some tribes have distributed per capita payments from revenues they received in compensation for natural resource sales or as retribution for lands taken by treaty, many rural residents believed that this was a routine occurrence for all Indians. Many thought as well that Indian people did not have to work or did not want to work, and that they did not want the education or training needed to take advantage of work opportunities. When they saw, for example, that Indians had a high rate of unemployment compared to Whites, and that over 90% of the Colstrip White students graduated, compared to only about two-thirds of Indian students, their beliefs about the differences between Indians and Whites were confirmed.

Another important source of information for Colstrip residents was the area newspaper, the *Billings Gazette*. This newspaper has a long history of sensationalizing stories about Indians, especially those that have involved violence. For example, a 1988 story about a murder of an Indian woman in downtown Billings showed a picture of the dead woman's body. Showing a murder victim's picture was unprecedented, but the newspaper approved it in the case of an Indian murder. Such publicity, along with stories about tribal government corruption and other illegal or violent events, highlighted the negative behaviors of Indian people.

Another story about several members of the Northern Cheyenne Tribe published in 1987 similarly caused a tremendous public reaction against Indians in the rural area of southeastern Montana that includes Colstrip. The story concerned the murder of a White man by several Indians in Miles City, Montana, a town located about one hundred miles east of Colstrip. The facts of the story were that two Indian males engaged in a conflict with the White man in a bar. The Indians later took him out into the country and killed him. A young Indian woman accompanied them. The two Indian men, from Busby, were convicted of murder. For her role in the murder, the Indian woman, who became a witness for the state, received a long sentence in a state women's prison. A letter I received from this woman, who saw a story about this dropout research project in the newspaper, stated that her high school experiences were similar to those of many other Indian women; she was bored and did not have the aspiration to finish, so she dropped out. At that time, she was working on her GED in prison.

The occurrence of violence against a White person by Indians apparently struck terror in the hearts of many Whites in rural towns of Montana close to Indian reservations. As a response to this event in 1987, a number of stores and restaurants posted "No Indians" signs in their windows, and Indian students attending the large community college in Miles City reported numerous experiences with overt prejudice and discrimination. Such actions as these indicate the level of apprehension about Indians that pervaded the large rural area in which Colstrip is located. Without opportunities for routine interaction with reservation residents and for obtaining information about Indian people and their circumstances, White parents were left with little to inform their judgments other than what the media and their neighbors provided. Thus, stereotypes about Indian people set the tone for the interaction that occurred.

Summary

To summarize the analyses presented for Colstrip High School, the evidence showed that individual attributes (gender and ethnicity) have important effects on school performance. The effect of gender for the total student population at Colstrip is a departure from the previous findings for the Indian students attending Colstrip. These new findings suggest, in fact, that gender is more a factor for White students than for Indian students. Thus, the major individual characteristic influencing Indian students' school performance at Colstrip is their ethnicity.

On the other hand, school experience variables for the total school population closely resemble the model for Colstrip Indian students in their effects on school performance. School transfers, absences, and suspensions from school all negatively influenced school performance, while extracurricular activity involvement positively influenced school performance.

The model for dropout behavior for all Colstrip students reveals that extracurricular activity involvement and a higher mean GPA both negatively affected dropping out. Again, these findings are similar to the model for Indian students. However, once again, individual characteristics

CHAPTER SEVEN

positively influenced dropout behavior such that females and Indian students were more likely to drop out of high school.

Without the family background variables for all Colstrip students, this analysis could not make a systematic evaluation of these types of influences on school performance and completion. However, qualitative data regarding the effects of the variables in the models suggest that families had a great deal of influence on students attending Colstrip. For example, community residence, family attitudes, and resources influenced how much Indian students could participate in school activities, how far they were bused, and whether or not students had an adult advocate if there were problems at school.

The information provided by parents, teachers, and students also suggested that the social environment was one in which Indian students experienced school in a very different way than Whites. While Indian students took advantage of activities offered if they were willing to travel long distances, they were excluded from the leadership positions associated with school clubs and other social groups. For the cohorts included in this study, there were no special Indian student clubs or social activities that acknowledged the value of Indian culture and history. The academic environment likewise did not show any particular leniency toward Indian students in terms of grading. While many Indian students had problems with the school requirements at Colstrip, others responded positively to the more challenging academic environment and opportunities for school involvement. In relation to cultural issues, the school made few systematic attempts to incorporate Indian culture or history in the high school curriculum.

Overall, the information revealed a negative social bias against Indian students that translated into intimidation for some, tension and pressure for others, and a general agreement that Indian students faced an academic and social climate at Colstrip High School that had to be reckoned with in some way. For some students the answer was to try to fit in with their White peers, while others struggled with the need to belong to both groups, and still others remained isolated from the majority of students or dropped out altogether. Students also coped with academic demands in a variety of ways, some accepting the academic requirements, others negotiating minimal levels of success, and still others resisting school and opting to drop out. However, the percentage of students who chose to drop out was somewhat smaller at Colstrip than at St. Labre or Busby. The qualitative data suggest that the reasons for this were based in the school environment, which provided for a wide variety of academic opportunities, greater levels of participation in school activities, and a more challenging set of expectations from teachers, peers, and administrators. Parents of many Indian students at Colstrip, however, offered their children few resources or effective strategies for helping them succeed. Thus, Indian students were often on their own in negotiating their journey through the schooling process. Among parents, students, and teachers, there was an ongoing, but mostly invisible, struggle about how the school environment should assist Indian students to make that journey more successful.

The implications of these findings for evaluating relevant theory and empirical results concerning ethnic differences in school completion are addressed in chapter 8.

CHAPTER EIGHT
CONCLUSION: NATIVE CAPITAL AND NORTHERN CHEYENNE DROPOUT RATES

The objectives of this study included, first, analyses of the schooling processes for Indian students overall and within three different school populations and, second, comparisons of schooling processes of Indian and non-Indian students within a single school context. In reference to these objectives, the following discussions will relate our research findings to relevant theoretical concepts and previous empirical findings on American Indian schooling. This will be followed by a discussion that shows how students experience the multiple contexts examined in this study and make decisions about graduating and dropping out in this reservation context. Finally, the chapter ends with a discussion of policy considerations, both for the Cheyenne Nation and for schools and communities that experience similar dropout problems.

School Performance

Individual and Family Characteristics Related to School Performance

This analysis began with the use of descriptive statistics for this population of Indian and White students to assess the school performance levels of these groups. These statistics generally confirmed the difference between Indian and White students' school performance found by previous studies of Indian educational achievement. Specifically, Indian students had lower GPAs than White students.

Other individual characteristics relevant to school performance, gender, community residence, and reservation origins, were examined as well.

CONCLUSION

While the initial analyses indicated that gender had little effect on Indian students' performance levels overall, the analyses for Colstrip Public School found that being female had a very positive effect on school performance within that school population; however, analyses showed further that this effect was stronger for White students. These findings support studies showing that girls have higher grades than boys.

Students' community residence, which provides a general indication of the influence of cultural, family, and geographic groups within the Northern Cheyenne reservation, was found to have important effects on school performance. Specifically, residence in the more homogeneous community of Busby had a positive effect on performance compared to Lame Deer, a more heterogeneous community. Residence in Lame Deer had a negative effect on performance in Busby Tribal School, but the effect was somewhat more positive for students attending St. Labre Catholic School and Colstrip. Similarly, school performance was negatively affected by being from the Crow reservation (compared to Northern Cheyenne). These results suggest that individual attributes related to community and reservation associations affect the schooling of Indian students. Parents and children are located within community and reservation contexts that define the meaning of schooling, its relationship to economic activities, and the process of acquiring social status and provide relevant sanctions. Variation in these sociocultural structures by community offers different types of social contexts that influence both parents and students. That is, some family/community structures provide more supportive environments for schooling than others; thus, they vary in levels of native capital and other resources.

While other studies of schooling in Indian communities have indicated the importance of ethnic group membership for school performance, few studies have investigated the role of intragroup (intratribal or intertribal) differences in explaining school performance. Most studies have suggested that traditional culture has a negative effect on performance. The findings of this study are important because they indicate the effects of intragroup cultural and social differences that typically have not been measured in achievement research for this ethnic group. Additionally, the research shows that traditional cultural resources, especially at the community level, can have positive effects on schooling. Unlike the "cultural deprivation" or "cultural difference" approaches used to assess the role of

CHAPTER EIGHT

culture in schooling, this research shows that variations in individual experiences and school outcomes can be better understood by examining (1) the specific meaning of schooling and its relation to the cultural knowledge and the social relations within family, community, and reservation groups and (2) how these different social and cultural groups relate to schooling.

In contrast to previous studies of the influences of family background characteristics on student achievement, this study found that two characteristics of families—parents' high school education and employment status—had little effect on students' academic performance levels. Since we had only a few measures of family background, it is possible that these measures were not the most meaningful within this reservation context. On the other hand, family structure and family support for schooling had important effects on performance; family structure (single-parent home) effects were negative, and family support for schooling was positive.

Because we expected that family background variables (parental education and employment status) would be important, we looked to the ethnographic data for some possible explanations for the absence of effects of these family characteristics. Key sources of information on family background and attitudes about education in the home revealed that parents using traditional parenting styles (and others concerned with personal or other problems) were less involved with students' schooling in terms of supervising homework or helping with school assignments. While parents agreed that education was important for their children, specific efforts to support this goal were often limited. This can be attributed to several influences: adults' lack of experience or success with education; lack of role models; cultural biases against the "White man's" education; permissive parenting styles; perceptions concerning the lack of connections between job opportunities and educational credentials; substance abuse and family problems.

Ethnographic data were particularly useful for indicating that the cultural resources (values and behaviors meaningful within the reservation setting) that children acquired from family members often did not directly support, or even contradicted, school performance. Although the noninterference parenting style used by some parents provided general guidance to teenagers, it did not involve monitoring of schoolwork. Thus, even when parents had relevant educational experiences, children did not always benefit from them. Support for education also varied among adults and extended family members in the larger community contexts. These findings support studies of other minority communities in which schooling has been problematic. The concept of native capital suggests that parents and family members bring different types and levels of cultural and social resources to their parenting responsibilities and to the support they provide for their children's schooling.

School Experiences and School Contexts

Findings from this study may be evaluated in light of the research by Coleman and Hoffer (1987) about the different effects of private and public schools on school achievement. For example, their study found that Catholic, private school contexts had a more positive effect on minority student achievement growth than other private schools or public schools. Similarly, our findings showed higher levels of school performance (as measured by mean GPA) among Indian students attending the tribal school and the Catholic Indian school than the public school. These results support the findings of the Coleman and Hoffer study.

Moreover, school experiences were found to have the most influence on school performance within the context of the public school. That is, problems such as higher levels of school transfers and absences were more likely to negatively affect Indian students' performance at the public school than at the Indian schools. Additionally, extracurricular activity involvement played a positive role in improving school performance at St. Labre and Colstrip. These results generally support other schooling studies that have focused on the effects of school experiences and differences in the types of schools that serve Indian students.

Qualitative data suggested that important school context influences on performance levels included differences in curricular offerings, academic expectations, and orientations toward Indian students. In the Indian schools, academic expectations were sometimes lowered as a result of demands made by Indian parents on behalf of students, often in relation to maintaining eligibility for extracurricular activities. Ethnographic information also suggested that such factors as the less restrictive policies at the tribal school for participation in extracurricular activities may have contributed to the absence of the expected effect of this type of school involvement on school performance. In contrast, the St. Labre Catholic School environment more closely resembled that of Colstrip in terms of

CHAPTER EIGHT

academic requirements for participation in school activities such as sports teams. In both Indian schools academic expectations were tempered by the special missions of these schools to support Indian students. The Catholic school's academic expectations were somewhat higher than the tribal school's due to its relatively well-paid staff and faculty who had fairly high agreement on educational goals. At the tribal school, on the other hand, teacher expectations were highly influenced by the political and cultural climate of the reservation and were therefore subject to pressures toward minimal effort and risk. The tribal school was much less likely to use suspensions in response to discipline problems than St. Labre.

Analyses of the Colstrip Public School population provided some additional insights into contextual factors within this organizational environment. The public school, which offered somewhat higher academic expectations and greater opportunities for Indian students to succeed, also had some important contextual elements that reduced these benefits. In particular, school personnel were less receptive to negotiation of solutions to Indian students' problems with Indian parents, suggesting some degree of prejudice or discrimination. Such findings also suggest the possible relevance of such notions as "symbolic violence" (Bourdieu and Passeron 1977) for understanding the relations of Indian students to this school context; that is, the differences between Indian students and the overall culture of the school created a social and cultural chasm between Indian students and others in the public school environment that undermined their success relative to White students.

The school performance findings indicate that, in general, for Indian students from communities of the Northern Cheyenne reservation, attending the Indian Catholic private school may have had a more positive effect on school performance levels than attending the other two schools. Problems with schooling seemed to be handled in ways that were generally more favorable to Indian student performance. Also, the school climate, specifically including greater encouragement for Indian students to become involved with extracurricular activities, increased their engagement with school and improved school performance levels.

Some continuity between the students' community residence and the school context also appeared to be important. For example, residence in a more homogeneous, traditional community positively influenced school performance. In particular, student performance benefited more when Indian students resided in Busby than Ashland. Students from Busby and Ashland also benefited more from attending their local school than one outside their community. However, Indian students from Lame Deer benefited from attending either St. Labre or Colstrip and had less academic success at Busby. In contrast, Crow reservation origins negatively affected performance.

Dropout Behavior

The Role of Individual and Family Characteristics in School Completion

Other studies of Indian school completion have suggested that Indian girls and boys are equally likely to drop out. Additionally, research comparing White and Indian students has found Indians to have a higher dropout rate than most other students. This study confirmed that Indian girls were just about as likely as boys to drop out, except within the context of the tribal school, where girls were more likely to drop out. Our findings are consistent with previous studies suggesting that Indian students have higher dropout rates than White students.

Results related to the effects of community and reservation residence indicate that residence patterns, again, had an important effect on this school outcome. For example, although we do not know the specific dimensions of community residence that positively affected finishing school in Busby compared to other communities, we do know that Busby had one of the highest percentages of high school and GED graduates among adults on the reservation. In contrast, we have also noted the negative effect of living in Lame Deer on school performance and on high school graduation from Busby Tribal School. This could explain why Busby Tribal School had the highest dropout rate, and yet Busby residence had a positive effect on students' performance and graduation compared to residence in Lame Deer: Lame Deer students attending Busby school were more likely to drop out than students from Busby.

Again, our ethnographic data suggested possible reasons for the different effects of living in these communities on dropping out of high school. Students from Busby were located in a community in which extended families offered encouragement, especially regarding graduation. The community had considerable pride in their tribally controlled school. On the other hand, where family support was not forthcoming for students, the pressures toward dropping out were often overwhelming. This

CHAPTER EIGHT

mix of factors created low family support for some students but greater community-level support for education. Similarly, some students from Ashland experienced lower levels of support for education from family and social networks. On the other hand, some family networks involved in recovery from alcohol abuse and adults with higher levels of education provided support for schooling. Additionally, Crow students residing at St. Labre were isolated from their families; many also had problems at home and poor academic experiences prior to high school. Both of these last two groups of students had higher dropout rates than students from other communities.

Students from Lame Deer were located in the most heterogeneous community on the reservation. Although there was a wide range of incomes, Lame Deer had the largest percentages of the poor and unemployed and the lowest levels of high school education of any community on or near the reservation. Consequently, students from Lame Deer had relatively lower levels of community support, although somewhat higher family support, for education. Students also were exposed to family and peer pressures for drug abuse and other illegal activities that distracted many from schooling.

With regard to family background characteristics, the findings generally upheld previous research concerning the role of family structure in the school completion process. These results can be contrasted with the school performance analyses in which the family variables had less influence on students' performance levels. The finding that students from single-parent homes were more likely to drop out is consistent with other studies of the influence of family traits. However, this influence was more important at Busby Tribal School than at the Catholic or public school. Busby students in single-parent households were less likely to receive support for schooling and, therefore, were comparatively disadvantaged. This pattern is consistent with the suggestion made above that students in Busby benefited from the extended family or community members who offered support for completion of school.

The effect of parents' education on dropout behavior is also consistent with previous research concerning the influence of parents' education on the educational attainment of their children. However, the effect of parents' education varied by school and was most important at the two Indian schools. Students attending these schools needed more adult support for education to help them graduate. Since the education levels of adults were not generally high, parents who had educational credentials had an important effect on their children's school completion. This is supported by ethnographic data indicating that Indian parents with high school diplomas or GEDs were more likely to place demands on the Indian schools when graduation of their children was at risk.

Although parents' education had significant effects on dropping out, in contrast to most studies, parents' employment status did not affect either of the school outcomes. The reasons for this finding are related to the adaptations of this population to the reservation economic opportunity structure. Specifically, opportunities for employment in this reservation context were very limited. However, we also observed a widespread strategy of combining part-time or seasonal work with support from extended family networks, welfare, and other types of subsistence activities, legal and illegal (e.g., drug trafficking), for obtaining income. Such adaptations to the opportunity structure provided reservation residents with sources of support that did not necessarily require extensive educational attainment and also allowed the pursuit of lifestyles that were not organized around regular work hours.

These findings support research by Snipp and Sandefur (1988) and Brown et al. (2001) that found limited job opportunities for Indians in most rural reservation areas, as well as the work of Jensen and Tienda (1989), which showed that poorer Indians were more likely to rely on family and community resources than welfare. The evidence presented here concerning the effects of households, family networks, and communities on schooling is an interesting parallel to evidence presented on low-income, ethnic communities in urban areas, such as Chicago (Wilson 1987, 1996). Similar to these studies, our research revealed the crucial influences not only of adults' education but also their relations to family and community networks. These relations (social capital) provided information or other resources needed to access scarce opportunities (e.g., jobs). In this context family mutual assistance and use of a variety of economic strategies are often necessary for survival. Thus, economic isolation for some reservation residents reflects the lack of social capital.

Additionally, family residence patterns have an important effect on economic survival. For example, Lame Deer is characterized by greater social diversity, and families in Lame Deer had the least attachment to the labor market and to education compared to the other communities. Thus, Lame Deer students' households were among the most isolated

CHAPTER EIGHT

from economic resources. Residents of other communities had relatively more education and homogeneous social networks to help them access opportunities. The concept of native capital suggests that in this context the conventional forms of social capital and human capital often were in short supply or could not be readily converted into valued employment and wages. Therefore, cultural and social resources specific to this reservation community were called upon to meet the needs of local residents and members of this ethnic group for survival and for achieving meaningful goals (J. Hall 1992). However, these forms of native capital both interacted with and conflicted with schooling and labor market institutions at specific points. In some cases, they overlapped; for example, cultural norms that support knowledge and family assistance and guidance for school success contributed to personal achievement. However, in other cases they conflicted with typical American values; for example, Western notions that school credentials are more important than family loyalty or traditional activities contradicted important Cheyenne ideals.

These patterns indicate that reservation adaptations to structural deficiencies in the local economy (such as low wages and lack of jobs) were influenced not only by the social resources available to individuals and families but also by cultural orientations and norms that differed from the dominant society and surrounding population's values and norms for school and work. Importantly, native capital translated into economic benefits, sometimes at higher rates than education credentials and other forms of human capital. However, those lacking native capital were likely to be the most economically vulnerable. The use of a variety of strategies to support families ensured that all survived, albeit many in poverty. These strategies also provided the flexibility for some reservation community members to pursue traditional activities valued by the larger community.

The Effects of School Contexts

Finally, we can consider the dropout results in relation to studies focusing on the effects of school experiences and school contexts. The findings of this study contradict in some ways the expected results, based on the Coleman and Hoffer (1987) study, that the dropout rate would be higher at the public school rather than the two (independent) Indian schools. In this study, the public school and the Catholic Indian school had lower levels of dropping out among Indian students than the tribal school.

CONCLUSION

The variables that affected dropout behavior were generally similar at the three schools. However, the different effects of ethnicity, community residence, and family background among the three schools indicated that different processes were operating in the three school populations. These results suggest that school contexts were a factor in school completion. However, unlike the findings of Coleman and Hoffer, the most supportive school environment for completion of high school within the reservation context was not necessarily found in the Catholic private school. A slightly smaller percentage of Indians left public school than the other two schools. In the public school environment, being Indian had an important effect on whether a student graduated, even after taking into account school engagement factors and performance. However, Indian students' performance in the public school was not affected by whether they received support for schooling at home or whether they were from a two-parent family.

In the Indian schools, dropping out was more likely despite the fact that, overall, Indian students' performance levels were positively affected by attending these schools compared to the public school. Of particular importance in these contexts was support for schooling from adults at home. Also, positive school experiences, particularly, academic success and involvement with extracurricular activities, made a difference in graduation. These were of special significance at the Catholic school. In contrast to findings by Coleman and Hoffer that greater support for disadvantaged students in Catholic schools ameliorated the effects of low family support, our findings indicated that school experiences contributed the most to students' successful academic performance in the Catholic school environment. Parental influences were more important in relation to graduation. In the Indian schools, students without parental support or positive school experiences were more likely to drop out. This suggests that neither the Catholic nor the tribal school was able to provide Indian students who had low academic ability or family support with sufficient help to improve their school performance or to graduate.

Family, Community, and School Connections

Our research findings on factors that contribute to dropping out indicate the significance of the intersection of school contexts with students' family resources and networks, and community contexts. Coleman's (1988) research on family–school relations revealed two critical dimensions that

CHAPTER EIGHT

increase the effectiveness of the school: the existence of a functional community involving both schools and parents, and the availability of family support for schooling. Where families lack the kinds of relationships or resources to support schooling, a school in a functional community can make up the difference.

In our previous look at the adults in the households of students in our study, we established, first, that many Indian parents and guardians lacked educational credentials, experience, or the information needed to support school processes. Second, we established that other adults in family networks also varied in the cultural and social resources that they contributed to the support of school goals. However, adults (typically those with education) brought resources into action in relation to graduation rather than school performance. Thus, while some students who received this assistance graduated, large percentages of students without such family or community support dropped out. These findings indicate possible weaknesses within family networks that limited the mobilization of resources to support education. However, our data also suggested that the lack of conventional social and cultural capital within some Cheyenne families did not preclude the support of students' graduation; in some cases, traditional cultural resources and community relations played a key role in the support for schooling.

The schools also varied in the resources and orientations they offered to the communities they served. While Colstrip had the highest level of resources for instructional and social activities, it had the least commitment to Indian education. In contrast, St. Labre and Busby schools had high levels of commitment to Indian education, albeit for different reasons, and differing approaches and levels of resources to devote to serving Indian students' needs. Thus, the three schools varied in their contributions to a school community in which the Indian students and parents could freely participate.

The agreement on educational goals and values between schools and their constituencies also varied. For example, while the Catholic mission school and Catholic parents may have had certain religious values in common, school personnel and Indian families often differed in their views of the importance of schooling and how schooling should be done. Even though a social structure existed in the form of the Catholic Church in which all could participate, the "mission" of the church shaped contributions of Indian community members. In other words, Indian families had to conform to the church's requirements as it fulfilled its mission to educate and assimilate Indians and convert them to Catholicism. The cultural incongruity between the community and the Catholic Church, which the St. Labre Mission existed to address, created barriers to a truly functional community for the school. When St. Labre School and the parents found common ground for the education of Indian children, a functional community acted as a resource for students. However, our findings indicate that the variance between the community and the school orientations also created tensions that worked against forming a functional school community.

Negative views of the "White man's" school are indicated by reports that as recently as forty years ago, persons who left the reservation to attend college were considered by some tribal members to be lost to the tribe. While this attitude is no longer prevalent, remnants of suspicion remain in many quarters. Elders often quote the cultural hero of the Cheyenne, Sweet Medicine (Grinnell 1923), who said,

> At last those people will ask for your flesh . . . but you must say 'No.' They will try to teach you their way of living. If you give up to them your flesh [your children], those that they take away will never know anything. They will try to change you from your way of living to theirs, and they will keep at what they try to do. They will work with their hands. They will tear up the earth, and at last you will do it with them. When you do, you will become crazy, and will forget all that I am teaching you.

On the other hand, others quote the Cheyenne chief, Dull Knife, for whom the tribal college is named, who promoted education for the Cheyenne, saying, "We need a new way of life." Importantly, however, Cheyenne leaders who supported schooling also warned against loss of the Cheyenne language and culture (Risingsun 1988). Such differences in attitudes represent the variations in cultural views that are brought to the interactions with schools.

Thus, the Catholic school, like the tribal school, is faced with a dilemma: as reservation community members continue to experience obstacles to using school credentials to access economic opportunities, the meanings they give to schooling continue to diverge from those of the educational institutions serving the communities. The Indian schools have had the highest level of familiarity with and concern for Indian community members. And yet, they have lacked the political, ideological, and financial resources to improve the local opportunity structures that influence the links between schooling and the labor market. Nor do the schools effectively draw on local cultural resources to make schooling more relevant to community life.

Busby School has been especially vulnerable to the social, cultural, and political pressures of the reservation that often work against schooling. St. Labre has similarly faced cultural and social obstacles to achieving its schooling goals, despite its resources and longevity in the reservation community. Thus, these schools have been handicapped to some extent by the nature of their relationships to the community: Busby School as a tribal institution mandated to serve the tribal community's interests over its own school goals, and St. Labre as a religious institution mandated to compete with cultural values and practices of the tribal community.

These observations raise the question of why Colstrip Public School was somewhat more successful overall in retaining Indian students through graduation. Colstrip was different from the Indian schools in terms of its orientation toward Indian students. It was less concerned with Indian students in general, but it was also less constrained by the cultural orientation of the Lame Deer community it served. Again, it is useful to consider the nature of each community, in particular the social and cultural resources it contributed to the schooling process. Where Busby and St. Labre students were typically embedded in cultural groups and family networks that may have reduced the support for schooling unless education was a priority among some adults in the social network, Lame Deer students were relatively more isolated from these influences. That is, Lame Deer students may have been more independent of the cultural and social influences in this diverse community. In essence, while they may not have received the benefits that can come from such networks, some students were also able to stay removed from social pressures that detract from schooling. Thus, for these students the school context may have been the greatest source of support for schooling. While Colstrip did not have a strong commitment to Indian education, it did value quality education for its students. Moreover, it promoted educational achievement, rewarded students for participation and meeting high standards, and did not openly conflict with the basic values of most students' families. Thus, in the absence of a strong community orientation (in Lame Deer, where most of the Indian students lived) that clearly valued and supported education,

Colstrip provided an educational environment that some students from Lame Deer could embrace, and they could even overcome the negative social bias or other academic handicaps that Indian students faced.

We may conclude from our analyses that the public school had somewhat more of the characteristics associated with a supportive school context that Coleman and Hoffer (1987) identified in the private Catholic schools in their research. In contrast to their findings, an important finding of this study is that community–school links were tenuous, and Indian students at the public school still suffered disadvantages as minority students. They were more likely to perform at lower levels and drop out than White students, but their dropout rate was lower than for Indian students at the Catholic school.

Implications of the Findings for the Actions of Students

Our findings indicate that contextual elements are important to the explanation of the lower dropout rate of Indian students attending the public school compared to the Indian schools. Indian students are located in family networks and social groups that make up the communities served by the schools, and these family/community structures differ in the social and cultural resources they contribute to the schooling of children and to their relations with the different school contexts. Figure 8.1 provides a visual representation of the multiple layers of social contexts or nested structures (Powers et al. 2003)—household, family/social network, school, community, reservation—each including relationships that support or detract from educational performance and completion. It is important, at this point, to examine these findings about the social contexts associated with school outcomes from the point of view of students making decisions about schooling.

The first, reservation context, is particularly meaningful for Northern Cheyenne schooling patterns because it represents the continued cultural integrity of the tribe. The continued use of the Cheyenne language among a substantial proportion of the tribal members and the persistence of collective traditions provided students in this study with important sources of information about and experience with their cultural heritage. Champagne's discussion of Cheyenne institutions (1996) supports the importance of considering the congruence of tribal structures with dominant

CHAPTER EIGHT

American institutions. For example, the tribe's decision to severely limit coal development represents the values placed on sovereignty and natural resource preservation, which conflict with the interests of energy development corporations to meet the consumption needs of Americans.

While tribal agencies and local schools support these important values of the tribe, modern reality also makes difficult the realization of development goals to provide jobs and sustainable economic activities without exploitation of the tribe's coal and other natural resources. For students, the impact of limited development is felt through their awareness of the generally poor opportunity structure on the reservation. Students are aware that their ability to attain scarce jobs is affected by their family group's access to work opportunities as well as by their school credentials. Additionally, their experiences with prejudice and racism through interactions with non-Indian instructors and/or students at school and in encounters off the reservation often erode students' confidence and indicate the limitations of opportunities for Indians off the reservation as well. Thus, the reservation context has both positive and negative effects for students: while it promotes a positive cultural identity, it also negatively affects high school students' confidence and expectations that high GPAs and graduation will be rewarded in local labor markets.

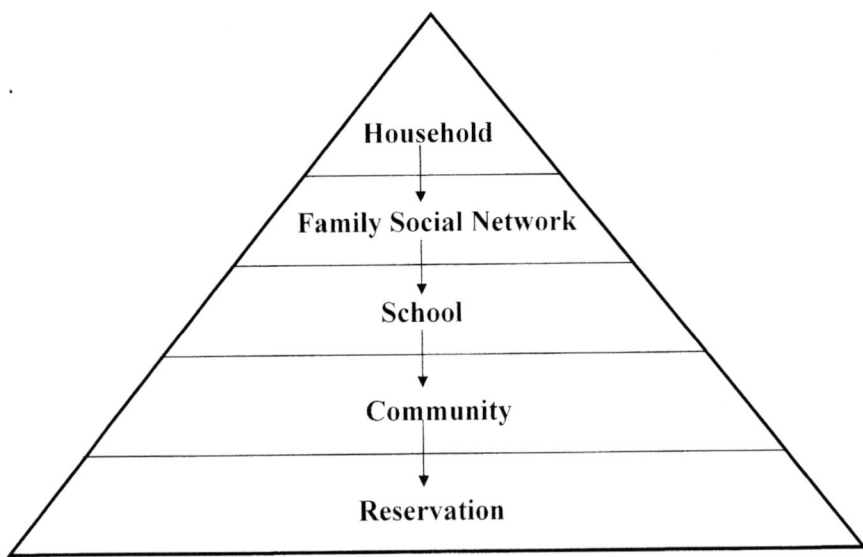

Figure 8.1. Social and Cultural Contexts in which Indian Students Are Located

CONCLUSION

The second layer of social context that affects Indian students is community. Community life is significant because it is within these local structures that students live their daily lives. This influence represents not only the cultural legacy of the Cheyenne bands that settled specific geographic areas that make up the official districts of the reservation today but also the effects of different local social environments. Each community has its own history, family groups, and social networks, as well as resources and organizations. These community environments include important social ties that may provide support to students in their schooling as well as activities that can distract students from school participation. In Busby, local community support appears to be particularly important, since Busby residence reduces the chances of dropping out. Additionally, Busby's history includes important tribal leaders (e.g., Chief Dull Knife) as well as the development and continued presence of the tribal school. Such cultural resources are a significant element of the community support for schooling that encourages students' school performance and results in their being more likely to graduate than students from other communities (Ward 1995). Living in Ashland—a border town that includes a significant Cheyenne population—modestly enhances the school performance of students attending the local Indian school, St Labre. Similarly, students residing in Lame Deer (who had no local Indian high school to attend in the late 1980s) also had modest benefits from attending St. Labre Catholic Indian School.

Since reservation communities differ from each other and are served by different schools, it is not surprising that these communities have different types of relations with the schools that serve them. For example, Busby community members have a closer relationship with the local tribal school than is typical of the relationship of Lame Deer residents to the schools their children attend outside of Lame Deer—Colstrip Public, Busby Tribal, and St. Labre Catholic schools. Similarly, Ashland residents have unique expectations of and experiences with St. Labre based on the long history and relationship of the Catholic Church missions to the Northern Cheyenne people. Ethnographic data show that the different relations between communities and schools result in different levels of support for schooling; for example, while Busby and Lame Deer parents generally showed low levels of support for schooling, Busby community effects were particularly positive for its students, and Lame Deer community residence indirectly enhanced graduation for its students attending Colstrip.

CHAPTER EIGHT

A third context that affects students is the school they choose to attend. In the reservation setting, the Indian schools acted as community schools in much the same way that public schools are community schools in most areas of the country. In other words, students generally attended the school that served the community in which they lived. In Ashland and Busby, although students were offered different kinds of opportunities by the local schools, the schools had similar approaches that may have lowered academic standards and expectations for the Indian students. Students in these two schools perceived similar levels of expectations of their academic performance, which affected not only their academic aspirations but also their occupational goals. Along with the perceptions of the poor opportunity structure for the Indian community overall, students also faced school environments in which high aspirations may well have been perceived as irrelevant or futile. Additionally, distractions from academic pursuits (such as drug use and other peer pressures) were a prevalent element of Indian community and school environments.

The schools responded to student involvement in drugs and alcohol abuse in different ways. While Busby School did not have the orientation or resources to adequately address students' problems with substance abuse, St. Labre provided assistance to students with drug or alcohol problems and enforced sanctions against substance abuse. Although such problems were not absent from the communities served by the other schools, St. Labre had the only long-term school program integrated into the curriculum designed to help secondary school students with drug and alcohol problems. Through its actions St. Labre indicated to students and parents alike that drug and alcohol use would not be tolerated. Similarly, students attending the Catholic school faced the potential requirement to leave school should they decide to become part of the drug and alcohol social groups. Such a requirement was not enforced at the other schools.

While Busby School had Indian administrators and staff (although few Indian teachers), most of St. Labre's administrative personnel and teachers were White. This created qualitatively different sets of relationships between students, teachers, and administrators. Students in Busby had the benefit of seeing a larger number of Indian role models within the school structure than St. Labre students. Additionally, the contributions of these personnel may have resulted in a somewhat higher degree of cultural sensitivity within the Busby School context than the Catholic school.

CONCLUSION

Finally, these two schools served community constituencies with interests that diverged from those of the school to some extent, either in terms of educational or cultural goals. Since these communities had the power to place demands on the school, the school environments included actors from the school and community who represented diverse perspectives on school problems and solutions. While the range of perspectives may have been somewhat narrower at St. Labre, neither this school nor Busby Tribal School could be characterized as a "functional" school community. Students, therefore, experienced schooling that was politicized on issues of school policies and practices.

Colstrip Public High School was, in some ways, more similar to a private school, or "value" community. It was located outside the communities where its Indian students resided and offered a wider range of programs and services and opportunities for participation. Importantly, the school did not face many conflicting pressures or demands from Indian parents, since it had not created the opportunity for significant influence by reservation residents. School personnel assumed a high level of agreement on school policy and practices on the part of parents. Reservation students were somewhat less tied to a cultural or social community that impeded their participation in schooling if they chose to take advantage of what Colstrip offered. Thus, the public school environment appears to have some of the same kinds of effects on improving Indian student performance and school completion expected from a private school.

From the perspective of students, these differences in the social environments of schools as well as their academic programs provided important influences on choices about schooling. While the public school context provided some elements of the type of school that could enhance performance and completion, it also provided for ethnic conflict, which had consequences for students' self-esteem. Ethnographic information indicates that Indian students who experienced prejudice typically were negatively affected, such that they had lower expectations of themselves and lower self-confidence. Many Indian students felt uncomfortable being with White students for this reason. This affected students' decisions about schooling: many opted to simply "get by" until they graduated; others were challenged to excel; and still others looked for options outside of school—dropping out to start a family, becoming involved with drugs or illegal activities, or taking part in cultural pursuits. Except for the drug use and illegal activities, these were acceptable courses of action within the diverse social atmosphere of the reservation.

The fourth context, the influences of family or social networks, generally affected the range of choices that students perceived as well as how they evaluated and acted on them. In particular, the implications of our research findings are that the more tightly students were integrated into households, family, and social networks (even those in homogeneous, traditional communities) that favored school completion, the more likely they were to graduate.

The new cultural variables added to the analysis indicated the importance of the family and household contexts. While previous research suggested the significance of adults' high school graduation and family structure for dropping out, this analysis showed the importance of family traditionality and parental support for schooling. Although the evidence showed negative direct effects of traditional cultural resources of parents, student fluency in Cheyenne reduced the chances of dropping out. Thus, the effects were complex and were mediated by parental education and family support for schooling. These findings support studies (e.g., Deyhle 1995) showing that traditional cultural resources do not necessarily conflict with schooling in Indian populations. For Cheyenne students, this statistical finding is consistent with ethnographic data (Ward 1996, 1998a) indicating that traditional families and social networks support the development of wisdom and knowledge, two respected traits in Cheyenne culture (Stands In Timber 1967; Rowland 1994). In the modern context, such support involves the efforts of immediate and extended family to emphasize that schooling can be an important way for students to pursue personal development goals. Additionally, this support reflects both family and community interest in students' contributing to the resources needed for survival and well-being. Some students were located in family groups and communities that had the means to help them realize rewards for their investment in schooling, while other students were more isolated from such opportunities and rewards. Thus, students' decisions about school completion reflected important differences among family and community cultural, social, and economic resources as well as their own perceptions of the relevance of schooling to their futures.

While this research did not collect attitude data for the individual-level analyses, ethnographic data obtained through interviews and participant observation raise some questions regarding the development of social psychological responses of students to these diverse school settings, and the links between students' evaluations of school and their decisions about school performance and graduation. In this line of inquiry, future research could benefit from work in the area of juvenile deviance. In particular, a study by Kaplan, Martin, and Johnson (1986) concerning "self-rejection and the explanation of deviance" offers some interesting possibilities. For example, self-rejection defined as global self-derogation, the lack of desirable attributes, and experiences of rejection and failure in family and school seem especially relevant given the prejudice and school failure experienced by many Indian students as well as the problems related to substance abuse and other family problems. In relation to the latter, research on family stress and its contributions to adolescent problem behaviors suggests a promising area for linking household dynamics to students' school outcomes (Barber 1992). Additionally, research that examines dimensions of community-level social disorganization suggests that social networks, social control of adolescents, and organizational participation are relevant for understanding varying levels of deviant behaviors across communities (Sampson and Groves 1989; Sampson 1998). This approach also supports the importance of identifying linkages between community social structures and individual behaviors.

Summary and Discussion

This research has used a holistic approach, advocated by Cleary and Peacock (1998), to identify characteristics associated with the three school contexts, the communities they serve, and the effects on dropping out described above. These are summarized in table 8.1, which brings together the results of the quantitative analyses of dropout behavior and the conditions suggested by the ethnographic data. For the three schools, the first panel shows characteristics of the school contexts, including relations between Indians and Whites (i.e., discrimination), the resources and opportunities of the school, the level of academic expectations, and the degree to which Indian parents are involved with the school. For example, minus signs in the areas of resources and expectations for Colstrip School indicate that they negatively affect dropping out within this school compared to the other two schools.

CHAPTER EIGHT

Table 8.1. Summary of Individual and Contextual Variable Effects on Dropping Out Using Quantitative and Qualitative Data

	Busby	St. Labre	Colstrip
School Contexts			
1. Discrimination	0	0	+
2. Resources	+	−	−
3. Expectations	+	+	−
4. Parent involvement	−	−	0
5. Lame Deer/Indian students[a]	+	−	+
Family/Background Characteristics			
Parents/Adults			
1. Education[a]	−	−	0
2. Employment[a]	0	+	0
3. Substance abuse	+	+	+
4. Cultural resources	−	−	0
Family/Community			
1. Nonintact family[a]	+	0	0
2. Family relations	−	−	0
3. Norms (education)	−	+	0
4. Information (education)	+	+	−
Student Variables			
1. Residence[a]	−	0	+
2. School involvement[a]	0	−	−
3. Performance[a]	−	−	−
4. Native language	−	−	0
Dropout Rate	54%	44%	42%

Key: 0 = no effect on dropping out
    + = increases probability of dropping out
    − = reduces probability of dropping out
[a] Effects based on quantitative analyses of dropping out.

Next, family background characteristics are displayed in two parts. The first part concerns attributes of parents or other adults in the household: the education and employment status variables analyzed in the models of school outcomes. Two other variables are shown that represent the effects of the cultural milieu in which parents and other adults in the community are located. These include the extensiveness of substance abuse and the cultural integration of adults. The second set of variables refers to family and community characteristics, since these are integral aspects of the local social structures. These include the effects of the family structure variable as well as additional variables based on ethnographic data. The latter refer to the presence and effects of extended family networks, the community's norms, and information related to education.

CONCLUSION

The intention of this table is to provide a visual representation that summarizes the array of information presented. These discussions have identified the influences of both structural and cultural variables on school outcomes. In particular, we have seen the importance of social and structural characteristics of households in which students reside. However, we have also found that cultural views of schooling based in family networks and communities mediate the responses of adults and students to the reservation opportunity structure and schooling. Given this information, we can ask the same question asked by Gambetta (1987) in his research on school completion of Italian students: "Were they pushed or did they jump?" Similar to his answer, this research suggests that social structural constraints are relevant to students' actions and personal preferences to leave school early, while social and cultural orientations can offer crucial support for Indian students' school performance and decisions to graduate.

The students of this case study are influenced by the adaptations of their families and communities to the poor economic opportunities of the reservation, which create a lack of meaning and connection between educational attainment and participation in the labor force overall. In particular, they are influenced to varying degrees by cultural views about social status within the community, such that the range of statuses is limited, and the acquisition of those statuses is determined by criteria that include family group membership as well as achievement-based criteria. Views of schooling, work, and ways of life among the members of their household, family network, social groups, and community shape their choices about schooling as well. Importantly, however, students are typically expected to navigate the journey through schooling with little direct assistance from Cheyenne adults, who, for a variety of reasons, are not likely to intervene.

While in a more homogeneous community views toward education may be either predominantly negative or positive, in a more heterogeneous community the changing attitudes and behaviors related to schooling, as well as the prevalence of alternatives to school, create a social environment in which individual students may form their own preferences, relatively free of social pressures. Thus, the influences of family and community structures on students may be placed along two continua, one related to the level of cultural homogeneity and the other representing the social and structural support for schooling. Push-pull influences, however, may change weight and direction within the social environment of each community.

CHAPTER EIGHT

These two dimensions are integral to the concept of native capital, which represents the potential for conflict between a community's cultural views and practices and the demands of the larger society and its institutions, including human capital development. Although social capital within Cheyenne families and communities supports human capital formation, the cultural environment also reinforces the rights of adolescents to make their own choices and to learn from those decisions, even when adults do not approve of the choices. Adults in this situation often provide guidance but not strict monitoring of children's human capital development.

The use of human capital occurs in a socioeconomic and cultural environment that does not value the accumulation of personal wealth or conspicuous consumption to the extent seen in many non-Indian communities. Local work may or may not provide opportunities for individuals to demonstrate valued skills or to enhance personal status and achievement; these are often realized in other family and community activities. But work does provide for the support of families, one of the highest priorities in the Cheyenne community. To use human capital in another way would mean rejection of important elements of Cheyenne culture and community life. Thus, acquisition of human capital represents for some assimilation to middle-class American society—essentially a choice between different cultural paths.

Within the changing sociocultural context of the reservation, students from a more homogeneous cultural community (e.g., Busby) that is generally supportive of education have a higher probability of school success due to the "pull" for school completion. In Busby, where native capital is high, local cultural and social resources are more likely to be used to adapt the educational process to the needs of students and parents. In other words, key actors make local concerns and interests into priorities over outside interests as they confront the demands made by institutions such as public schooling and the labor market. This may be seen as a form of resistance to cultural and social forces that subordinate the Cheyenne; however, a more diverse community, such as Ashland, lacks sufficient resources to adapt the schooling process to help students acquire skills that are locally meaningful and lead to success. Therefore, students in Ashland not only lack significant "pulls" for school completion but also may be encouraged—or pushed—to find alternatives to schooling. That is, their preferences for dropping out may be socially or culturally supported due to the prevalence

CONCLUSION

of substance abuse or the negative views of the "White man's" education. Finally, within a more heterogeneous community (Lame Deer), students may have less access to native capital in their families and community and, therefore, may be comparatively less affected by these resources. Thus, they may respond in a variety of ways to the demands and challenges of the school environment. In this situation, although a relatively larger proportion complete school, many students still choose to leave school, and they have little in their social environment that can prevent such actions.

Assuming the generally similar effects of the student performance variable in the three schools, the summary information shown in table 8.1 reveals that the primary differences in the school experiences of students rest with the nature and level of involvement of the students with the school, and the family/social network structure associated with their community of residence. Within this reservation context, approaches of the schools and the relations of parents and community members to the schooling of students become pivotal to the students' school outcomes. These relations are conditioned by the cultural orientations and resources that Indian families and school personnel bring to their interactions with Indian children and schooling. The types of social interactions that students are primarily engaged in, at school and in their homes and communities, have important effects on the choices they make about graduating or dropping out of high school. An important school factor is that Indian students cannot escape some form of negative social bias or racism within the school context, whether it takes the form of paternalism by school personnel or prejudice from other students. Such attitudes influence the way that opportunities for learning and participating in school are structured. Given the importance of the prevailing orientations to schooling found in families and communities served by the schools, the interaction of schooling opportunities with these attitudes and behaviors provides for important sets of social influences that affect students' decisions regarding school performance and completion. This case study indicates that the combined influences affecting many students are primarily negative for school outcomes, performance, and completion. Thus, this study indicates the utility of the various dimensions explored in this research effort to comprehend the school completion process. That is, we can now more fully understand the experiences and actions of the students as indicated by their location in households, family networks, and communities, as well as different school contexts.

In summary, the data presented for these dimensions suggest the importance of social structures and cultural orientations affecting schooling outcomes for Indian students as well as the form and content of social relations within specific school settings. For the Indian population of this study, the findings indicate that the high school attended is a crucial factor in students' academic success in school as well as their chances for completion versus dropping out. However, equally important for each high school setting are the family and community orientations that influence students' perceptions of the meaning of school, their range of choices, and the extent to which they experience social pressures to meet school-related goals. Additionally, the intersection of family and community orientations to schooling with those of the school context influences how schools respond to Indian students and, in turn, whether students are successful enough to graduate.

Policy Implications

Programmatic actions considered by the public school to improve school performance may address problems with school experiences of Indian students by increasing the extracurricular activity involvement of Indian students prone to absence or suspensions, or who do not participate. Such actions should be designed to improve the accessibility of social activities to Indian students as well as provide for academic opportunities. These efforts should help address the negative effects of being "outsiders" based on either cultural or social differences.

In addition to efforts to improve the school experiences and engagement of Indian students, special attention to the social relationships or climate within the school is important for improving school performance. Because each school has a different set of relationships within its unique context, different types of actions or activities may be appropriate. However, the point in each case would be to address differences that negatively affect school performance levels. Whether the distinction is between Indians and Whites at Colstrip, between students from different reservations at St. Labre, or between residents of different towns on the reservation at St. Labre and Busby, efforts to improve understanding, social relations, and academic opportunities for all these groups may well enhance school involvement and performance. New research on students' experience with prejudice and racism should contribute to school and community efforts to address these issues. Additionally, much greater efforts must be made by school personnel to understand and respond to the cultural orientations, social structures, and needs of the communities they serve. Improvement of relations between parents and all three schools may help to bring the orientations of the community and school personnel closer together.

The Cheyenne Nation and other reservation organizations offer unique resources to assist in the processes outlined above. Similar to the situations described in chapter 3 in which the Tribe took precedent-setting actions to protect its natural resources and to gain control over schooling in the 1960s and 1970s, this type of action may now be needed to improve the schooling of Northern Cheyenne students.

This study demonstrates both the important relationship between the local schools and reservation communities and the ways in which non-Indian institutions have shaped reservation organizations, including the tribal school. While the Tribe has shown that it can successfully influence American political structures to preserve its natural resources, it has been less successful in protecting the cultural resources and traditions of the Northern Cheyenne people. And yet, the Northern Cheyenne have been one of the more successful tribes in terms of opening opportunities for cultural preservation within school settings.

This suggests not only that tribal sovereignty is limited in its power and effectiveness but also that these limitations create potentially serious problems for communities on the Northern Cheyenne reservation. Without the appropriate support of the central tribal government structures, communities face many difficulties in creating solutions to their problems or meeting their needs. In schools, Cheyenne cultural orientations come into conflict with some of the goals and styles of the schools serving the reservation students. However, tribal-level solutions have not been successful in alleviating this problem (Ward 1998a). Communities in which the schools are located, families involved in the schools, and the schools themselves must be encouraged to find ways to address the communities' needs and interests. Different solutions may be required for different communities and the schools that serve them. Cheyenne communities must find new solutions either by initiating them or by negotiating with the institutions that serve the community, whether they are non-Indian (e.g.,

CHAPTER EIGHT

schools, law enforcement agencies, health care, etc.) or Northern Cheyenne institutions. One Cheyenne institution that can provide significant resources to schools and communities is Chief Dull Knife College, where language and cultural programs are currently helping to preserve Cheyenne identity and prevent Cheyenne language loss (Littlebear 2003). Faculty members are also developing new ways to draw on Cheyenne cultural practices to increase the involvement of students in learning and improve their school performance in meaningful ways. (See Cajete 1994 for more information on this approach.)

The implications of this study for Indian education nationally are that Indian students, their families, and communities continue to suffer from isolation that impedes access to opportunities for education and labor force participation. Additionally, they continue to experience social interaction in schools that includes prejudice and racism. When schools are structured to provide for the equal participation of Indian students in a schooling process that leads to economically, socially, and culturally rewarding roles, barriers to school success may be overcome and the "tragedy of Indian education" eliminated. As Indian communities continue to adapt to their changing social, economic, and political circumstances, it will be necessary for schools serving such communities not only to recognize the needs of Indian students as a group but also to relate to the intragroup differences of this population. While greater recognition of the cultural complexity of Indian communities may be only a start in making schooling more relevant, it is likely that such efforts will be rewarded with greater participation from both students and parents. However, such participation is likely to be forthcoming only if Indian students' and parents' investment in schooling is taken seriously by schools and is perceived as meaningful within the social environment of these students and their families.

REFERENCES

Akom, A. A.
    2003   "Reexamining Resistance as Oppositional Behavior: The Nation of Islam and the Creation of a Black Achievement Ideology." *Sociology of Education* 76 (October): 305–325.

Aldrich, J. H., and F. D. Nelson
    1984   *Linear Probability, Logit, and Probit Models*. Beverly Hills, CA: Sage.

Alexander, K. L., and B. K. Eckland
    1975   "The Wisconsin Model of Socioeconomic Achievement: A Replication." *American Journal of Sociology* 81:324–342.

Alwin, D. F., and A. Thornton
    1984   "Family Origins and the Schooling Process: Early versus Late Influence of Parental Characteristics." *American Sociological Review* 49:784–802.

Antell, W.
    1979   *Source Book of Equal Educational Opportunity*. Chicago: Marquis Academic Media.

Apple, M. W., and L. Weis
    1986   "Seeing Education Relationally: The Stratification of Culture and People in the Sociology of School Knowledge." *Journal of Education* 168 (1).

Ashabranner, Brent
    1982   *Morning Star, Black Sun: The Northern Cheyenne Indians and America's Energy Crisis*. New York: Dodd, Mead.

Astone, N., and S. McLanahan
    1991   "Family Structure, Parental Practices and High School Completion." *American Sociological Review* 56:309–320.

REFERENCES

Backes, John S.
    1993   "The American Indian High School Dropout Rate: A Matter of Style?" *Journal of American Indian Education* 32 (3): 16–29.

Bailey, Robert. (Busby School superintendent.)
    1988   Interview by author. Busby, MT. March.

Baird-Olson, Karren, and Carol Ward
    2000   "Recovery and Resistance: The Renewal of Traditional Spirituality among Native American Women." *American Indian Culture and Research Journal* 24 (4): 1–35.

Barber, B. K.
    1992   "Family, Personality, and Adolescent Problem Behaviors." *Journal of Marriage and the Family* 54:69–79.

Beaulieu, L. J., and G. D. Israel
    1996   "Strengthening Social Capital: The Challenge for Rural Community Sustainability." In *Rural Sustainable Development in America*, ed. Ivonne Audirac. New York: John Wiley.

Beaulieu, L. J., and D. Mulkey
    1995   *Investing in People: The Human Capital Needs of Rural America*. Boulder, CO: Westview.

Beauvais, F., E. L. Chavez, E. R. Oetting, J. L. Deffenbacher, and G. R. Cornell
    1996   "Drug Use, Violence, and Victimization among White American, Mexican-American, and American Indian Dropouts, Students with Academic Problems, and Students in Good Standing." *Journal of Counseling Psychology* 43 (3): 292–299.

Benson, P. L.
    1996   *Developmental Assets among Minneapolis Youth*. Minneapolis: Search Institute.

Bidwell, C. E., and N. Friedkin
    1988   "Sociology of Education." In *Handbook of Sociology*, ed. Neil Smelser. Beverly Hills, CA: Sage.

Bielby, W. T.
    1981   "Models of Status Attainment." *Research in Social Stratification and Mobility* 1:3–26.

Bixby, Norma. (Chairwoman, Indian Parent Advisory Committee, Colstrip Public Schools, and chairwoman, Northern Cheyenne Education Commission.)
    1990   Interview by author. Lame Deer, MT. May.

Blalock, Hubert M.
    1989   "Comparing Individual and Structural Levels of Analysis." *Research in Sociology of Education and Socialization* 8:57–86.

REFERENCES

Blauner, R.
    1972   *Racial Oppression in America*. New York: Harper & Row.

Bonvillain, N.
    1988   "Gender Relations in Native America." *American Indian Culture and Research Journal* 13 (2): 1–28.

Bourdieu, P.
    1979   *La Distinction. Critique Social du Jugement*. Paris: Minuit. Published in English as *Distinction: A Social Critique of the Judgement of Taste*, trans. Richard Nice (Cambridge, MA: Harvard University Press, 1984).
    1986   "Forms of Capital." In *Handbook of Theory and Research for the Sociology of Education*, ed. John Richards. New York: Greenwood.
    1993   *Sociology in Question*. London: Sage.

Bourdieu, P., and J. Passeron
    1977   *Reproduction in Education, Society and Culture*. London: Sage.

Bowker, A.
    1992   "The American Indian Female Dropout." *Journal of American Indian Education* 31 (3): 3–20.
    1993   *Sisters in the Blood: The Education of Women in Native America*. Newton, MA: WEEA Publishing Center.

Bowles, S., and H. Gintis
    1976   *Schooling in Capitalist America: Educational Reform and the Contradictions of Economic Life*. New York: Basic Books.
    2002   "Schooling in Capitalist America Revisited." *Sociology of Education* 75 (January): 1–18.

Braddock, J. H., R. L. Crain, and J. M. McPartland
    1984   "A Long-Term View of School Desegregation: Some Recent Studies of Graduates as Adults." *Phi Delta Kappan* 66:259–264.

Brandt, E. A.
    1992   "The Navajo Area Student Dropout Study: Findings and Implications." *Journal of American Indian Education* 31 (3): 3–20.

Brint, Stephen
    1998   *Schools and Societies*. Thousand Oaks, CA: Pine Forge.

Brinton, Mary
    1988   "The Social-Institutional Bases of Gender Stratification: Japan as an Illustrative Case." *American Journal of Sociology* 94 (September): 300–334.
    1993   *Women and the Economic Miracle*. Berkeley: University of California Press.

Brown, E. F.
    1973   "A Comparative Study of Alaskan Native Adolescent and Young Adult Secondary School Dropouts." In *A Perspective of the Alaskan Native School*

REFERENCES

Dropout, ed. B. E. Oviatt. Salt Lake City: Social Service Resource Center of Utah.

Brown, Eddie F., Leslie Whitaker, Melinda Springwater, Stephen Cornell, Mirian Jorgensen, Michelle Hale, and Ami Nagle
    2001   "Welfare, Work, and American Indians: The Impact of Welfare Reform." A Report to the National Congress of American Indians. St. Louis, MO: Kathryn M. Buder Center for American Indian Studies, George Warren Brown School of Social Work, Washington University; and Native Nations Institute for Leadership, Management and Policy, Udall Center for Studies in Public Policy, University of Arizona.

Bryan, W. L., and W. P. Yellowtail
    1985   "Future High School Education Options for the Northern Cheyenne Tribe: An Education Planning and Strategy Study." Report prepared for the Northern Cheyenne Tribe. Bozeman, MT: Bureau of Indian Affairs, Office of Indian Education Programs, U.S. Department of the Interior. 1988. *Report on BIA Education: Excellence in Indian Education through the Effective School Process*. Washington, DC. (ERIC Document Reproduction Service no. ED 297 899.)

Bureau of Land Management
    1989   *Economic, Social and Cultural Supplement: Powder River I Regional EIS*. U.S. Department of the Interior, Miles City District Office.

Cajete, Gregory
    1994   *Look to the Mountain: An Ecology of Indigenous Education*. Skyland, NC: Kivaki.

Carrier, J. G.
    1986   "Sociology and Special Education: Differentiation and Allocation in Mass Education." *American Journal of Education* 32:281–327.

Champagne, Duane
    1996   "Sociological Responses to Coal Development: A Comparison of the Crow and Northern Cheyenne." In *American Indian Economic Development*, ed. Carol Ward and Matthew Snipp, 131–146. Greenwich, CT: JAI.

Cheng, Simon, and Brian Starks
    2002   "Racial Differences in the Effects of Significant Others on Students' Educational Expectations." *Sociology of Education* 75 (October): 306–327.

Chestnut, Steve
    1979   "Coal Development on the Northern Cheyenne Reservation." In *Energy Resource Development*, U.S. Commission on Civil Rights, 159–183. A selection of papers presented at a consultation sponsored by the Colorado, Montana, North Dakota, South Dakota, Utah and Wyoming Advisory Committee.

REFERENCES

Cicourel, A. V., and H. Mehan
    1985 "Universal Development, Stratifying Practices, and Status Attainment." In *Research in Social Stratification and Mobility*, ed. R. Rubinson. Greenwich, CT: JAI.

Cleary, Linda Miller, and Thomas Peacock
    1998 *Collected Wisdom: American Indian Education*. Needham Heights, MA: Allyn and Bacon.

Coggins, Kip, Edith Williams, and Norma Radin
    1997 "The Traditional Tribal Values of Ojibwa Parents and the School Performance of Their Children: An Exploratory Study." *Journal of American Indian Education* 36 (3): 1–15.

Coladarci, T.
    1983 "High School Dropouts among Native Americans." *Journal of American Indian Education* 23 (1): 15–22.

Coleman, James S.
    1961 *The Adolescent Society*. New York: Free Press of Glencoe.
    1988 "Social Capital in the Creation of Human Capital." Supplement, *American Journal of Sociology* 94:S95–S120.

Coleman, J. S., and T. Hoffer
    1987 *Public and Private Schools: The Impact of Communities*. New York: Basic Books.

Collins, R.
    1977 "Functional and Conflict Theories of Educational Stratification." In *Power and Ideology in Education*, ed. J. Karabel and A. H. Halsey. New York: Oxford University Press.

Cornell, S.
    1984 "Transformations in American Indian Ethnicities." Paper presented at Conference on Ethnicity, University of Chicago.
    1988 *The Return of the Native: American Indian Political Resurgence*. New York: Oxford University Press.

Cornell, S., and J. P. Kalt
    1990 "Pathways from Poverty: Economic Development and Institution-Building on American Indian Reservations." *American Indian Culture and Research Journal* 14:89–125.

Crawford, J.
    1987 "The Special Case of Bilingual Education for Indian Students." *Education Week* 6 (16).

Crosnoe, Robert
    2001 "Academic Orientation and Parental Involvement in Education during High School." *Sociology of Education* 74 (July): 210–230.

REFERENCES

Crosnoe, Robert, Shannon Cavanagh, and Glen H. Elder Jr.
  2003 "Adolescent Friendships as Academic Resources: The Intersection of Friendship, Race, and School Disadvantage." *Sociological Perspectives* 46 (3): 331–352.

Davids, D. W.
  1963 "An Analysis of the State Department of Public Instruction Reports to the Federal Government Relative to Milwaukee, Wisconsin." ERIC Document Service, no. ED 070537.

Davis, John, Kirk Anderson, and Samina Jamal
  2001 "Culture and Community in Canada's Isolated Schools." Paper presented at the annual meeting of the Canadian Association for the Study of Educational Administration, Quebec, QC, Canada, May 25.

Day, Jennifer C., and Eric C. Newburger
  2002 *The Big Payoff: Educational Attainment and Synthetic Estimates of Work-Life Earnings.* Special Studies. Current Population Reports. Washington, DC: Bureau of the Census, Economic and Statistics Administration, U.S. Department of Commerce.

Deloria, Vine, Jr., and Daniel R. Wildcat
  2001 *Power and Place: Indian Education in America.* Golden, CO: Fulcrum Resources.

deMarrais, Kathleen B., and Margaret D. LeCompte
  1995 *The Way Schools Work: A Sociological Analysis of Education*, 2nd ed. New York: Longman.

Development Associates
  1983 *Final Report of the Evaluation of the Impact of the Part A Entitlement Program, Title IV of the Indian Education Act.* Arlington, VA: Development Associates.

Deyhle, Donna
  1986 "Break Dancing and Breaking Out: Anglos, Utes and Navajos in a Border Reservation High School." *Anthropology and Education Quarterly* 17:111–127.
  1989 "Pushouts and Pullouts: Navajo and Ute School Leavers." *Journal of Navajo Education* 6 (2): 36–51.
  1991 "Empowerment and Cultural Conflict: Navajo Parents and the Schooling of Their Children." *Qualitative Studies in Education* 4 (4): 277–297.
  1992 "Constructing Failure and Maintaining Cultural Identity: Navajo and Ute School Leavers." *Journal of American Indian Education* 31: 24–47.
  1995 "Navajo Youth and Anglo Racism: Cultural Integrity and Resistance." *Harvard Educational Review* 65 (3): 403–444.

Deyhle, Donna, and Karen Swisher
  1997 "Research in American Indian and Alaska Native Education: From Assimilation to Self-Determination." In *Review of Research in Education*, vol. 22, ed.

REFERENCES

Michael W. Apple, 113–194. Washington, DC: American Educational Research Association.

DeYoung, Alan J.
  1987 "The Status of American Rural Education Research: An Integrated Review and Commentary." *Review of Educational Research* 57:123–148.

Dodd, John M., Mike Hermanson, J. Ron Nelson, and Jerome Fischer
  1990 "Tribal College Faculty Willingness to Provide Accommodations to Students with Learning Disabilities." *Journal of American Indian Education* 30 (1): 8–16.

Dodd, John M., and J. R. Nelson
  1989 "Learning Disabled Adults: Implications for Tribal Colleges." *Journal of American Indian Education* 10:31–39.

Dornbusch, S. M., P. L. Ritter, H. Leiderman, D. F. Roberts, and M. J. Leiderman
  1987 "The Relation of Parenting Style to Adolescent School Performance." *Child Development* 58:1244–1257.

Dornbusch, S. M., P. L. Ritter, and L. Steinberg
  1991 "Community Influences on the Relation of Family Statuses to Adolescent School Performance: Difference between African-Americans and Non-Hispanic Whites." *American Journal of Education* 99:543–67.

Dumais, Susan A.
  2002 "Cultural Capital, Gender, and School Success: The Role of Habitus." *Sociology of Education* 75 (January): 44–68.

Dunaway, Wilma
  1996 "Incorporation as an Interactive Process: Cherokee Resistance to Expansion of the Capitalist World System." *Sociological Inquiry* 66 (4): 445–470.

Eberhard, D. R.
  1989 "American Indian Education: A Study of Dropouts, 1980–1987." *Journal of American Indian Education* 11:32–40.

Ekstrom, R. B., M. E. Goertz, J. M. Pollack, and D. A. Rock
  1986 "Who Drops Out of High School and Why? Findings from a National Study." *Teachers College Record* 87:356–373.

Elliott, R., and A. C. Strenta
  1988 "Effects of Improving the Reliability of the GPA on Prediction Generally and Comparative Predictions for Gender and Race Particularly." *Journal of Education Measurement* 25 (4): 333–37.

Elliott, D.S., W. J. Wilson, D. Huizinga, A. Elliott, and B. Rankin
  1996 "The Effects of Neighborhood Disadvantage on Adolescent Development." *Journal of Research in Crime and Delinquency* 33:389–426.

REFERENCES

Epstein, J. L.
   1990   "School and Family Connections: Theory, Research, and Implications for Integrating Sociologies of Education and Family." *Marriage and Family Review* 15:99–126.

Erickson, Bonnie
   1996   "Culture, Class and Connections." *American Journal of Sociology* 102:217–51.

Erickson, F.
   1987   "Transformation and School Success: The Politics and Culture of Educational Achievement." *Anthropology and Education Quarterly* 18:335–357.

Farkas, G.
   1996   *Human Capital or Cultural Capital?* New York: Aldine De Gruyter.

Feeney, M., C. Kroll, E. Quigley, and C. Villalva
   1986   *Social and Economic Effects of Coal Development on the Northern Cheyenne Tribe.* Report by Mara Feeney and Associates for the U.S. Bureau of Land Management, Billings, MT.

Fernandez-Kelly, M. P., and R. Schauffler
   1996   "Divided Fates: Immigrant Children and the New Assimilation." In *The New Second Generation*, ed. Alejandro Portes. New York: Russell Sage Foundation.

Fine, Michelle
   1991   *Framing Dropouts: Notes on the Politics of Urban Public High School.* Albany: State University of New York Press.

Foley, D.
   1991   "Reconsidering Anthropological Explanations of Ethnic School Failure." *Anthropology and Education Quarterly* 22:60–94.

Fordham, Signithia
   1996   *Blacked Out: Dilemmas of Race, Identity and Success at Capital High.* Chicago: University of Chicago Press.

Frase, M.
   1989   *Dropout Rates in the United States: 1988.* (NCES 89-609.) National Center for Education Statistics, U.S. Department of Education, Office of Educational Research and Improvement. Washington, DC: U.S. Government Printing Office.

Fuchs, E., and R. J. Havighurst
   1972   *To Live on This Earth: American Indian Education.* New York: Doubleday.

Furstenberg, F. F., and M. E. Hughes
   1995   "Social Capital and Successful Development Among At-Risk Youth." *Journal of Marriage and the Family* 57:580–592.

REFERENCES

Gambetta, D.
  1987 *Were They Pushed or Did They Jump? Individual Decision Mechanisms in Education*. New York: Cambridge University Press.

Gamoran, A., and R. D. Mare
  1989 "Secondary School Tracking and Educational Inequality: Compensation, Reinforcement, or Neutrality?" *American Journal of Sociology* 94:1146–1183.

General Accounting Office
  2000 "BIA and DOD Schools: School Achievement and Other Characteristics Often Differ from Public Schools." Report to Congress (GAO-01-934). Washington, DC: GAO.

Giddens, Anthony
  1979 *Central Problems in Social Theory: Action, Structure and Contradiction in Social Analysis*. Berkeley: University of California Press.

Giroux, Sharon S.
  1997 "The Experiences That Contributed to the Attrition Decisions of Lac du Flambeau High School Students." Ph.D. dissertation, University of Minnesota.

Gloria, Alberta M., and Sharon E. Robinson Kurpius
  2001 "Influences of Self-Beliefs, Social Support, and Comfort in the University Environment on the Academic Nonpersistence Decisions of American Indian Undergraduates." *Cultural Diversity and Ethnic Minority Psychology* 7 (1): 88–102.

Goodluck, Alda. (Talent Search coordinator, Crow Tribe.)
  1988 Interview by author. Crow Agency, MT.

Granovetter, M.
  1985 "Economic Action and Social Structure: The Problem of Embeddedness." *American Journal of Sociology* 91 (3): 481–510.

Greenbaum, S. D.
  1985 "Nonverbal Differences in Communication Style between American Indian and Anglo Elementary Classrooms." *American Educational Research Journal* 22:101–115.

Gregory, Robert, Annie C. Abello, and Jamie Johnson
  1996 "The Individual Economic Well-Being of Native American Men and Women during the 1980s: A Decade of Moving Backwards." In *Changing Numbers, Changing Needs: American Indian Demography and Public Health*, ed. Gary D. Sandefur, Ronald R. Rindfuss, and Barney Cohen. Washington, DC: National Academy Press.

Grinnell, George Bird
  1923 *The Cheyenne Indians: Their History and Ways of Life*. 2 vols. New Haven: Yale University Press.

REFERENCES

Guest, Andrew, and Barbara Schneider
2003 "Adolescents' Extracurricular Participation in Context: The Mediating Effects of Schools, Communities, and Identity." *Sociology of Education* 76 (April): 89–109.

Hale, Lorraine
2002 *Native American Education: A Reference Handbook*. Santa Barbara, CA: ABC-CLIO.

Hall, John R.
1992 *The Capital(s) of Cultures: A Nonholistic Approach to Status Situations, Class, Gender, and Ethnicity*. Chicago: University of Chicago Press.

Hall, Thomas D.
1986 "Incorporation in the World-System: Toward a Critique." *American Sociological Review* 51:390–402.
1988 "Patterns of Native American Incorporation into State Societies." In *Public Policy Impacts on American Indian Economic Development*, ed. C. Matthew Snipp. Development Series 4. Albuquerque, NM: Native American Studies.

Hanushek, E., and J. Jackson
1977 *Statistical Methods for Social Scientists*. New York: Academic Press.

Hauser, R. M., S. Tsai, and W. J. Sewell
1983 "A Model of Stratification with Response Error in Social and Psychological Variables." *Sociology of Education* 56:20–46.

Hirshman, C., and M. Wong
1981 "Trends in Socioeconomic Achievement among Immigrant and Native-Born Asian-Americans, 1960–1976." In *Majority and Minority: The Dynamics of Race and Ethnicity in American Life*, 4th ed., ed. Norman Yetman. Boston: Allyn and Bacon.

Hobbs, D.
1995 "Capacity Building: Reexamining the Role of the Rural School." In *Investing in People: The Human Capital Needs of Rural America*, ed. L. J. Beaulieu and D. Mulkey. Boulder, CO: Westview.

Hoffmann, John P.
2004 *Generalized Linear Models: An Applied Approach*. Boston: Pearson Education/Allyn and Bacon.

Horvat, Erin McNamara, and Kristine S. Lewis
2003 "Reassessing the 'Burden of "Acting White"': The Importance of Peer Groups in Managing Academic Success." *Sociology of Education* 76 (October): 265–280.

Huff, D. J.
1997 *To Live Heroically: Institutional Racism and American Indian Education*. Albany: State University of New York Press.

REFERENCES

Huffman, Terry
    2001   "Resistance Theory and the Transculturation Hypothesis as Explanations of College Attrition and Persistence among Culturally Traditional American Indian Students." *Journal of American Indian Education* 40 (3): 1–23.

Huffman, T.E., M. L. Sill, and M. Brokenleg
    1986   "College Achievement among Sioux and White South Dakota Students." *Journal of American Indian Education* 25:32–38.

Hurn, C. J.
    1993   *The Limits and Possibilities of Schooling: An Introduction to the Sociology of Education*. 3rd ed. Boston: Allyn and Bacon.

James, K., E. Chavez, F. Beauvais, R. Edwards, and G. Oetting
    1995   "School Achievement and Dropout among Anglo and Indian Females and Males: A Comparative Examination." *American Indian Culture and Research Journal* 19 (3): 181–206.

Jencks, C., J. Crouse, and P. Mueser
    1983   "The Wisconsin Model of Status Attainment: A National Replication with Improved Measures of Ability and Aspirations." *Sociology of Education* 56:3–19.

Jensen, L., and M. Tienda
    1989   "Nonmetropolitian Minority Families in the United States: Trends in Racial and Ethnic Economic Stratification, 1959–1986." *Rural Sociology* 54:509–532.

Johnson, Monica Kirkpatrick, Robert Crosnoe, and Glen H. Elder Jr.
    2001   "Students' Attachment and Academic Engagement: The Role of Race and Ethnicity." *Sociology of Education* 74 (October): 318–340.

Jones, W. M.
    1977   "The Impact on Society of Youths Who Drop Out or Who Are Underedu-cated." *Educational Leadership* 34:411–416.

Jordan, K. Forbis, and Teresa S. Lyons
    1992   "Financing Public Education in an Era of Change." Research Report. Bloomington, IN: Phi Delta Kappa Education Foundation.

Jordan, W. J., J. Lara, and J. M. McPartland
    1996   "Exploring the Causes of Early Dropout Among Race-Ethnic and Gender Groups." *Youth and Society* 28 (1): 62–94.

Jorgensen, Joseph G.
    1978   "A Century of Political Economic Effects on American Indian Society, 1880–1980." *Journal of Ethnic Studies* 6:1–82.

Kaplan, H., S. Martin, and R. Johnson
    1986   "Self-Rejection and the Explanation of Deviance: Specification of the Structure among Latent Constructs." *American Journal of Sociology* 92:384–411.

REFERENCES

Kerckhoff, A. C.
   1986 "Family Position, Peer Influences, and Schooling." In *Handbook of Theory and Research for the Sociology of Education*, ed. John Richards. New York: Greenwood.

Kim, Kwang Chung
   1981 "Job Information Deprivation in the U.S.: A Case Study of Korean Immigrants." *Ethnicity* 9:219–232.

Kingston, Paul W., Ryan Hubbard, Brent Lapp, Paul Schroeder, and Julia Wilson
   2003 "Why Education Matters." *Sociology of Education* 76 (January): 53–70.

Kitchen, Richard S., Diane Torres Velásquez, and John Myers
   2000 "Dropouts in New Mexico: Native American and Hispanic Students Speak Out." Paper presented at the annual meeting of the American Educational Research Association, New Orleans, April.

Kleinfeld, J.
   1973 *A Long Way from Home: Effects of Public High Schools on Village Children Away from Home*. Fairbanks, AK: Institute of Social, Economic, and Government Research.

Kleinfeld, J., G. W. McDiarmid, and D. Hagstrom
   1989 "Small Local High Schools Decrease Alaska Native Drop-out Rates." *Journal of American Indian Education* 28:24–30.

Kohn, Melvin L., and Carmi Schooler
   1969 "Class Occupation and Orientation." *American Sociological Review* 34 (October): 659–78.

Kroskrity, P.
   1986 "Ethnolinguistics and American Indian Education." In *American Indian Policy and Cultural Values: Conflict and Accommodation*, ed. Jennie R. Joe. Contemporary American Indian Issues Series 6. Los Angeles: American Indian Studies Center, University of California, Los Angeles.

Kunisawa, B.
   1988 "A Nation in Crisis: The Dropout Dilemma." *National Education Association* 6:61–65.

LaFromboise, T. O., A. M. Heyle, and E. J. Ozer
   1990 "Changing and Diverse Roles of Women in American Indian Cultures." *Sex Roles* 22 (7/8): 455–476.

LaFromboise, T. O., and D. N. Rudes
   1981 "American Indian Perception and Trustworthiness in a Counseling Interview." *Journal of Counseling Psychology* 28:135–139.

Lamont, M., and A. Lareau
   1988 "Cultural Capital: Illusions, Gaps and Glissandos in Recent Theoretical Developments." *Sociological Theory* 6 (2): 153–168.

REFERENCES

Lareau, A.
    1989   *Home Advantage: Social Class and Parental Intervention in Elementary Education.* London: Falmer.

Ledlow, S.
    1992   "Is Cultural Discontinuity an Adequate Explanation for Dropping Out?" *Journal of American Indian Education* 31 (3): 21–36.

Lee, V. E., and A. Bryk
    1988   "Curriculum Tracking as Mediating the Social Distribution of High School Achievement." *Sociology of Education* 61:78–94.

Levin, H.
    1972   *The Costs to the Nation of Inadequate Education.* Report to the Select Committee on Equal Educational Opportunity, U.S. Senate. Washington, DC: U.S. Government Printing Office.

Lichter, D. T., G. T. Cornwell, and D. J. Eggebeen
    1993   "Harvesting Human Capital: Family Structure and Education among Rural Youth." *Rural Sociology* 58 (1): 53–75.

Littlebear, Richard E.
    2003   "Chief Dull Knife Community Is Strengthening the Northern Cheyenne Language and Culture." *Journal of American Indian Education* 42 (1): 75–84.

Looker, D. E., and P. C. Pineo
    1983   "Social Psychological Variables and Their Relevance to the Status Attainment of Teenagers." *American Journal of Sociology* 88:1195–1219.

Lopach, J. J., M. H. Brown, and R. L. Clow
    1990   *Tribal Government Today: Politics on Montana Indian Reservations.* Boulder: Westview.

Mare, Robert
    1979   "Social Background Composition and Educational Growth." *Demography* 16:55–71.
    1981   "Change and Stability in Educational Stratification." *American Sociological Review* 46:72–87.

Marsh, H. W.
    1987   "The Big Fish-Little Pond Effect on Academic Self-Concept." *Journal of Educational Psychology* 79 (3): 280–295.

May, Phillip A.
    1996   "Overview of Alcohol Abuse Epidemiology for American Indian Populations." In *Changing Numbers, Changing Needs: American Indian Demography and Public Health,* ed. Gary D. Sandefur, Ronald R. Rindfuss, and Barney Cohen. Washington, DC: National Academy Press.

REFERENCES

McDill, E. L., G. Natriello, and A. M. Pallas
    1986   "A Population at Risk: Potential Consequences of Tougher School Standards for Student Dropouts." *American Journal of Education* 94:135–181.

McDill, E. L., L. Rigsby, and E. D. Meyers Jr.
    1969   "Educational Climates of High Schools: Their Effects and Sources." *American Journal of Sociology* 74:567–568.

McDonald, A.
    1978   "Why Do Indian Students Drop Out of College?" In *The Schooling of Native America*, ed. Thomas Thompson. Washington, DC: American Association of Colleges for Teacher Education.

McInerney, Dennis M., and Karen Gayton Swisher
    1995   "Exploring Navajo Motivation in School Settings." *Journal of American Indian Education* 34 (3): 28–51.

McLaughlin, Daniel
    1994   "Critical Literacy for Navajo and Other American Indian Learners." *Journal of American Indian Education* 33 (3): 47–59.

Mensch, B. S., and D. B. Kandel
    1988   "Dropping Out of High School and Drug Involvement." *Sociology of Education* 61:95–113.

Mickelson, R. A.
    1990   "The Attitude-Achievement Paradox among Black Adolescents." *Sociology of Education* 63:44–61.

Mingione, Enzo
    1991   *Fragmented Societies: A Sociology of Economic Life beyond the Market Paradigm.* Oxford: Basil Blackwell.
    1994   "Life Strategies and Social Economies in the Postfordist Age." *International Journal of Urban and Regional Research*, March, 24–45.

Montana
    1985   *1980 Profile of the Montana Native American.* Helena, MT: State Department of Statistics.
    1994   *1990 Profile of the Montana Native American.* Helena, MT: Office of Indian Affairs.
    2003   Montana Code Annotated 2003. Available at data.opi.state.mt.us/bills/mca/85/20/85-20-301.htm.

Montana Public Hearings on Northern Cheyenne Petition for Public High School.
    1991   February and March. Forsyth and Hardin, MT.

Moore, John H.
    1987   *The Cheyenne Nation.* Lincoln: University of Nebraska Press.

REFERENCES

Münch, Richard
    1994 *Sociological Theory: Development since the 1960s.* Chicago: Nelson-Hall.

Nabokov, Peter
    1978 *Native American Testimony.* New York: Harper & Row.

Nagel, J.
    1996 *American Indian Ethnic Renewal: Red Power and the Resurgence of Identity and Culture.* New York: Oxford University Press.

Nagel, J., and C. M. Snipp
    1993 "Ethnic Reorganization: American Indian Social, Economic, Political and Cultural Strategies for Survival." *Ethnic and Racial Studies* 16:203–235.

National Assessment of Educational Progress
    1985 Report. Science and Engineering Indicators-1985 (N.S.B. 85-1). Washington, DC: U.S. Government Printing Office.

National Center for Education Statistics
    1994 *The Condition of Education 1994.* Washington, DC: U.S. Department of Education.

National Institute on Drug Abuse
    1987 "Drug Use Among Indian Students on the Northern Cheyenne Reservation." Western Behavioral Studies, Colorado State University. Fort Collins, CO.

Ness, Jean E.
    2002 "Crossing the Finish Line: American Indian Completers and Non-completers in a Tribal College." *Tribal College Journal* 13 (4): 36–40.

Nordstrom, Jean
    1977 "The Northern Cheyenne Tribe and Energy Development in Southeastern Montana. Volume I: Social, Cultural, and Economic Investigations." Research Report. Crow Impact Study Office, MT.

Northern Cheyenne Education Commission
    1990 Report of Education Survey Findings. Lame Deer, MT.

Northern Cheyenne Follow Through
    1980 Program Proposal to the U.S. Department of Education to Fund Northern Cheyenne Follow Through Program. Lame Deer, MT.

Northern Cheyenne Tribal Action Plan
    1994 Plan Prepared for the Northern Cheyenne Tribe. Lame Deer, MT.

Northern Cheyenne Tribal Committee on 638 Funding
    1988 Minutes. Lame Deer, MT.

REFERENCES

O'Brien, Eileen
    1990   "Demise of Native American Education." *Black Issues in Higher Education*, March 15, 19–36.

O'Connell, Joanne C., ed.
    1987   *A Study of the Special Problems and Needs of American Indians with Handicaps Both on and off the Reservation*. Vol. 2. Flagstaff and Tucson: Northern Arizona University Native American Research and Training Center and University of Arizona Native American Research and Training Center.

Ogbu, John U.
    1978   *Minority Education and Caste: The American System in Cross-Cultural Perspective*. New York: Academic Press.
    1988   "Class Stratification, Racial Stratification, and Schooling." In *Class, Race, and Gender in American Education*, ed. Lois Weis, 163–182. Albany: State University of New York Press.
    1989   "The Individual in Collective Adaptation: A Framework for Focusing on Academic Underperformance and Dropping Out among Involuntary Minorities." In *Dropouts from School: Issues, Dilemmas, Solutions*, ed. Lois Weis, E. Farrar, and H. G. Petrie. Albany: State University of New York Press.

Parcel, Toby L., and Mikaela J. Dufur
    2001   "Capital at Home and at School: Effects on Child Social Adjustment." *Journal of Marriage and Family* 63 (February): 32–47.

Philips, Susan
    1983   *The Invisible Culture: Communication in Classroom and Community on the Warm Springs Indian Reservation*. New York: Longman.

Pipho, Chris
    1988   "Dropout Statistics: The Unreliable Indicator." *Education Week* 7 (38).

Platero, P. R., E. A. Brandt, G. Witherspoon, and P. Wong
    1986   *Navajo Students at Risk: Final Report for the Navajo Area Student Dropout Study*. Window Rock, AZ: Platero Paperwork.

Portes, A., and J. Sensenbrenner
    1993   "Embeddedness and Immigration: Notes on the Social Determinants of Economic Action." *American Journal of Sociology* 98 (6): 1320–1350.

Powers, Kristin, Sandra J. Potthoff, Linda H. Bearinger, and Michael D. Resnick
    2003   "Does Cultural Programming Improve Educational Outcomes for American Indian Youth?" *Journal of American Indian Education* 42 (2): 17–49.

Quay, H. C., and L. B. Allen
    1982   "Truants and Dropouts." *Encyclopedia of Educational Research*. Vol. 5. New York: Wiley.

REFERENCES

Reyhner, J.
   1992a   "American Indians out of School: A Review of School-Based Causes and Solutions." *Journal of American Indian Education* 31 (3): 37–56.
   1992b   "Adapting Curriculum to Culture." In *Teaching American Indian Students*, ed. Jon Reyhner, 97–103. Norman: University of Oklahoma Press.

Risingsun, Ted. (Northern Cheyenne tribal elder.)
   1988   Interview by author. Lame Deer, MT. October.
   1989   Interview by author. Lame Deer, MT. Spring.

Roderick, M.
   1993   *The Path to Dropping Out: Evidence for Intervention*. Westport, CT: Auburn House.

Rosenbaum, James E.
   1986   "Institutional Career Structures and the Social Construction of Ability." In *Handbook of Theory and Research of the Sociology of Education*, ed. John G. Richardson, 139–172. New York: Greenwood.

Rossi, R. J.
   1994   *Schools and Students at Risk: Context and Framework for Positive Change*. New York: Teachers College Press.

Rowland, Franklin Clay
   1994   "Tribal Education: A Case Study of Northern Cheyenne Elders." EdD dissertation, Montana State University.

Rowland, Ted. (Administrator, St. Labre Catholic Mission School.)
   1989   Interview by author. Lame Deer, MT. May.

Rumberger, R. W.
   1983   "Dropping Out of High School: The Influence of Race, Sex, and Family Background." *American Educational Research Journal* 20:199–220.
   1987   "High School Dropouts: A Review of Issues and Evidence." *Review of Educational Research* 57:101–121.
   1995   "Dropping Out of Middle School: A Multilevel Analysis of Students and Schools." *American Educational Research Journal* 32 (3): 583–625.

Sack, W. H., M. Beiser, G. Clarke, and R. Redshirt
   1987   "The High Achieving Sioux Indian Child: Some Preliminary Findings from the Flower of Two Soils Project." *American Indian and Alaska Native Mental Health Research* 1:37–51.

Sahlins, Marshall
   1976   *Cultural and Practical Reason*. Chicago: University of Chicago Press.

Sampson, R.
   1998   "How Do Communities Undermine Human Development? Relevant Context and Social Mechanisms." From the national symposium *Does It Take a*

REFERENCES

    Village? Community Effects on Children, Adolescents, and Families. Pennsylvania State University, November 5–6.

Sampson, R., and W. Groves
    1989 "Community Structure and Crime: Testing Social-Disorganization Theory." *American Journal of Sociology* 94:774–802.

Sandefur, Gary D.
    1988 "Blacks, Hispanics, American Indians, and Poverty—and What Worked." In *Quiet Riots*, ed. Fred Harris and Roger Wilkins. New York: Pantheon.

Sandefur, G. D., and A. Sakamoto
    1987 "American Indian Household Structure and Income." *Demography* 25:71–80.

Sandefur, G. D., and W. J. Scott
    1983 "Minority Group Status and the Wages of Indian and Black Males." *Social Science Research* 12:44–68.

Sandefur, G. D., and M. Tienda
    1988 "Social Policy and the Minority Experience." Introduction to *Divided Opportunities: Minorities, Poverty and Social Policy*, ed. G. Sandefur and M. Tienda, 1–19. New York: Plenum.

Sawyer, K.
    1993 *Women's Choices about Family and Work: Three Generations of Northern Cheyenne Women*. Master's thesis, Brigham Young University.

Schmid, Carol L.
    2001 "Educational Achievement, Language-Minority Students, and the New Second Generation." Extra issue, *Sociology of Education*, 71–87.

Schofield, J.
    1982 *Black and White in School: Trust, Tension, or Tolerance?* New York: Praeger.

Scott, W. A.
    1967 *New Mexico State Indian Student Dropout Study, First Year Report 1966–67*. Santa Fe, NM: State Department of Education.
    1986 "Attachment to Indian Culture and the 'Difficult Situation': A Study of American Indian College Students." *Youth and Society* 17:381–395.

Seipel, M.
    1996 "Community Social Capital and School Effectiveness in Rural, Missouri High Schools." Dissertation, University of Missouri.

Smerdon, Becky A.
    2002 "Students' Perceptions of Membership in Their High Schools." *Sociology of Education* 75 (October): 287–305.

REFERENCES

Smith, Jeanne Jacoby
    1998   "The Gifted High School Dropout." Article inset in "Anatomy of a High School Dropout: Pulitzer Prize Winner Donald Murray," 312–313. *World and I* 13 (July): 306–319.

Snipp, C. Matthew
    1986   "The Changing Political and Economic Status of the American Indians: From Captive Nations to Internal Colonies." *American Journal of Economics and Sociology* 45:145–157.
    1988   *Public Policy Impacts on American Indian Economic Development*. Albuquerque: University of New Mexico.
    1989   *American Indians: The First of This Land*. New York: Russell Sage Foundation.
    1995   "The Educational Attainments of American Indians." In *Investing in People: The Human Capital Needs of Rural America*, ed. L. J. Beaulieu and D. Mulkey. Boulder, CO: Westview.

Snipp, C. Matthew, and G. D. Sandefur
    1988   "Earnings of American Indians and Alaskan Natives: The Effects of Residence and Migration." *Social Forces* 66:994–1008.

Snipp, C. Matthew, Hayward D. Horton, Leif Jensen, Joane Nagel, and Refugio Rochin
    1993   "Persistent Rural Poverty and Racial and Ethnic Minorities." In *Persistent Poverty in Rural America*, 173–199. Boulder, CO: Westview.

Sooktis, Ruby. (Northern Cheyenne Follow Through staff member.)
    1988   Interview by author. Lame Deer, MT. February.

Spang, Alonzo. (Instructor, Chief Dull Knife College.)
    2004   Interview by author. Lame Deer, MT.

Stands In Timber, John, and Margot Liberty
    1967   *Cheyenne Memories*. New Haven, CT: Yale University Press.

Stanton-Salazar, Ricardo D., and Sanford M. Dornbusch
    1995   "Social Capital and the Reproduction of Inequality: Information Networks among Mexican-Origin High School Students." *Sociology of Education* 68 (2): 116–135.

Steinberg, L. D., P. Blinde, and K. Chan
    1984   "Dropping Out among Language Minority Youth." *Review of Educational Research* 54:113–132.

St. Germaine, R.
    1995   "Drop-Out Rates among American Indian and Alaska Native Students: Beyond Cultural Discontinuity." *Eric Digest*. EDO-RC-96-1.

Swisher, K., and M. Hoisch
    1992   "Dropping Out among American Indians and Alaska Natives: A Review of Studies." *Journal of American Indian Education* 31 (2): 3–23.

REFERENCES

Szasz, Margaret C.
    1974   *Education and the American Indian*. Albuquerque: University of New Mexico Press.

Takie, Y., P. Lynch, and G. M. Charleston
    1988   "Drink or Not to Drink: The Indian Adolescents' Choice between Friends and Family." *Journal of American Indian Education* 27:1–9.

Talbot, Steve
    1981   *Roots of Oppression: The American Indian Question*. New York: International.

Tierney, W. G.
    1992   *Official Encouragement, Institutional Discouragement: Minorities in Academe; The Native American Experience*. Norwood, NJ: Ablex.

U.S. Bureau of the Census
    1993   Social and Economic Characteristics, Montana. Washington, DC: U.S. Government Printing Office.

U.S. Congress
    1969   *Indian Education: A National Tragedy—A National Challenge*. Special Senate Subcommittee on Indian Education. Washington, DC: U.S. Government Printing Office.

Valenzuela, A., and S. M. Dornbusch
    1994   "Familism and Social Capital in the Academic Achievement of Mexican Origin and Anglo Adolescents." *Social Science Quarterly* 75 (1): 18–36.

Valli, Linda
    1983   "Becoming Clerical Workers: Business Education and the Culture of Femininity." In *Ideology and Practice in Schooling*, ed. M. W. Apple and L. Weis. Philadelphia: Temple University Press.

Van Fossen, B., J. Jones, and J. Spade
    1987   "Curriculum Tracking and Status Maintenance." *Sociology of Education* 60:104–122.

Velez, William
    1989   "Why Hispanic Students Fail: Factors Affecting Attrition in High School." In *Schools and Society: A Unified Reader*, 2nd ed., ed. Jeanne H. Ballantine, 380–388. Mountain View, CA: Mayfield.

Wacquant, Loic J. D., and W. J. Wilson
    1989   "The Cost of Racial and Class Exclusion in the Inner City." In *Majority and Minority: The Dynamics of Race and Ethnicity in American Life*, ed. Norman R. Yetman. Boston: Allyn and Bacon.

Wagenaar, Theodore C.
    1987   "What Do We Know about Dropping Out of High School?" *Research in the Sociology of Education and Socialization* 7:161–190.

REFERENCES

Ward, Carol
    1992   "Social and Cultural Influences on the Schooling of Northern Cheyenne Youth." PhD dissertation, Department of Sociology, University of Chicago.
    1993   "Explaining Gender Differences in Native American High School Dropout Rates: A Case Study of Northern Cheyenne Schooling Patterns." In special issue on the Native American family, ed. Carol Ward, *Family Perspective* 27 (4).
    1995   "American Indian High School Completion in Rural Southeastern Montana." *Rural Sociology* 60 (3): 416–434.
    1996   "Key Actors in American Indian Human Capital Formation: The Northern Cheyenne Case." In *American Indian Human Capital and Economic Development*, vol. 10, ed. C. Matthew Snipp and Carol J. Ward, 41–68. Greenwich, CT: JAI.
    1998a   "Community Resources and School Performance: The Northern Cheyenne Case." *Sociological Inquiry* 68 (1):83–113.
    1998b   "The Importance of Context in Explaining Human Capital Formation and Labor Force Participation of American Indians in Rosebud County, Montana." *Rural Sociology* 63 (3): 451–80.

Ward, Carol, and C. Matthew Snipp
    1996   "An Introduction to American Indian Human Capital and Development." In *American Indian Human Capital and Economic Development*, vol. 10, ed. C. Matthew Snipp and Carol J. Ward, 1–16. Greenwich, CT: JAI.

Ward, Carol, and D. Wilson
    1985   "Northern Cheyenne Adult Education Survey." Report to Dull Knife Memorial College, Northern Cheyenne Tribe, Lame Deer, MT.
    1989   "Educational Census of the Northern Cheyenne Reservation." Report for the Northern Cheyenne Tribe, Lame Deer, MT.
    1991   Annual Evaluation of the Adult Education Program. Report for Dull Knife Memorial College, Northern Cheyenne Tribe, Lame Deer, MT.
    1992   Annual Evaluation of the Adult Education Program. Report for Dull Knife Memorial College, Northern Cheyenne Tribe, Lame Deer, MT.

Wax, M. L.
    1980   *When Schools Are Desegregated: Problems and Possibilities for Students, Educators, Parents and the Community*. New Brunswick, NJ: Transaction.

Wax, M. L., R. H. Wax, and R. V. Dumont
    1964   "Formal Education in an American Indian Community." Supplement, *Social Problems: Official Journal of the Society for the Study of Social Problems* 2:1–116.

Wehlage, G. G., and R. A. Rutter
    1986   "Dropping Out: How Much Do Schools Contribute to the Problem?" *Teachers College Record* 87:374–392.

REFERENCES

Wehlage, G. G., P. Lipman, and G. Smith
    1989   "Empowering Communities for School Reform: The Annie E. Casey Foundation's New Futures Initiative." Paper prepared for National Center on Effective Secondary Schools.

Whitbeck, Les B., Dan R. Hoyt, Jerry D. Stubben, and Teresa LaFromboise
    2001   "Traditional Culture and Academic Success among American Indian Children in the Upper Midwest." *Journal of American Indian Education* 40 (2): 48–60.

Wilson, William J.
    1987   *The Truly Disadvantaged: The Inner City, the Underclass, and Public Policy.* Chicago: University of Chicago Press.
    1996   *When Work Disappears: The World of the New Urban Poor.* New York: Knopf.

Wood, P. B., and C. Clay
    1996   "Perceived Structural Barriers and Academic Performance among American Indian High School Students." *Youth and Society* 28 (1): 40–61.

Yellowbird, Michael, and C. Matthew Snipp
    1994   "American Indian Families." In *Minority Families in the United States*, ed. Ronald Taylor. Englewood Cliffs, NJ: Prentice Hall.

Young, Beth Aronstamm
    2003   *Public High School Dropouts and Completers from the Common Core of Data: School Year 2000–01.* Washington, DC: National Center for Education Statistics, U.S. Department of Education, Institute of Education Sciences. NCES 23004-310.

Zhou, M., and C. L. Bankston
    1994   "Social Capital and the Adaptation of the Second Generation: The Case of Vietnamese Youth in New Orleans." *International Migration Review* 28 (4): 821–845.

INDEX

Abello, Annie C., 6, 49
academic expectations, 138–40
African American achievement levels, 3–4, 31
Akom, A. A., 38
alcohol abuse: Northern Cheyenne, 86, 91, 124–26, 128, 130, 133, 144, 161–62, 180, 196–99, 211, 224, 227, 231; studies of, 26, 28–29, 77–78
Aldrich, J. H., 115
Alexander, K. L., 32
Allen, L. B., 25
Alwin, D. F., 30, 112
American Indian political resurgence, 8
Anderson, Kirk, 34
Antell, W., 44
Apple, M. W., 12–13, 30
arts and crafts production, native, 159–60
Ashabranner, Brent, 69–70, 76
Ashland, description of, 131
assimilation, 7, 38, 51–54, 63, 67, 131, 230
Astone, N., 31

"at-risk" students, 47, 51
attendance, 142, 196
attitude-achievement paradox, 16

Backes, John S., 27, 39
Bailey, Robert, 89
Bankston, C. L., 48
Barber, B. K., 31, 227
Bearinger, Linda H., 13, 22, 221
Beaulieu, L. J., 48
Beauvais, F., 27, 29, 35
Beiser, M., 34
Benson, P. L., 28
BIA Johnson-O'Malley Program, 66, 78
Bidwell, C. E., 25, 30, 37
Bielby, W. T., 38
Billings Gazette, 204
Bixby, Norma, x, 200
Blalock, Hubert M., 114
Blauner, R., 16
Blinde, P., 26
boarding school, 8, 63, 66, 88, 123, 132
Bourdieu, P., 12–13, 212
Bowker, A., 28, 34, 50

INDEX

Bowles, S., 13–14, 33
Braddock, J. H., 42
Brandt, E. A., 34
Brint, Stephen, 2, 12, 24
Brinton, Mary, 14
Brokenleg, M., 51
Brown, E., 7, 34
Brown, M. H., 71
Bryan, W. L., 19, 64–66, 68, 70, 73
Bryk, A., 43
Bureau of Land Management Study, 58, 72, 73–75
Busby Tribal School, descriptions of, x, 88, 128–29
busing, 196–97

Carrier, J. G., 42
Catholic school, effects of, 47
Cavanagh, Shannon, 25
Champagne, Duane, 8
Chan, K., 26
Charleston, G. M., 28
Chavez, F., 27, 29, 35
Cheng, Simon, 30
Chestnut, Steve, 57
Chief Dull Knife. *See* Dull Knife, Chief
Chief Dull Knife College, xi, 234
Cicourel, A. V., 33
Clarke, G., 34
Clay, C., 35
Clow, R. L., 71
Coladarci, T., 34
Coggins, Kip, 34
Coleman, James, 12, 15–16, 28, 31, 38, 43, 47, 216–17, 221
college attendance: first-generation students, 160; Whites, American Indians, African Americans, 4

college completion, American Indian, 3, 28
Collins, R., 33
Colstrip Public Schools, description of, x, 84
community context, 116–17, 154, 166, 173–74, 189, 209, 213–15, 220, 223, 228–29
community-school relations, 47–55, 165, 168–69, 171, 181, 184, 221, 223, 231
congressional enactment and funding of Indian education initiatives, 8
contrast coding, 144, 149, 156, 171
Cornell, G. R., 27, 29, 35
Cornell, Stephen, 7, 8, 49
Cornwell, G. T., 48
Council of Forty-four, 70–71
Crain, R. L., 42
Crawford, J., 9, 27, 42
crime, 130, 132, 225–26
critical theory tradition, 13
Crosnoe, Robert, 25, 31, 42–43
Crouse, J., 30
Crow Reservation, 65, 86, 132, 142, 154, 166, 209, 213–14
Crow students, 94, 129, 133
cultural awareness programs, 8
cultural capital, 12, 32, 51, 218
cultural differences, theory of, 39, 43
cultural discontinuity, theory of, 34–35, 50
cultural renewal, 8
cultural tradition, analysis of, 143–47

Davids, D. W., 28
Davis, John, 34
Day, Jennifer C., 2
Deffenbacher, J. L., 27, 29, 35

INDEX

Deloria, Vine, Jr., 1
DeMarrais, Kathleen B., 24, 38
Department of Education, Office of Educational Research and Improvement, ix, 20, 90–91
desegregated schools, 42, 189
Deyhle, Donna, 1, 34–35, 39, 40, 50–51, 122, 226
DeYoung, Alan J., 15–16
discrimination, 200, 203–5, 212
Dodd, John M., 27, 42, 45
Dornbusch, S. M., 31, 33, 112
dropout rates: American Indian, Latino, African American, White rates, 4; American Indian rates, 5, 21, 44; analysis of, 150–58, 165, 170, 173–74, 213–17; community effects, 151; costs of, 2; definitions of, 92–94, 202; reasons for, 25–29. *See also* school completion
Dufur, Mikaela J., 31
Dull Knife, Chief, 36, 122, 219, 223
Dumais, Susan A., 26
Dumont, R. V., 7
Dunaway, Wilma, 52

Eberhard, D. R., 33
Eckland, B. K., 42
ecological approach, 11
economic practices, Northern Cheyenne, 164
economic strategies, 163–64
educational attainment, influences on, 24–29; enrollment, 4–5; intergenerational gaps, 5, 123; urban vs. rural, 4–7
educational attainment by ethnic groups, 3
Edwards, R., 27, 35

"effective schools" literature, 43
Eggebeen, D. J., 48
Ekstrom, R. B., 25–26, 38
Elder, H., 25, 42–43
Elliot, A., 15
Elliot, D. S., 15
Elliot, R., 112–13
embeddedness approach, 53–54
employment, 125, 156–58, 160, 162, 216; comparisons between ethnicities, 6; meaning of, 160
Epstein, J. L., 14, 31
Erickson, Bonnie, 12, 16
ethnicity, effect of, 192, 194–95, 199
ethnographic methods, 18–19, 81–84
extracurricular activities, 38, 40, 137, 150–88, 154, 169, 173–74, 181, 184, 190, 193–194, 196, 211–12

family characteristics, 168, 171, 174, 176–77, 184, 208, 213–15, 228–29; effects of, 150–88; studies of, 30–36
family networks, 177–78
family structure, 125–26, 155, 177, 184, 210
Farkas, G., 11, 18, 31
federal policies, 7, 8, 16; government assimilation policies, 8, 16; self-determination, 7
Feeney, M., 57
Fernandez-Kelly, M. P., 14
Fine, Michelle, 13
Foley, D., 33
Fordham, Signithia, 39
foster care, 125–26
Frase, M., 4, 28, 44
Friedkin, N., 25, 30, 37
friendship and kinship ties, 157–58

INDEX

Fuchs, E., 8, 39
Furstenberg, F. F., 12

Gambetta, D., 229
Gamoran, A., 41
GED, 128, 130–31
gender, 159, 174–75, 190, 192–94, 209
Giddens, Anthony, 26
Gintis, H., 13–14, 33
Giroux, Sharon S., 34
giveaways, 163. *See also* spending patterns
Gloria, Alberta M., 28
Goertz, M. E., 25–26, 38
Goodluck, Alda, 65
Granovetter, M., 18
Greenbaum, S. D., 27
Gregory, Robert, 6, 49
Grinnell, George Bird, 219
Groves, W., 227
Guest, Andrew, 38

Hagstrom, D., 44
Hale, Lorraine, 27
Hale, Michelle, 7
Hall, Thomas D., 7, 14, 18, 216
Hanushek, E., 115
Hauser, R. M., 30
Havighurst, J., 8, 39
Heyle, A. M., 50
High School and Beyond study, 4
Hirshman, C., 33
Hobbs, D., 16, 48
Hoffer, T., 12, 15–16, 28, 38, 43, 47, 216–17, 221
Hoffmann, John P., 115
Hoisch, M., 1, 39
Horvat, Erin McNamara, 39

housing, 161
Hoyt, Dan, 39
Hubbard, Ryan, 2
Huff, D. J., 49
Huffman, Terry, 39, 51
Hughes, M. E., 12
Huizinga, D., 15
human capital, 11, 14, 18, 47, 49, 53, 61, 126–127, 157, 164–165, 216, 230
Hurn, C. J., 13

immigrant minority groups, 14, 32, 38, 39, 48; involuntary minority, 14, 32, 38, 39; voluntary minority, 14, 48
income, 49, 73, 93
Indian preference ordinance, 157
Indian Reorganization Act (IRA), 71
Indian schools, academic demands of, 178
Indian Self-Determination Act of 1975, 68–69
informal economy, 160–61
internal colonies, 7
Israel, G. D., 48

Jackson, J., 115
Jamal, Samina, 34
James, K., 27, 35
Jencks, C., 30
Jensen, L., 49
Johnson, Jamie, 6, 42–43, 49
Jones, J., 41
Jones, W. M., 25
Jordan, K. Forbis, 2
Jordan, W. J., 25
Jorgensen, Mirian, 7

Kalt, P., 7, 49
Kandel, D. B., 26
Kennedy, Edward, 1
Kerckhoff, A. C., 25
Kim, Kwang Chung, 33
Kingston, Paul W., 2
Kitchen, Richard S., 34
Kleinfeld, J., 40, 44
Knows His Gun, Sylvester, 76
Kohn, Melvin, 31
Kroll, C., 57
Kroskrity, P., 27
Kunisawa, B., 4

labor force participation, 156
labor market opportunities, 49
LaFromboise, T. O., 39, 50
Lame Deer, description of, 128, 130
Lamont, M., 16
Lapp, Brent, 2
Lara, J., 25
Lareau, A., 16, 31
learning disabilities, 39, 42, 45, 85
LeCompte, D., 24, 38
Ledlow, S., 35
Lee, V. E., 43
Leiderman, H., 31, 112
Leiderman, M. J., 31, 112
Levin, H., 2
Lewis, Kristine S., 39
Lonebear, Juanita, x–xii
Lichter, D. T., 48
Lipman, P., 16, 43
Littlebear, Richard, xi–xii, 234
Looker, D. E., 30
Lopach, J. J., 71
Lynch, P., 28
Lyons, Teresa S., 2

Mare, Robert, 30, 41
Marsh, H. W., 112–13
May, Phillip, 28
McDiarmid, G. W., 44
McDill, E. L., 38, 43
McDonald, Art, ix, 44
McInerney, Dennis M., 28
McLanahan, S., 31
McLaughlin, Daniel, 14
McPartland, J. M., 25, 42
Mehan, H., 33
Mensch, B. S., 26
Meyers, E. D., Jr., 43
Mickelson, R. A., 16, 33
Mingione, Enzo, 18, 53
Montana Public Hearings on Northern Cheyenne Petition for Public High School 1991, 194–97, 201
Montana state documents, 20, 70, 74–75
Moore, John M., 52, 129
Mueser, P., 30
Mulkey, D., 48
Munch, Richard, 52
Myers, John, 34

Nabokov, Peter, 8
Nagle, Ami, 7
Nagel, Joane, 8, 51
National Center for Education Statistics (NCES), 1, 4, 44
National Institute on Drug Abuse, 28, 76–77, 133
native capital, 19, 52–53, 127, 156–57, 159, 162, 165, 185, 209, 216, 230–31; definition of, 53
native language fluency, 26–27, 35, 39, 42, 45, 85, 142, 180–81, 184–85, 221, 226, 234

INDEX

Natriello, G., 38
NCES Common Core data, 4
Nelson, F. D., 115
Nelson, J. Ron, 27, 42, 45
Ness, Jean E., 28
Newburger, Eric C., 2
noninterference parenting style, 124, 136, 155, 210
Nordstrom, Jean, 70
Northern Cheyenne Area Chamber of Commerce, 161
Northern Cheyenne communities, 56–62
Northern Cheyenne dropout study, description of: cohorts included, 102–11; dropout definition, 93–94; mean GPA definition, 99–101, 112–13; school outcome, 102–11; variables, 95–100
Northern Cheyenne Educational Census, 60–62, 94, 122
Northern Cheyenne Education Commission, ix, 19, 78, 85, 91–92; description of, 83–84
Northern Cheyenne Education Department. *See* Northern Cheyenne Education Commission
Northern Cheyenne reservation, description of, 19, 56–62; health characteristics, 75–76; income, 72–75; labor force, 72–75; language use, 61; political organization, 69–71; poverty, 20, 35–36, 65, 74; social structure, 56–60; unemployment, 20; women's roles, 129, 133–34

O'Brien, Eileen, 44
O'Connell, Joanne C., 42
Oetting, G., 27, 29, 35
Ogbu, John U., 16, 32–33, 38
oppositional cultural frame, 16
Ozer, E. J., 50

Pallas, A. M., 38
Parcel, Toby L., 31
Passeron, J., 13, 212
Philips, Susan, 27, 35
Pineo, P. C., 30
Pipho, Chris, 93
Platero, P. R., 34
policy implications, Northern Cheyenne dropout study, 232–34
Pollack, J. M., 25–26, 38
Portes, Alejandro, 14, 47, 61
Potthoff, Sandra J., 13, 22, 221
poverty, 35–36, 49, 65, 74
Powers, Kristin, 13, 22, 221
prejudice, 43, 46, 86, 157, 197, 199–200, 203–5, 212, 222, 225, 227, 233–34
Public Law 874, 66

Quay, H. C., 25
Quigley, E., 57

racism, 222, 231
Radin, Norma, 34
Rankin, B., 15
Red Power movement, 8
Redshirt, R., 34
reservation, economic conditions, 49, 52–53; income, 49, 73, 93; poverty, 35–36, 49, 65, 74; unemployment, 6, 36, 49, 65, 72, 74–75, 136, 156, 164
reservation economy, 156, 219–20
reservation system, 7. *See also* trust relationship

Resnick, Michael D., 13, 22, 221
Reyhner, Jon, 13, 35, 100
Rigsby, L., 43
Risingsun, Ted, x, 63, 67, 71, 219
Ritter, P. L., 31, 112
Roberts, D. F., 31, 112
Robinson Kurpius, Sharon E., 28
Rock, D. A., 25–26, 38
Roderick, M. 25, 112
Rosenbaum, James E., 41
Rowland, Franklin Clay, 122, 226
Rowland, Ted, 64
Rumberger, R. W., 12, 25, 30–31
rural schools, 15–16
Rutter, R. A., 25, 38

Sack, W. H., 34
Sahlins, Marshall, 26
Sakamoto, A., 35
Sampson, R., 15, 227
Sandefur, Gary D., 6–7, 35, 49, 215
Sawyer, K., 133
Schauffler, R., 14
Schmid, Carol L., 33
Schneider, Barbara, 38
Schoefield, J., 42
school climate, 42–43, 147, 197, 199, 201, 212, 225. See also school context
school completion, 3, 25, 37–40. See also dropping out
school context, 17, 40–46, 178–79, 211, 216, 224, 231; ability groups, 41–42, 45; tracking, 41–42, 47. See also school climate
Schooler, Carmi, 31
school experience, 37, 39, 46, 137, 150–88, 168–69, 173, 190–91, 193–94, 196, 211
school membership, 16, 38

school performance, 25–28, 118–22; analysis of, 118, 150–88, 153–54, 169, 184, 190, 192, 194, 208–10, 212, 217
school progress, 4
school relations, 225
schools, Northern Cheyenne, description of, 83; Busby Tribal School, x, 66–68, 88, 128–29; Chief Dull Knife College, xi, 68–69, 234; Colstrip Public School, x, 65–66, 84; St. Labre Catholic School, x, 63–65, 86, 100
Schroeder, Paul, 2
Scott, W. J., 7, 27
Seipel, M., 48
self-esteem, 198, 222, 225
Sensenbrenner, J., 14, 47, 61
Sewell, W. J., 30
sexual activity and pregnancy: Northern Cheyenne, 175–76; studies of, 26
Sill, M. L., 51
Smerdon, Becky, 38
Smith, G., 2, 16, 43
Snipp, Matthew C., 1, 3–7, 13, 28, 35, 49, 51, 62, 215
social capital, 12, 15, 47–48, 51, 61, 134, 156, 178, 215–16, 218, 230
socioeconomic attributes, 171
Sooktis, Ruby, 124
sovereignty, 222, 233
Spade, J., 41
Spang, Zane, x–xii, 70
Special Senate Subcommittee on Indian Education, 1
spending patterns, Northern Cheyenne, 161, 163–64
Springwater, Melinda, 7

INDEX

standardized tests, 100
Stands In Timber, John, 133, 226
Stanton-Salazar, Ricardo D., 33
Starks, Brian, 30
status attainment approach, 11, 18
status equalization, 163
Steinberg, L. D., 26, 112
St. Germaine, R., 13
St. Labre Catholic Mission School, description of, x, 86
Strenta, A. C., 112–13
Stubben, Jerry, 39
student views of school, Northern Cheyenne, 195
subsistence strategies, 159, 164
substance abuse: Northern Cheyenne, 86, 91, 124–26, 128, 130, 133, 144, 161–62, 180, 196–99, 211, 224, 227, 231; studies of, 26, 28–29, 77–78
suicide, 198
Sweet Medicine, 219
Swisher, Karen, 1, 28, 39
Szasz, Margaret C., 9, 10, 40

Talbot, Steve, 7
Talkie, Y., 28
teacher-parent relations, 199–203, 212
theories: critical theory, 13; cultural differences theory, 39, 43; cultural discontinuity theory, 34–35, 50; embeddedness approach, 53–54
Thornton, A., 30, 112
Tienda, M., 6, 49
Tierney, W. G., 13, 27, 51
Title IV Indian Education program evaluation, 27–28

traditional culture: Northern Cheyenne, 127, 136, 151, 180–81, 184, 209, 218, 221, 226; studies of, 27, 50, 39; tribal affiliation, 34, 129
transfer, definition of: out of region, 93–94, 142; school switching, 94, 142
tribal college enrollment, 160
trust relationship, 7. *See also* reservation system
Tsai, S., 30
types of school, 40, 44, 46, 134–37, 174, 221, 217, 220; analysis of, 116–18; private, 15, 43, 21; public, 15, 43, 211

unemployment, 6, 36, 49, 65, 72, 74–75, 136, 156, 164
unemployment rate, 156–57

Valenzuela, A., 112
Valli, Linda, 38
Van Fossen, B., 41
Velasquez, Diane Torres, 34
Velez, William, 25
Villalva, C., 57

Wacquant, 15
Wagenaar, Theodore C., 25, 38
Ward, Carol J., 1, 3–5, 7, 20, 60, 62
Wax, M. L., 7, 42
Wax, R. H., 7
Wehlage, G., 16, 25, 38, 43
Weis, Lois, 12–13, 30
Whitaker, Leslie, 7
Whitback, Les, 39
Wildcat, Daniel R., 1
Williams, Edith, 34

Wilson, Julia, 2
Wilson, William J., 15, 20, 60, 62
Wisconsin model of status
    attainment, 11, 18
Witherspoon, G., 34
Wong, M., 33
Wong, P., 34

Wood, P. B., 35
Woodenlegs, John, 36

Yellowtail, P., 19, 64–66, 68, 70, 73
Young, Beth, 1, 4

Zhou, M., 48

ABOUT THE AUTHOR

Carol J. Ward grew up in Fort Worth, Texas, and attended North Texas State University for her bachelor of arts degree and master of arts degree in sociology. After receiving her master's degree she went to Washington, D.C., where she worked for the Administration for Native Americans (U.S. Department of Health and Human Services) for five years as a research specialist. Carol then moved to Lawrence, Kansas, where she worked for Native American Research Associates. She entered the PhD program at the University of Kansas but transferred to the PhD program at the University of Chicago and finished there in 1992. About this same time Carol started her own consulting business working with Indian tribes and organizations. She moved from Chicago to Lame Deer, Montana, in 1987 to work at Chief Dull Knife College, the tribal community college of the Northern Cheyenne Indian Tribe of southeastern Montana. There she was the director of research and a member of the faculty. It was at Dull Knife that Carol completed a study of American Indian school completion. In 1990 she joined the sociology faculty at Brigham Young University. She has continued to work with Dull Knife on many different projects and to conduct research on education issues, recovery from alcohol and substance abuse, the effects of welfare reform, and food assistance programs. She teaches classes in racial and ethnic relations, sociology of education, sociology of rural communities, qualitative methods, and survey methods.